# The
# CHARACTER
## of our
# COMMUNITIES

# The
# CHARACTER
## *of our*
# COMMUNITIES

*Toward an Ethic of Liberation for the Church*

# Gloria H. Albrecht

*ABINGDON PRESS*

*Nashville*

THE CHARACTER OF OUR COMMUNITIES
TOWARD AN ETHIC OF LIBERATION FOR THE CHURCH

*This book is printed on recycled, acid-free paper.*

**Library of Congress Cataloging-in-Publication Data**

Albrecht, Gloria H.
    The character of our communities : toward an ethic of liberation for the Church / Gloria H. Albrecht.
        p.    cm.
    Includes bibliographical references.
    ISBN 0-687-00283-4 (pbk : alk. paper)
    1. Sociology, Christian.    2. Hauerwas, Stanley, 1940—
-Contributions in Christian sociology.    3. Sociology, Christian-History—20th century.
4. Christian ethics—Presbyterian authors.    5. Social ethics.    6. Feminist theology.
7. Liberation theology.    8. Feminist ethics.    I. Title.
BT738.A418 1995
261—dc20                                                                                    95-18112
                                                                                                    CIP

Unless otherwise noted, Scripture quotations are from the New Revised Standard Version Bible. Copyright © 1989 by the Division of Christian Education of the National Council of the Churches of Christ in the USA. Used by permission.

The poem on page 157 is reprinted by permission from *The Window of Vulnerability* by Dorothy Soelle, copyright © 1990 Augsburg Fortress.

95 96 97 98 99 00 01 02 03 04 05 — 10 9 8 7 6 5 4 3 2 1

MANUFACTURED IN THE UNITED STATES OF AMERICA

*To my mother
Amalie Hafer Frank
pastor and pilot*

# ACKNOWLEDGMENTS

I feel deeply indebted to the many womanist and feminist voices that have helped me to find my own. Many of them you will find listed in the footnotes, but many others are known to me because the courage of their daily lives has graced my own life. I am also grateful for the consistent support and encouragement, over many years, of two pro-feminist colleagues and friends, Dr. John Raines and Dr. Thomas Schindler. Finally, it is to my children, Missy Albrecht and Jeffrey Albrecht, that I owe my passion for a better church and a better world, now.

# CONTENTS

# INTRODUCTION

This is a book about community, particularly Christian community, and the ethics that I think some of us need to practice in order to sustain community in the coming century. I approach the question of the contemporary task of Christian ethics, and especially the ethical character of the church, out of a particular context. First, I am a Presbyterian minister. I spent eight years in urban ministry before taking an academic position in an urban university. The churches I served were white, middle-class congregations whose members lived mostly in white, middle-class neighborhoods.[1] On Sundays we drove "in" to our church buildings which, due to the demographic and economic changes of the past fifty years, are architecturally magnificent buildings located in the center of a predominately poor and black city.

Each congregation supported a great deal of "mission": the provision of food, clothes, and shelter to the poor, mostly black, women, men, and children of the city. In each congregation "mission" was seen by some as taking resources away from our care of our "own"; a way of avoiding our responsibility for those closest to us. For others, mission was the core of our Christian faith. Yet, for many in both groups, the different race and class of those for whom the mission committee was responsible was accepted as significant in the explanation of why recipients of "mission" would not be interested in our other congregational activities. On the other hand, the different race and class of these persons was often emphatically denied as being relevant to their experience of poverty, homelessness, illiteracy, and ill health in our city.

In my experience, talk about "difference" in the context of analyzing social location was often met with an anxious hostility. Talk about the social power (or the lack of it) that adheres to social location was considered divisive, and being divisive was considered unchristian. In both my pastoral and academic experiences, middle- and upper-class white Christians, for the most part, do not admit to having a social location. We tend not to admit to the social prerogatives and privileges that are ours simply because we are white and middle class.

I believe that the unwillingness of many white middle- and upper-class folk to see the difference in social location that race, class, and gender make in U.S. society allows us to avoid a social analysis of the problems of racism, classism, and sexism and their concrete effects. I believe that it allows us to avoid the complicities and the "response-abilities" of our own social location with all its limits, its prerogatives, and its power. The question I raise here is whether this failure is a result of our not being "real" or "faithful" Christians, or whether there is something fundamentally wrong with Christianity itself—something that makes it incapable of forming people who are able to respond to human differences without fear and the need to ignore, destroy, or dominate.

I am also a white, middle-class, heterosexual, Christian feminist clergywoman: that is, one who is on the margins in some social relations and in the center of others. I cannot claim to be either "normative" or "marginal," but I am sometimes one, sometimes the other, and sometimes both—depending on the social context. Sharon Ringe describes this well:

> The sociological term for a North American, Caucasian, middle class clergywoman is "Status inconsistency." Most of the characteristics of that social location point to privilege and dominance in the world community, except for the fact of being female. With that one detail, the insider is also outside, the dominant is subordinate, and the privileged has to struggle to find her history, has to be vigilant over economic and civil rights at best grudgingly granted, and has constantly to search for her space, for "a room of her own."[2]

This metaphor of "margin" and "center" is a commonplace one. I use it to refer to social location; that is, the possession of or lack of social power which adheres to persons as members of social groups defined by class, sexual orientation, gender, and race. I am using it as informed by the theme developed by bell hooks in *Feminist Theory: From Margin to Center*. The point she makes in her preface is that those on the margins grow up knowing—having to know—that they are a part of the whole but not part of the center. They see the whole, by necessity, in order to survive. However, those at the center can live quite well without ever seeing or knowing the margins. They can, in fact, assume that their experiences of reality are universal, that is, true.[3] In the United States today, middle- and upper-class, white, heterosexual males are in the center. Middle- and upper-class, white, heterosexual females (including academic feminists) are not far off center.

Because I am a privileged white feminist academic, my reference to hooks's and to other womanists' experiences and works raises the acute issue of white feminists' appropriation of the work of women of color. This is an essential, ongoing discussion as we all attempt to understand how each of us participates in existing structures of oppression and how to resist that participation; how to identify our differences and use them to critique our own work; and how to identify our commonalities and make them a source of mutual strength. The following points explain my use of the works of women of color. (1) The value of womanist work does not depend upon it being referenced or used or found valuable by white women (or men). (2) There is a painful, unjust, ongoing practice of white women and white men using the work of women of color for purposes that obstruct their struggle for justice. Sometimes it is a way of again masking our racism by a "me, too" appropriation of others' experiences. Sometimes it is just another way of taking gain from others' labors. However, (3) the work of women and men with whom I differ in terms of race, culture, class, sexual orientation, ethnicity, and religious tradition is essential to my understanding of myself and my analysis of my participation both in what oppresses and in what liberates others. I believe that the challenge of the larger vision from the margin is an epistemological and moral necessity.[4] It is in that spirit that I intentionally choose to work with and learn from others as I write about the character of the white, middle- and upper-class Christian community.

Along with some other white Christian feminists (such as Thistlethwaite, Davaney, Welch, and McClintock Fulkerson), I have found poststructuralist theory helpful not only in understanding this personal experience of double-positioning, but also helpful in the fundamental task of creating a feminist ethics of liberation.[5] I believe that task involves using our particular locations of class, race, gender, and sexual orientation as critical categories by which to uncover the relationships of domination that exist within human society generally—and within Christianity particularly—for the purpose of transforming them. Essential to this task is the need to acknowledge the

13

differences between people and the different ways in which structural oppressions are experienced, while developing among those variously marginalized peoples enough trust and shared goals to work together. Both my experience in ministry and my experience in theorizing have led me to believe that Christian ethics must be rooted in an analysis of social locations, of differences.

As a Christian ethicist, Stanley Hauerwas has observed the ongoing fragmentation of U.S. society and its violence. He is quite angry at the church for its failure really to be the church in this society. He insists that Christian community is based on the uniquely truthful premises of the Christian narrative and should provide the world with a model of a nonviolent community which does not need to control or destroy those not like us. Hauerwas's turn to virtue, character, and community, his insistence on the risk of faith, his emphasis on nonviolence, and his challenge to the church to be a community of character caught my attention as a pastor.

While Hauerwas does not explicitly address the concerns raised by Christian feminists in his published writings, I share with him a concern for the character of Christian community, which includes women. It is important, therefore, for a feminist critical theory to ask how any proposal for Christian life and community functions for Christian women. Does it provide for the wholeness of women as full moral agents in the construction of ourselves, our church communities, and our societies? Does it clarify or obfuscate the relations of domination we have experienced in church and society? Does it provide a clarifying analysis for the diverse and fragmented world we experience? And does it point to an adequate praxis of transformation? These are the concerns with which I approach Hauerwas's ethics of Christian character and which guide my own thoughts about the character of the white, affluent Christian community in the U.S. at the advent of the twenty-first century.

A brief word about the structure of this book. Chapter 1 attempts to locate the broader social and theological context in which a conversation between Hauerwas's ethics of character and a feminist ethics of liberation occurs. In chapter 2, I present Hauerwas's description of the experiences that have shaped the basic assumptions he brings to the task of Christian ethics. I also describe his account of the human condition, the promise of the Christian narrative, and the character of the community which it shapes. In chapter 3, I contrast Hauerwas's experiences of community with those of women. I explore how these differing experiences seem to lead to alternative explanations of the violence and chaos of U.S. society and of our experiences of difference. Consequently, I end up with a different understanding of the task of Christian ethics. In chapter 4, using the analysis of social location as my tool, I re-view Hauerwas's proposal for Christian community to identify its social source, to discern its capacity to respond to the new voices within Christianity, voices differentiated by race, class, sexual orientation, and gender, and to evaluate its capacity to point to an adequate praxis of social transformation. Finally, in chapter 5 I return to my central questions, as pastor and ethicist. What should be the character of the Christian communities composed of people like myself, people privileged by race and class to be part of the dominant culture of the U.S.? And how can our communities shape characters of resistance to violence, both the violence of war and the violence inherent in all relationships of domination?

# CHAPTER 1

# DIVERSITY, FRAGMENTATION, AND COMMUNITY

In the last half of the twentieth century, a diversity of voices has demanded to be heard. Civil rights movements developed within the marginalized groups of the United States. European colonial powers were overthrown in Africa and Asia. Black South Africans stood in line for hours to cast their first free votes and elect Nelson Mandela president. Totalitarian governments were overthrown in eastern Europe. And revolutionary movements continued to challenge the ruling classes in the countries of Central and Latin America. Each movement, in its distinct way, challenged hegemonic political and economic powers and the ideologies supporting them.

These same movements are the sources of voices erupting within the practices of Christian theology and ethics: Asian voices, African voices, eastern European voices and voices from the Americas—Native Americans, black Americans, Hispanic Americans, white feminists, black womanists, gay men and lesbian women.[1] Each voice raises to sight and sound its own history of suffering, its story of repression and of resistance. Each, in its distinctive way, challenges the hegemonic powers of race, nation, class, gender, and sexual orientation within the Christian tradition with knowledges hitherto ignored or disqualified. No Christian denomination escapes the tensions created by the multitude of voices erupting from the pews.[2] As we Christians approach the end of our second millennium, we face our own diversity and the questions about truth and justice which it reveals. This context is not simply "interesting." In its prophetic possibilities, our context reveals multiple claims for justice intertwined with multiple accusations of oppression and multiple cries for deliverance. In its prophetic possibilities, the clamor could truly bring down some walls.

At the same time, the social context of the U.S. is interpreted by many commentators as one of profound fragmentation: human rela-

17

tions seem ruptured by the shrill demands of self-interest. The civil practice of governance is threatened by the conflicting and uncompromising demands of special interest groups. As we reach the end of the "American" century and witness the global threat of balkanization, we in the U.S. face our own internal social fragmentation. In recent years we have experienced this fragmentation and these challenges to tradition in such issues as civil rights and the remedy (or not) of the effects of past discrimination, quarrels over the academic canon,[3] the regulation (or not) of pornography,[4] the legalization (or not) of abortion,[5] and the debate over the definition of "family."[6] The point is not that we are faced with difficult moral issues, but that we do not seem to be able as a society to work our way through them.

The response from many differing social perspectives is a lament at our loss of a sense of the common good and a call for the reestablishment of communities of tradition and shared values. One of the first to articulate the modern dilemma was Daniel Bell in *The Cultural Contradictions of Capitalism*, a book Larry L. Rasmussen calls "an epiphany."[7] Bell describes a modern society of individuals, lost in an endless quest for self-gratification, driven by a constant demand for entitlements, and cut loose from any sense of self-sacrifice, self-denial, limits, or the tragic. He called this "Western society" or "bourgeois society" or culture.[8] Five years later, Alasdair MacIntyre published *After Virtue* and described the modern democratized self as an "emotivist self," who, in the name of freedom, has lost any social identity and lives amid moral fragments and chaos.[9] Then, in 1985, Robert Bellah and others published *Habits of the Heart*, a sociological study of individualism and social commitment. Their conclusion, similar in many respects to that of Bell and MacIntyre, is that "the citizen has been swallowed up in 'economic man'; that the every increasing, self-interested, consumptive appetite of American culture destroys the very ties necessary to the maintenance of community."[10] According to the book jacket, their study covered "the sweep of America's cultural history and . . . explores the ways in which *we* see ourselves" (*emphasis mine*). Actually, these authors were more restrained. They point out that their research was focused on white, middle-class Americans, a distinction often lost in the preceding and succeeding laments about "our" lack of shared values.[11]

The distinction was not lost on Larry Rasmussen in his recent work, *Moral Fragments and Moral Community*. Our modern U.S. society, he says, has become an open marketplace, one in which every aspect of human life is fashioned after the competitive, individualistic, self-interested, and instrumental relationships of a capitalist economy. He concludes: "Our society [the United States] currently lives from moral fragments and community fragments only, and both are being destroyed faster than they are being replenished."[12] Rasmussen is clear about that portion of U.S. society he is describing. Specifically, he is writing about "preponderantly middle-class white U.S. Americans heavily invested in the institutions and patterns of modernity."[13] He is writing about dominant U.S. culture. Bell's book was for Rasmussen an epiphany because Bell "was holding up to the light an X ray of white, middle-strata psyches and society."[14] In the debates about values and community now shaping secular culture, as well as Christian ethics, distinguishing the social location of race and class matters. There is a difference between the demands rising from the marginalized (the challenge of diversity) and the self-interested individualism of the dominant (the threat of fragmentation).

As the century comes to an end, the U.S. faces the question of the meaning and possibility of "community" in the midst of a fragmented and diverse secular society. Christians in the U.S. confront the question of the meaning and possibility of church "community," not only in our local parish or particular denomination, but globally, as we recognize both our diversity and our fragmentation. Today we Christians with white, middle-strata psyches live in the context of an often troubling diversity created by the emergence of once-silenced voices. We also live in the context of a morally fragmented dominant culture. The healing of that fragmentation, that is, the healing of the dominant, the healing of ourselves, must not be at the price of the silencing of that diversity. It is this diversity which reveals that the perceived unity of a simpler time, the remembered peace of traditions and shared values, was achieved at the price of justice. It is in this context of diversity and fragmentation that those of us who participate in dominant culture must reconsider the nature of our Christian communities and the task of our Christian ethics.


## THE CHALLENGE OF HISTORICAL PARTICULARITY

One result of the historical process we are experiencing is a fundamental challenge to the way European culture has, since the Enlightenment, understood such basic concepts as truth, knowledge, and power, and a challenge to its understanding of the relationship between self and community, through which truth, knowledge, and power function. In European history, the transition from a medieval world to a modern one required the dethroning of medieval sources of authority: church and king (himself divinely authorized). That transition to modernity raised its own crisis of community. If society was not to be ordered by the divine will expressed through the divinely established and hierarchical authorities of church and state, what would ensure social cohesion and stability?

The philosophers of the Enlightenment turned their trust to the optimistic pursuit of universal truths made accessible through human reason. Superstitions and prejudices, especially those of the religious mind, would be replaced with neutral, objective, and dispassionate studies by the rational mind. Truth, understood as the basic and unchanging structure of things, exposed by reason, would guide human progress. Knowledge, consisting of a direct, unmediated comprehension of these rational structures, would become the basis of authentic power. Authentic power would be gained through the acquisition of unbiased knowledge. Despite the difference in method between, for example, Jeremy Betham (utilitarianism) and Immanuel Kant (deontology), both would subscribe to the motto of the Enlightenment, *sapere aude,* that is, have the courage to use your own reason.[15]

A brief summary of the basic assumptions Western culture inherits from the Enlightenment spirit might be helpful at this point.[16] First, modern thought envisions the human self as a stable and independent entity gifted with the capacity of reason. Reason allows the self to analyze, with neutrality and objectivity, the law-driven processes of nature, of human society, and of human reason itself. With this understanding of reason, each self can be expected to detach itself from its embodied and historical particularity (emotions, needs, loyalties, ideologies, etc., as well as race, class, sex, and sexual orientation). The self can then pursue direct comprehension of the real, unchanging nature of a thing. Science, especially the "hard" sciences, and the scientific method express the epitome of this Enlightenment faith.[17] The tool used to represent each real thing is language. Language is understood as the transparent signifier of a real thing. The right use of reason, expressed in language, is the source of truth. Rightful authority is guided by knowledge grounded in truth and justified by reason. When reason guides the use of power, all will benefit. These are the theoretical assumptions which give sense to (and morally justify) the concrete realities of U.S. modern society: faith in a rational individualism, unrestrained by traditional values or loyalties, which promotes the social good through a competitive and pragmatic spirit functioning freely in an open marketplace of things and ideas.[18]

These assumptions have been profoundly challenged by the growing awareness of our historical particularity; an awareness created in large part by the cacophony of voices challenging traditional truth claims. Simply put, all fields of knowledge must now wrestle with the implications of theories exposing the "social construction of knowledge." From the work of Clifford Geertz in anthropology, to the work of Thomas Kuhn in identifying scientific paradigms, to the literary criticism of Umberto Eco and Jacques Derrida, the defense of reason as that which provides a truth which can unify human community has become increasingly difficult. In post-Enlightenment theories, the definition of knowledge has shifted from knowledge as a clear and impartial description of reality (what a thing is in itself) to knowledge as a cultural-linguistic expression of culturally devised meanings (what a thing means in a particular social location). Consequently across a number of fields—including theology, scripture studies and religious ethics—a sense of suspicion greets whatever labels itself as natural, essential, or universal.[19]

In *Theology at the End of Modernity*, editor Sheila Davaney describes the late twentieth century as a time when Christian theology must be reevaluated in light of this "radical historicist perspective."[20] Taking seriously the historical context of all human capacities, including reason, and of all human knowledge, including theology, presents a radical challenge to traditional ways of justifying Christian truth claims. On the one hand, the faith of liberal Christians in a common, God-given reason has allowed Christians to engage others in the pursuit of shared values for the maintenance of a just, secular community. It grounds the U.S. experiment in religious plurality and religious freedom. However, if there is no transcultural basis for human unity—in reason or natural law—how can Christians dialogue with others without losing what it means to be a Christian? Do we not lose uniquely Christian values when we enter into the value systems of these others in order to make dialogue possible?

On the other hand, a radical historicity also challenges the faith of literalist fundamentalists who believe that Scripture contains truths which are immediately accessible to anyone reading the text.[21] If Scripture is the text of a historically particular tradition which embodies the meaning system through which Scripture is rightly read, then Scripture loses any claim to universal accessibility. Its truth can only be fully understood by those who are a part of the community it has produced. Must Christianity be relegated, then, to the margins of the world as a sect which insists upon a truth that is not verifiable by external criteria, only affirmed by believers?

The current crisis facing theology, then, is the issue of how to account for truth, knowledge, and community in what Richard Lints calls a "postpositivistic" age. Lints suggests that the issue can be understood as the choice between two competing methodologies. Each makes a "post"-positivistic move while dragging one foot behind in modernity.[22] Lints uses the term "postliberal" to refer to those who reject the liberal claim that human reason can lead to beliefs that all right-thinking people can embrace. Therefore, postliberals also reject the liberal Christian project of finding a correlation between Christian beliefs and public meanings. For the postliberal, the Christian message is not "true" because it can speak to contemporary society's interests or explain something common to all humans. If human reason itself is shaped by the narrative of a particular community, claims to truthfulness (or reasonableness) can only be made within that narrative and can only be justified within the life of the community shaped by this narrative. To postliberals, the Christian tradition is such a narrative of stories and language and practices that creates a community that lives a life faithful to this narrative. Scripture, particularly the story of Jesus, provides the narrative that Christians live as our own.

For example, George Lindbeck calls for a "postliberal theology" that grounds itself in its particular cultural-linguistic community. Christians need to be formed by the power of the biblical text, he says. We need to renounce the temptation to be relevant in secular society at the price of losing our unique tradition.[23] In this sense, postliberals maintain a concept of nonrefutable truth (the dragging foot), but acknowledge that it is verifiable only within a particular narrative. Consequently, the emphasis of some postliberal theologians is on the formation of a Christian community faithful to the Christian narrative, despite the existence in the surrounding world of communities with diverse and conflicting identities.[24]

According to Lints, postliberals include Stanley Hauerwas, George Lindbeck, David Kelsey, and Hans Frei, although because of other differences such a grouping could be contested. I am using Lints's structure as a convenience to place Hauerwas among those who share the turn to narrative traditions as the form theology and ethics must now take in a postpositivistic era. In his recent writings Hauerwas has focused on the character of the church as that community that shapes Christian selves to live uniquely as Christians in a fragmented and violent world. What it means to be uniquely Christian is a matter of strong disagreement among postliberals (and others). Hauerwas will argue that the primary characteristic revealed by the Jesus story, around which the life of Christians must be shaped, is the nonviolent love of God. With these two emphases, narrative and pacifist, he can be compared to two other Christian ethicists: the Mennonite John Howard Yoder, by whom Hauerwas has been strongly influenced, and the Baptist James William McClendon, Jr. Yet it is probably impolite to impose labels on folk who have not claimed the label for themselves, and it is here that we see the slipperiness of all such labels. For example, Yoder refers to "my post-modern acceptance of the particularity of the Christian story without subjecting it either to the claimed objectivity of general consensus or to that of some specific 'scientific method.' "[25] By Lints's usage Yoder is postpositivistic in the "postliberal" sense. When Yoder asserts that "The church precedes the world epistemologically," asserting a unique Christian claim to truth, he exhibits the foot-dragging I mentioned above.[26] Because of this, some would argue that he is not "post" anything. McClendon also emphasizes the narrative basis of truth claims: the story "enables us to see what *we* mean by 'truth.' " And in holding out the possibility of finding a real truth that will bring divergent peoples together on the basis of the quality of life this truth exhibits, he also displays the postliberal refusal to relinquish a claim to the real truth.[27] What the three hold in common, despite differences I will note at other points, is their insistence that nonviolence is at the core of the Christian faith and their acceptance of narrative as the form which Christian truth claims must take.

The opposing "postpositivistic" methodology that Lints identifies is the "postmodern" alternative. While admitting the diversity within the ranks of those who call themselves "postmodern," Lints argues that this alternative can generally be characterized by its rejection of modernity's faith in an objective and neutral reason, while retaining the belief (foot-dragging) that some common ground can be found for the influence of Christian values within public debate. Lints includes among Christian "postmodern" theologians David Tracy, Gordon Kaufman, Edward Farley, and Sally McFague. For "postmoderns," all truth, all theology—including Scripture and the Christian stories—arises out of some historically located, and therefore limited, cultural context. It is perhaps this stress on the common condition of historical limits and finitude which allows postmoderns to sense a more porous nature to the boundaries between traditions. As Linell Cady argues, most people inhabit a diversity of traditions.[28] This keeps alive the possibility of some sort of social rationality and dialogue among diverse communities. As a self-named "postmodern," Mark Kline Taylor suggests that North American Christian theologies must respond to a "postmodern trilemma" of needs/demands that stand in tension: a rootedness in a particular tradition, a celebration of diversity, and Christian resistance to structures of domination.[29]

The challenge of historical particularity, this realization that there are no forms of human experience, no knowledges, that are not affected by the particular social and historical location of the knower, raises at least two fundamental inquiries. (1) If all human knowing is, at best, partial, are not all truth claims, including those of Christianity, suspect? Is Christian theology ideology? This is the issue of epistemology. How do we "know"? What can we "know"? What truth should claim our lives? (2) If community depends upon allegiance to shared traditions and values, what do we do about diversity? If we recognize/allow/support diversity, are we doomed to moral relativity and social chaos? And if communities of tradition and shared values are necessary for the formation of individual moral character, must we not clearly define ourselves as this and not that, or experience the social fragmentation that destroys community? This is a question of ethics. How can we live well, and truthfully, together?

## ENGAGING THE DIALOGUE

Stanley Hauerwas has made his mark in contemporary Protestant ethics by taking seriously the implications of a self formed by community. He describes his own journey as one that began in a working-class Texas Methodist family. He went from Texas to Yale, where he was influenced by Barth and Wittgenstein and learned about theology as a "tradition-determined activity" without becoming tradition-determined himself. Hauerwas spent fourteen years teaching at Notre Dame, where Roman Catholic theology nurtured his interest in an ethics of character and the kind of community necessary to sustain such an ethics. His first book, *Character and the Christian Life*, brought the Aristotelian-Thomistic tradition of virtue and character into dialogue with Protestant ethics.[30] Hauerwas identifies the work of John Howard Yoder as being the first to make him see the necessity of beginning all critical reflection from the place of being already engaged in a tradition.[31] Consequently, Hauerwas has helped to shift the focus of ethical conversation from the Enlightenment image of a rational agent at the moment of moral decision to the social process in the formation of character.

His emphasis on the importance of character for the moral life has led him to merge issues of ethics with issues of ecclesiology. As a Christian ethicist he has increasingly turned his attention to the nature of the church as that community which shapes Christian character. He charges that the church in the U.S. is held captive by its allegiance to the liberal ideals of our modern, secular culture: freedom, democracy, individualism. This current captivity to "America" is a consequence of the church's 1600-year-old seduction by Constantinianism: the desire to control history for God by gaining secular power. The result for the contemporary church, he argues, is that gospel concepts such as love, or freedom, or peace, or justice, become defined from within the liberal tradition of the U.S. rather than out of the Christian narrative. Christians have lost the uniqueness of their own story of nonviolence while trying to be relevant to those in a society that does not share this story. Hauerwas challenges the church to the political task of being the church, a resident alien in a violent world.

There are important areas of convergence between Hauerwas's ethics of character and the feminist ethics of liberation which I use (and will explain more fully in chapter 3). Our methodologies agree that humans are socially constructed; that all human knowledge is historically situated; and that the character of the communities which shape us is a central concern for doing Christian ethics. We share a critique of liberal theory with its image of the isolated, individual, rational self who freely selects this belief or that value from the marketplace of rootless ideas. We agree that there is no separation of public and private spheres; we each take seriously the public nature of "private" morality (sexuality, marriage, and procreation). And we will both find the church in the U.S. captive to unfaithful ideologies.[32]

However, despite these similarities, Hauerwas and I end up in very different places. It was this unexpected result that made me want to find out what happened. Others have engaged Hauerwas in an external criticism of his theological ethics. For example, he can be legitimately questioned with regard to his doctrine of creation, or how his theology might affect Christian relations with Jews and with other religious traditions, or whether his ethics leads to a sectarian stance that marginalizes Christianity.[33] My intention is to begin with what might be called an internal critique; that is, I want to accept the terms of his argument, at least initially, in order to disclose the concerns, values, and perspectives which give rise to these "truths."

Rather than beginning by debating "truth," I first want to reveal the social location in contemporary American culture in which such truths are at home.

I will argue that differences of experiences caused by differences of social location, particularly the difference it makes growing up as a white male rather than as a white female in a gendered and sexist church and society, lead to differing themes about the human condition. I will argue that Hauerwas, from a particular social location which he does not explore, develops a view of "the human" through which he then interprets the Christian story. His allegiance to this interpretation requires him finally to abandon the full implications that a radical historicity brings to the Christian narrative and the Christian church. Ultimately, he chooses not to see the difference that historical particularity makes within the church and its narrative(s), differences caused by race, class, ethnicity, gender, and sexual orientation. This results in two internal contradictions: (1) his narrative-based ethics becomes the new foundation for the assertion of universal truth, and (2) his commitment to nonviolence functions to justify the violence of domination. At this point, what began as an internal criticism becomes external. From different social locations, challenges can be raised to "truths" Hauerwas asserts as universal, or, at least, universally Christian.

What I will emphasize is the importance of recognizing the relationship between social power and the defining of cultural and theological meanings. I want to bring to bear in Christian ethics an analysis of the social, economic, and political power of dominant groups to name as "true" their own historically located assumptions and perspectives. I will argue that this analysis needs to be applied to any claim about Christian ethics, including my own. From the work of Paulo Freire in the politics of education to the work of Evelyn Fox Keller in the politics of science and the work of Michel Foucault in the politics of culture, the interplay in society of knowledge and power has been exposed.[34] This development has not come about simply through the practice of "better science."[35] It has come about because there has been a fundamental shift in the social location of those who are thinking about knowledge and its relationship to power. As people of color in the U.S., white women, and spokespersons from the marginalized of the two-thirds world have begun to gain access to the social positions from which what has been labeled "truth" is traditionally produced, the political dimension of "knowledge" is revealed.

Historically in the U.S., suspicion about claims to truth has arisen from those who have experienced, in concrete ways, the "rational" or "God-given" conclusions of such claims: specifically white women, African slaves and their descendants, Native Americans and Hispanic Americans. Both Bentham and Kant reasoned, for example, that (white) women are not capable, by nature, of the necessary objectivity for public responsibilities or the exercise of intellectual, legal or economic power. Since (white) women were determined to be incapable of disinterested reason, they could be "reasonably" denied access to the roles and opportunities of (white) male, adult moral agents.[36] Similarly, the liberal, white, male authors and signers of the U.S. Constitution could justify the slavery of black men and women through a theory of contract embedded in a Kantian theory of rights.[37] Katie Cannon has artfully analyzed the basis for white Christians' defense of racial slavery in the interplay of the ideology which arose from their material existence and their doing of theology.[38] The point is that history shows how the best reasoning of good people in positions of social power remains captive to preexisting and unquestioned assumptions about others.

From the experiences in the U.S. of white women and people of color, especially, something in this history of claims to the truth seems untruthful. Others might identify the problem as ignorance, or faulty reason, or unfaithfulness. I argue that the assumption that the claims of reason or of narratives can be divorced from one's contingent existence has served to mask the actual embeddedness of each of us in particular social relations, particular social loyalties, particular commitments, and a particular historical partiality.[39] Most important, what is masked is the role that social and economic power plays in the ability of dominant groups to name what will be called "knowledge" and to proclaim what will be called "reasonable" or "the Christian story." The suspicions which inform the knowledges of marginalized groups require a critical, oppositional stance toward dominant groups in all institutions and against their power to legitimate and impose their particular knowledges as "truth." These suspicions need to be brought to the task of doing Christian ethics.

In a "postpositivistic" world there is no stable place to stand. "Postmoderns" court the danger of continuing our social and ecclesial fragmentation by relativizing all truth claims and reducing "truth" to power dynamics. They must answer the question of how to sustain the communities of shared values which are essential to shaping morally competent persons and to sustaining human society. And they must define what remains of the meaning of Christi-

27

anity when it seems that all anchors have been cut loose. However, the "postliberal" move to narrative theology also has to face issues of verification and charges of sectarianism. Moreover, postliberals have not faced the implications of an equally basic issue: the distortions in all truth claims that emerge from communities structured by narratives that embody relationships of domination and subordination.

These may seem like abstract issues. They are not. On a personal level, as a white, feminist Christian in the U.S., I find the opportunities for faithful Christian community sadly limited. To the old observation that 11:00 Sunday morning is the most segregated hour of the week, we can add that it is too often sexist, class segregated, and homophobic. So, like Hauerwas, I am left with the question of the character of our communities; that is, of our white, middle- and upper-class Christian communities. What follows is, I hope, a contribution to that character.

CHAPTER 2

# THE CHARACTER OF HAUERWAS'S COMMUNITY

## A Texan Epistemology[1]

*To say that one is "from Texas" is never meant just to indicate where one happens to be born, but represents for many of us a story that has, for good or ill, determined who we are.[2]*

For Stanley Hauerwas, the key word is "determined," for there are stories we do not choose that shape us in fundamental ways. Hauerwas was born male and a Texan; thus, he was given a particular history.[3] By his own description, to have a history is to have an identity. So to say that a person was born in Texas is not simply to state a fact, but to indicate who this person is. Being a "Texan" is the particular historical condition in which this person comes to be himself in the midst of a particular people. Becoming himself in Texas means, for Hauerwas, coming to know himself as part of his people, of their past and present generations. These are a people who understood the world in particular ways and, therefore, behaved in the world according to the wisdom and skills of "Texans." It means learning what it is to be human according to this story, this narrative account, which, to quote Hauerwas, "provide[s] an intelligible pattern that links the contingent events of our lives."[4] In doing so, it sets a direction out of which a person lives into the future, continuing to shape his or her self with these particular skills. Equally important, it is from this formative story that a person also gives shape to their world through the actions she or he chooses to take in accordance with the description of the world this story provides.

Hauerwas points out that there is not one story of Texas, or of what it means to be a Texan, but at least four: the official story of Texas, the story of Hauerwas's family in Texas, Hauerwas's story of being a Texan, and Hauerwas's story of being a Texan who no longer lives in Texas.[5] Yet he finds a continuity among these stories. The continuity is not found at the level of historical fact, but at the level of understanding what it means to be a Texan. The importance of these stories is not in their historical accuracy, but in the value a Texan gives to these stories as they provide the context for self-identity. Thus, Hauerwas appeals to William Humphrey's novel *The Ordways*, which is the fictional account of a family that moved to Texas.[6] Appropriating this story, Hauerwas expresses his own sense of continuity with being a Texan, a continuity that exists despite the passing of time and the changes that occur. It is a continuity that keeps him rooted with his ancestors. It is a continuity that keeps the past alive in understanding the present. The lament "We are not the men our fathers were" tells a male Texan what is being lost to change, what to resist, where to cling.[7] The past, with all of its stories, becomes a collection of "proverbs and prophecies, legends, laws, traditions of the origins and tales of the wanderings of his own tribe" passed down from father to son.[8]

From his own family history in Texas, Hauerwas remembers with pride his father's participation in one of the last cattle drives, his mother's hard work in escaping from the effects of being raised in a poor white family. He treasures the knowledge from his father's and grandfather's experiences that independence and pride are the gifts of hard work. He acknowledges the impact of the experience of prejudice, fear, and hate which is also a part of the story of being a Texan. Yet, the story of being a Texan provides him with clarifying boundaries between his people and others, a positive experience of being different. He experiences a story that is unique, valuable, and irreplaceable. He is a (white, male) Texan.[9]

However, experiences such as Hauerwas's do not exist as an unmediated source of knowledge. The recounting of one's experience is not a recitation of uninterpreted reality. Instead, a person's description of her or his experience is particularly important because it reveals what Paulo Freire calls the "themes" within which that person understands their world and gives intention to their actions. Themes, says Freire, are characterized by "a complex of ideas, concepts, hopes, doubts, values, and challenges in dialectical interaction with their opposites, striving toward plentitude" and "the concrete representation of many of these ideas, values, concepts, and hopes, as well as the obstacles." These themes, by their very existence, imply their opposite and indicate actions to be taken.[10]

Hauerwas's description of being a Texan will reveal to us the themes within which he has come to understand his world and his Christian faith. Thus, for example, we will see how this experience of being shaped (for better or worse) by a unified, empowering, cultural narrative becomes for him both a paradigm for the task of Christian ethics and the basis of his critique of American society and the Christian church. From the experience of his own social formation as a Texan, he has developed what he calls his "Texan epistemology":

> Because I was raised Texan—which is like being southern, only better—I knew I was never free to be "modern" and "self-creating." I would always be, for better or worse, Texan. It was my first lesson in particularity; as some would put it, being Texan made me realize early that the foundationalist epistemologies of the Enlightenment had to be wrong. . . . I prefer simply to have a Texan epistemology.[11]

From his description of being raised Texan and his adoption of a Texan epistemology, Hauerwas moves to a series of important assumptions for ethics. He will describe human subjectivity, the relationship between individuals and society, and the narrative nature of knowledge. The result, I will argue, is the reassertion of a theory of essential human nature which serves to tie all of his assumptions together.

However, as Hauerwas himself would admit, it is not that his ethics represents a more objective reading of reality. He would agree, I think, with Lee Cormie that an interdependent relationship exists between experience and theory:

> Social theories, whatever else they are, are also attempts by concrete individuals to make sense of their own experiences, beliefs, feelings, hopes. Each social scientific perspective is, then, both a logic and a morality, and is adhered to in part because it resonates with the theorist's own experiences and vision of the world.[12]

Similarly, every ethical theory is founded upon the ethicist's understanding of what can or cannot be said about humans and human community. Whatever the origin claimed for our theories, whether they are said to be derived from revelation, or natural law, or the narrative of a community, these are understandings that have taken shape in the interaction between the ethicist, with the particularities of her/his life, and the interpretive discourses available to him or her.[13] Often these basic assumptions about humans and human society remain mostly implicit. Yet, they are themselves of great ethical significance. It is from these views of what is humanly and socially possible that one's ethical system and arguments will emerge. And in acting upon them, a person creates, or attempts to create, the world which they imply. Presented as *descriptive*, as the way things are, they are in fact *prescriptive*, the way this person thinks things should be.

Hauerwas presents an account of how he was shaped as a Texan, with all the lessons and limitations of that particular story. His description reveals the themes through which he sees his world and interprets the Christian narrative: that is, he has adopted out of this particular historical location a complex of interwoven ideas, concepts, values, hopes, interpretations, and concerns in interaction with similar and opposing views operative in American culture and in contemporary Christian theology. What follows is my account of Hauerwas's theological ethics and the themes it presents. I will describe Hauerwas's understanding of the human condition and of human society in order to disclose what he identifies as the potential and the problem of human existence. I will describe how his definition of the problem leads him to his particular interpretation of the Christian narrative and to the assumptions that shape his ethics of character. And I will also show that his themes are not unlike those through which some contemporary secular theorists have attempted to understand human experience and the intentions of human actions in the context of the modern Western world.

Despite my attempt to follow Hauerwas's phrases closely, this is, of course, *my* reading of Hauerwas. My reading of Hauerwas arises out of my experience as a middle-class, educated, white, heterosexual woman living in the United States. It arises out of my experience as a clergywoman. And it arises from my commitments as a Christian feminist. I bring to Hauerwas's texts my experience of the issues and concerns that shape the lives of women like me in the church today. I cannot proclaim this to be a "true" reading of the texts. I do claim that it is an authentic interpretation of the way these texts could function in the formation of such women.

## THE HUMAN CONDITION

### The Tower of Babel

The story of the Tower of Babel (Genesis 11:1-9) serves Hauerwas as a paradigm for the universal human condition.[14] According to this myth, humans enjoyed an original position of social unity, in which all people of the earth had one language, sharing the same words. In this unity, the power of human cooperation was great. Nonetheless, as interpreted by Hauerwas, this unified people feared that their existence might be lost to the memory of future generations. Unable to face their own finitude, they desired to make a lasting name for themselves. The memorial they chose was a tower whose top would reach to the sky. Fearing that the success of this cooperative effort would lead them to believe that nothing would be impossible for them, God responded by confusing their languages and scattering them into separate peoples unable to understand one another. It was God's plan, according to Hauerwas, that by seeing the "otherness" of those different from themselves, each would see their own crea- tureliness, their own finitude, and learn that their existence was a God-given gift. Unfortunately, God miscalculated.

Although the biblical account does not draw this conclusion, it is Hauerwas's contention that "at Babel war was born."[15] Murder began with Cain and Abel. However, with the creation of the Other group, "fear of the other became the overriding passion" which causes groups to attempt to force their own ways upon others.[16] Human history has thus become a history of violence, as each group attempts to absorb or destroy the other in order to avoid facing the reality of its own limitedness. There is, according to Hauerwas, an "inherent necessity of all people to have or create an enemy."[17] All human relations are characterized by fear, distrust, and violence. We are, Hauerwas argues, more governed "by our hates and dislikes than by our loves." Wrongs done to us give us "a history of resentments that, in fact, constitute who I am. How would I know who I am if I did not have my enemies?"[18] The very existence of the other gives rise to fear and violence. "I know myself to be filled with violence," writes Hauerwas.[19] Ultimately, the story of Texas, or of any other group, provides an inadequate response to this violence; instead, it partici- pates in it.

Using arguments from Rousseau, as interpreted by Kenneth Waltz in *Man, the State and War: A Theoretical Analysis,* Hauerwas identifies coercion and war as arising from the very nature of human coopera- tion.[20] As people gather together, each must forgo his or her immedi- ate interests for the longer-term interests of the whole group; each must trust that others will do the same. Since this cannot simply be assumed, the acceptance of the possibility of the need for coercion, on behalf of the common good, is intrinsic to the purposes of human cooperation. Furthermore, when unity and cooperation among a people take the form of the political state, the particular history, goods, interests, and purposes of that state form one will in relation to other existing states. Thus, conflict between states does not necessarily arise from selfishness. According to Hauerwas, international conflict most often is experienced as arising from "our moral commitment to the good of others" with whom we share a history.[21] War arises, then, in defense of the common good for which our people have worked, fought, and even died. War becomes possible because we value our common life together, our common moralities, our past sacrifices, and our history. If we are Texans, we remember the Alamo. "All of which reminds us that our violence lies not in ourselves but in our loves."[22] Thus, Hauerwas concludes, "if we seek cooperation we must accept the possibility of war."[23] Human sociality, a necessity of human existence, is necessarily marred by coercion and violence.

Finally, according to Hauerwas, fear and violence are not limited only to relationships between groups of people or to the public interactions between members of the same group. Even intimate relations between persons offer no haven from a world of violence. "[W]e all know that we never lie more readily than we do to those who are the closest to us."[24] Put most succinctly: "to be human is to fear the other—the other color, the other language, the other culture, and, most deeply, the other sex."[25] It seems that, according to Hauerwas, all human relations are distorted by a fear of the differing other; a fear rooted in every human's fear of their own finitude.[26] This anxiety grounds our inherent violence, the violence that characterizes human history, the violence embedded in each human soul. From Hauerwas's description of the human condition, violence must be the primary issue for any Christian social ethic.[27]

Yet, Hauerwas also writes: "we know that we are not by nature violent people."[28] What is unclear, then, in Hauerwas's account is exactly what he means by an "inherent necessity" to have or create enemies; or that "to be human" is to fear the other; or "as the ties of cooperation are strong so is the possibility of conflict."[29] Is Hauerwas suggesting an aspect of the human which exists prior to all socialization? For example, Frederick Hartmann argues that fear and antagonism toward the "other" is rooted in a constitutive, psychological aspect of the human which causes all humans to divide into groups.[30] Is Hauerwas following the thought of those such as Freud and Lacan who see each individual human as invariably motivated by impulses and needs which are essentially antisocial? His use of Waltz's account of Rousseau might seem to imply such an understanding of a universally distorting impact of a biologically based, or psychologically based, individual self-interest upon all attempts at social organization. The correlative is that social groups necessarily function to curtail individual self-interest and are always experienced by individuals as restricting individual freedom on behalf of a greater good.

On the other hand, his thinking may be akin to that of sociologist Peter Berger. In Berger's account, the fact that humans enter the world unshaped and unguided by instincts lays the background for the greatest human fear, meaninglessness. Meaninglessness (anomy) is the threat which terrifies humans whenever an individual is separated from the social world she or he has internalized. According to Berger, "anomy is unbearable to the point where the individual may seek death in preference to it. Conversely, existence within a nomic world may be sought at the cost of all sorts of sacrifice and suffering—and even at the cost of life itself."[31] For Berger, it is at the "margins" that individuals approach the boundaries of the social order that gives them their place in the world. In a listing of such marginal situations, Berger includes those which "appear on the horizon of consciousness as haunting suspicions that the world may have another aspect than its 'normal' one, that is, that the previously accepted definition of reality may be fragile or even fraudulent."[32] Thus, the self at the margins finds itself facing its own fundamental emptiness and lack of form, that "dark ominous jungle" that Berger finds residing within the self.[33] The terror this looming, internal chaos incites is held at bay by giving one's own social order the status of a natural, ontological necessity, that is, reality; or of a divine mandate, Berger's "sacred canopy."

Hauerwas's theory of the human fear of finitude exhibits similarities with Berger's analysis of the human condition. We have seen that Hauerwas presents his experience of being a male Texan as an experience of receiving a unified and empowering sense of identity with a particular people. However, he also points out that such identities have fatal limits. Specifically, all such human identities require loyalties which are incapable of accounting for the tragedies that result from the human failures, cruelties, and injustices within their histories.[34] Rather than face these limits, such stories become ideologies that deny these sins. The human social context, therefore, is a babel of competing ideologies or stories, each attempting to avoid the reality of its own limitations and failures. When faced with an "other," people must protect the story that is their own identity. According to Hauerwas, they turn to violence and force to do so.[35] So, too, with Berger: it is the "other" who raises a suspicion that "the world may have another aspect than the 'normal' one."[36] According to both Berger and Hauerwas, this threat is so intolerable that humans must defend their self-understanding and worldview with violence. The other must be assimilated or annihilated: "better to die than to let the other exist."[37]

What is clear from this analysis is that human sociality itself is problematic for Hauerwas. He perceives all human relations as distorted by defensive self-interest. Being in relationship, a necessity for human life, is, at the same time, the source of human conflict, coercion, and violence. As I will show in the following chapters, women's experiences of human connectedness, of differences, and of violence provide a radical challenge to Hauerwas's assertions.

## Modern Babel

How, asks Hauerwas, did one Christian nation give rise to the Nazi Holocaust? Why did another drop atomic bombs on Nagasaki and Hiroshima? Why, he asks, are there nearly two million abortions each year in the United States? Why does a rich nation like the United States accept as necessary the poverty that abounds within it? Enormously important moral issues are not unique in any way to this age, but in raising these questions, Hauerwas asserts that American culture has entered a dark age of moral incommensurability.[38] People experience themselves in a world that is morally chaotic. We drift among fragments of past moralities with no means to resolve the chaos. Moreover, we live with a deep suspicion that there really are no firm grounds upon which to base our moral beliefs. Confronted with chaos, people in the U.S. respond to the threat of moral uncertainty (anomy) with a dogmatism that refuses to look at itself carefully and that turns too quickly to the violence of coercion in order to secure, amid this chaos, a peace that is no peace.[39] According to Hauerwas, a fragmented world becomes a violent world.[40] In this modern and violent world, there is no way to resolve the disunity in ourselves or in our society.[41]

From this description of modern American society, Hauerwas locates the root of the problem of our violent fragmentation in the moral contradiction upon which American society is based: the moral contradiction found within liberal political theory. Since Hauerwas's critique of liberal theory arises out of his theory of human subjectivity, I will turn first to that.

*A Theory of Human Subjectivity*

In 1975, Hauerwas published his first book, *Character and the Christian Life*. At that point, his concern was twofold: (1) to analyze the relationship between an agent and his or her action in order to challenge the emphasis on decision making, or quandaries, in Christian ethical thinking; and (2) to explicate the importance of individual character and the virtues in the development of moral life.[42] By his own admission, this early description of the self as agent was still indebted to the liberal assumption of an essential self which lies behind its character: an independent self capable of choosing the descriptions that would give intentionality to its actions. Self-determination, as the freedom to choose among many possibilities, was defended in this first book as essential in the development of character. For example: "Man's choices consist in limiting an indeterminate range of possibilities by ordering them in accordance with his intentions. To be free is to set a course through the multitude of possibilities that confront us and so impose order on the world and ourselves."[43] The character of this free agent would be formed through the repetition of actions which would result in the formation of habits, called virtues.[44]

Subsequently, under the influence of the work of Alasdair MacIntyre, Hauerwas began to reflect on the significance of the concept of intelligible action; that is, that the intelligibility of an action depends upon the existence of a community and its shared language that gives meaning to one's experiences and one's responses. In sharing a language, speakers share a view of the world expressed in language that is a symbolic representation of that world.[45] Thus, it is only by being within a community that human actions can take on meaning. Hauerwas states: "to be an agent means I am able to locate my action within an ongoing history and within a community of language users."[46] The very act of learning to speak initiates the individual into the habits, practices, and history of her or his community.

In moving away from an Enlightenment (modern) view of an essential self existing behind one's historical contingencies, Hauerwas now claims to posit a fully historical self. "It is our nature to be historic beings."[47] "The only way to be human is to be habitual—which is to say, historical."[48] In this usage, "historical" has two meanings. First, it means that humans are determined by biology, biography, accidents of birth, the context of the time and place in which we live, and by our past. "We are what we have been made to be."[49] Second, it means that human beings are intentional beings; that human actions become intelligible only as they are set within personal and communal narrative histories, a context of what was before and what is to come. Human action is intentional because it "makes sense." It "makes sense" because it is set within a narrative "that is sufficient to give me a sense of self, one which looks not only to my past but points to the future, thereby giving my life a telos and direction."[50] Self-consciousness is itself a product of participation in community.[51] It is worth quoting Hauerwas at length on this point:

> The self is fundamentally a social self. We are not individuals who come into contact with others and then decide our various levels of social involvement. We are not "I's" who decide to identify with certain "we's"; we are first of all "we's" who discover our "I's" through learning to recognize the others as similar and different from ourselves. Our individuality is possible only because we are first of all social beings. After all, the "self" names not a thing, but a relation. I know who I am only in relation to others, and, indeed, who I am is a relation with others.[52]

As Richard Bondi notes, Hauerwas has shifted his emphasis from the self-as-agent to the self-as-story.[53]

At the same time, Hauerwas has made a correlative shift in his emphasis on, and understanding of, community. In 1975, community served as the source of the public language that was necessary for making an act intelligible to the agent and to others.[54] It also served as the source of symbols, practices, and descriptions from which an agent could choose. The existence of this variety in any society provided the multitude of possible choices that resulted in a variety of characters within the same society. Hauerwas suggested only that an intentional community might create some boundaries by "suggesting the fundamental symbols that should give each man's character its primary orientation."[55]

Since 1975, in the shift from self-as-agent to self-as-story, in the assertion that "all existence, and in particular the human self, is narratively formed,"[56] community and its narrative have become central to Hauerwas's ethics of character. As we have seen above, this means that the construction of individual self-consciousness is dependent upon the individual's participation in the narrative of a community. Consequently, every aspect of human intelligence, every way of knowing, is dependent upon the process of internalization. Human reason cannot be freed from its embeddedness in particular communities and their descriptions of reality. Any attempt to isolate human reason from an agent's particularly situated interests, by, for example, "stepping back" to a nonhistoric position, obscures this essential human reality. Consequently, ethical reasoning can never be freed from particular narrative discourses.[57] The way humans describe situations depends upon understandings, analogies, convictions, and descriptions developed through their community's tradition. For example, in his discussion of abortion, Hauerwas denies that the issue is about what the fetus is "in fact." Rather, the issue is how one's imagination has been morally trained to see the fetus.[58] Similarly, feminist ethicist Beverly Harrison writes: "We stress that our knowledge itself is grounded in our agency or activity. We 'see' the world through the interests embedded in our action."[59]

The point is that there can be no tradition-free account of facts or reason.[60] There is no narrative-free way to "see" the world. For Hauerwas, this does not negate the importance of giving reasons for one's actions (the practice of casuistry). But it shifts attention again to the community in which such reasons are formed and given; to which such reasons are intelligible; and in which such reasons are acceptable.[61]

As an example of the way in which a community's language allows persons to see and describe their world, and to take actions appropriate to that description, Hauerwas describes the Nuer tribe in Africa.[62] According to Hauerwas, in Nuer traditions, any child born deformed or retarded is not "seen" as a Nuer. Linguistically, it is named and "seen" as a "hippopotamus." Consequently, believing that each type of creature is cared for best by its own kind, the Nuers place such children in the river to be cared for by the hippopotami. Hauerwas uses this story to illustrate how we learn to see the world through the language, habits, and feelings we have been taught in community. For Hauerwas, however, the point cannot be that all views are relative. Ultimately, the point is to recognize the importance of a "truthful" narrative and the community which embodies it. Situations and responses exist, or not, dependent upon our ability to see (create) them. It is the stories that comprise a community's living tradition that tell people the way things are, that underlie their principles, values, and prohibitions.[63] Without a singular, meaning-giving narrative, people become adrift in events without the power to place such events in a meaningful context. Such is the problem of U.S. society. But, without a truthful narrative, people remain captive to the violence inherent within humans and human society.[64]

*A Critique of Liberal Theory*

Such a situation is, according to Hauerwas, the context in which modern liberal society struggles. Originally, the project of the Enlightenment was a well-intentioned attempt to find a way to avoid the continuation of a history of conflict and violence based on particular religious loyalties. There was a need to find a way to develop moral norms for society that were not grounded in the uniqueness of any historically contingent community.[65] The response was the turn, in liberal political theory, to the priority of the individual: a self who is assumed to exist prior to his or her insertion into society. Thus, the private needs of the individual are the "only possible source of public authority" since individuals are "vested with a right to act according to self-defined standards of conscience and interest."[66] Therefore, the role of government in liberal political theory is limited to "the preservation of order through the management of conflict between such individuals."[67] This liberal theory of the self assumed that the relativism, subjectivity, and particularity that divide people could be avoided in public life by reference to the objective reason of a nonhistoric, noncontingent, human nature.

The social requirements for these assumptions were the separation of private life from public life and the separation of values from facts. In a pluralistic society, religion and values, as aspects of one's personal views, were placed in the private sphere. Social ethics would be based on "facts"; that is, that knowledge which all rational people can obtain and those subsequent conclusions upon which all rational people would agree. Objectivity then becomes a function of separating oneself from one's particular views so that one can see the "facts."[68] Thus, liberal political theory could assume that there is a human reason qua reason, a justice qua justice. It assumes that it is "always possible to communicate with another linguistic community"; it assumes "that we are able to understand everything from human culture and history no matter how alien."[69] It assumes that education can overcome miscommunication or perceived differences. Most profoundly, it assumes that a diverse people with no shared traditions can create a pluralistic society in which communication, understanding, and agreement are possible because under all our diversity we are somehow all the same.[70]

The effect of liberal political theory upon modern life, according to Hauerwas, is our present age of moral chaos. Without a true description of human subjectivity, liberal theory assumes, wrongly, that community can be created among strangers who have no common histories and who distrust one another; that a public can be composed of individuals in pursuit of their own self-interest. It assumes that a social order can be based upon a system of procedural rules that will guide and mediate the relationships of people who have no shared sense of the good. The liberal search for a common human "nature" renders irrelevant that which, in fact, creates human reason, facts, and reality: namely, the particular histories, traditions, feelings, and religious beliefs of a people. In denying the historical and communal specificity of human values, liberalism substitutes self-interest as the only possible motivation for human action. Society is to offer no help in evaluating the worth of such proclaimed needs, but is to provide the freedom for individuals to choose whatever they want. Thus, says Hauerwas, in liberal society all moral claims must be met with cynicism as people search for the self-interest behind them and resist surrendering themselves to any particular loyalty.[71] Freedom, understood as freedom from restraint upon individuals and their choices, becomes an end in itself, the center of moral life.

Consequently, according to Hauerwas, we are "condemned to freedom." We are confronted with too many versions of virtue and we have no means for choosing among them. Within this fragmented world, there is no way to resolve the disunity in the self or the disunity in society.[72] We live "always on the edge of violence" as we hunger for a peace and a unity which, inaccessible through public moral discussion, seems possible only through coercion.[73] "The problem with our society," says Hauerwas, "is not that democracy has not worked, but that it has, and the results are less than good."[74] Along with Peter Berger and Daniel Bell, Hauerwas locates the problem of American society in this social contradiction.[75] An emphasis on individual freedom, grounded in a belief that all individuals participate in an ahistorical human capacity for reason, has resulted in the destruction of the social bonds which require shared cultural meanings and shared values.[76]

Furthermore, this mistaken emphasis on the dignity and equality of everyone (the common man) serves to destroy the real differences in people's social roles and their contributions to community. Such differences are the basis for any concept of honor as that virtue which gives us constancy in the face of threats. A concept of honor is critical to an ethics of character. Thus, in the destruction of shared, communal values, and in the destruction of any sense of honor sustaining our commitment to such values, individuals are thrown back into their unformed emptiness and unconstrained needs. Hauerwas quotes George Will:

> Politics should be citizens expressing themselves as a people, a community of shared values, rather than as merely a collection of competing private interests inhabiting the same country. Instead, politics has become a facet of the disease for which it could be part of the cure. The disease is an anarchy of self-interestedness, and unwillingness, perhaps by now an inability, to think of the public interest, the common good.[77]

The inability of the American government to develop comprehensive polities in energy or economics or health care, for example, is the result of every public issue being seen as an arena of competing interests. Modern public policies require a coalition of interests, usually justified in terms of meeting the needs of most, but, according to Hauerwas, more often meeting the needs primarily of the powerful. Hauerwas concludes: "Liberalism thus becomes a self-fulfilling prophecy; a social order that is designed to work on the presumption that people are self-interested tends to produce that kind of people."[78]

The paradoxical result is that government becomes more intrusive through its expanding bureaucracies, a result not solely of the complexity of modern industrialized society, but of its individualism.[79] In liberal society, Hauerwas argues, bureaucracies are necessary as a means of social control. Bureaucracies produce and act upon the "value-free" data that become the "facts" that shape the public world. The authority of bureaucratic experts is assured by the distinction made between values (subjective and personal) and facts (objective and public). Thus, in defense of individual freedom, liberal society creates the modern state which is "more intrusive than the most absolute monarch" as it is called upon to be the guarantor of each person's pursuit of happiness.[80] Without a community of shared beliefs, liberal society is actually a threat to liberty. Either government must act without social consensus or it creates crises that stimulate a false assent.[81] Finally, the price of citizenship in this modern order is the requirement of military service. The state, and particularly the liberal, democratic state, has become the god for which citizens, as citizens, are asked both to die and to kill.[82]

# THE HEALING OF BABEL

## Empowering Community

As an ethicist, Hauerwas argues that what is needed is an ethics that can account for moral agency. What is needed is an account by which people can learn to claim their actions as being truly their own, products of their own self-identity. From the perspective of a Texan epistemology, this self-possession is possible only through a community which can sustain for us a narrative which gives an account of the purposes for which we and the community are to live. In such a narrative, the skills or virtues necessary for being that sort of people are practiced and passed on. We, who are so fully historical in nature, are given our selves by the community and the story it embodies.[83] Through "living into" this narrative, through the practicing of these particular skills, we develop the character which sustains our personal identity and integrity. We become a history which we can claim as our own and from which we have the power to resist what others would impose upon us. More important, we have the power to choose actions which are consistent with who we are. In this way, we are empowered to participate in the naming and shaping of our world.[84]

Thus, for Hauerwas, the healing of our modern Babel lies in an empowering community. An empowering community gives us a past, an ongoing history, and a language within which we can locate, describe, understand, and intend our actions. The power of the moral agent in such a community is the power to describe what we see—a social skill learned within the narrative of the community in which we find ourselves.[85] Freedom is the "second nature" one develops from dependence upon the habits acquired as one embodies the skills of the narrative carried by one's community. It is the purposeful power of the character we develop in the habitual practice of these skills or virtues that grants us freedom.[86] "From the perspective of an ethic of virtue, therefore, freedom is more like having power than having a choice. . . . For the virtuous person, being free does not imply a choice but the ability to claim that what was or was not done was one's own."[87]

What is needed, then, is a community that will tell its young that they do not yet have minds worth making up. In this community the first object of education is to make students think like the community. It is training that "involves the formation of the self through submission to authority that will, if done well, provide people with the virtues necessary to be able to make a reasoned judgment."[88] Hauerwas argues: "To encourage students to think for themselves is therefore a sure way to avoid any meaningful disagreement. That is the reason that I tell my students that my first object is to help them think just like me."[89] Thus, learning to be a moral agent will require apprenticeship to a master; it requires daily practice in imitation of the master. It requires immersion into the skills and history and language of the community which sustains these skills. It requires the transformation not only of what we know, but of what we think we need to know.[90]

## The One Truthful Story

But an empowering community is not sufficient. We are still lost in a world that is fragmented and violent. "We are," says Hauerwas, "caught in a web of warring communities."[91] Amid this violence there is only one source of healing. Amid the fragmentation of ideologies there is only one source of unity: a truthful story which can face the limits and failures that are a part of human life without resorting to violence. Freedom itself depends upon the truthfulness of the narrative. Only through a truthful narrative is one given the skills to live with integrity and consistency through the diversity of life's experiences and the limits of our historically particular traditions.[92] As a Christian ethicist, Hauerwas finds this truthful story in the story of Israel and of Jesus; stories which witness to the nonviolent love of God who creates and redeems all people. "If you want to be for peace—and most will not—you will need the God Christians worship."[93]

According to Hauerwas, after Babel God chose not to relate to humankind as united. Rather, God called Abraham out of his particular tribe and made a covenant with him in order to create a people who, through their living, would witness to the nonviolent love and forgiveness of God for all creation.[94] Nonviolence is "the way of God with the world."[95] Nonviolence is not chosen because it is an effective strategy, nor is it merely one value among others drawn from Scripture. It is at the very heart of the Christian understanding of God. To the extent that Israel did not try to take history into its own hands by trying to bring about the promises of God through its own power, Israel faithfully carried God's story.[96]

However, "the resurrection of Jesus is the absolute center of history."[97] The nonviolent kingdom of God became present in the life of Jesus manifesting the power of God to create a people capable of living peaceably in this violent world.[98] In Jesus' death, his "ultimate dis-possession," and in his resurrection, God has already conquered the coercive forces of the world and makes available to all the power to live peaceably through the power of God's love and forgiveness.[99] In accepting God's forgiveness, people confront and accept our own powerlessness; we learn to give up the need to control our lives. A forgiven people welcome strangers, love enemies, and risk life without securities because we know that history is God's story. We know that God has already determined the end of history, that evil is already under the rule of God, and that the peaceable kingdom is already present.[100] Love for this God is the source of our capacity for a nonviolent acceptance of the other. By accepting God's forgiveness and love, there is no need to fear the other.[101] Hauerwas concludes: "the non-resistant character of Christian community, which is often sadly absent, is a crucial mark of the power of the Christian story to form a people in a manner appropriate to the character of God's providential rule of the world."[102]

At Pentecost such a people were created. In a multitude of languages, Jews of the Diaspora heard the story of Jesus and were united in a common understanding. Babel began to be healed as God created a people capable of living nonviolently in a violent world. This people bear within their living the true story which the world cannot know without them, and which the world must know for its salvation:

> God in Jesus has defeated the powers so that as disciples we can confidently live as a cruciform community in a world that has chosen not to be ruled by such love. . . . If we say, outside the church there is no salvation, we make a claim about the very nature of salvation—namely that salvation is God's work to restore all creation to the Lordship of Christ. Such a salvation is about the defeat of powers that presume to rule outside God's providential care. Such salvation is not meant to confirm what we already know and/or experience. It is meant to make us part of a story that could not be known apart from exemplification in the lives of people in a concrete community.[103]

Thus, for Hauerwas, a faithful Christian church is an ontological necessity. Its very existence is necessary as proof of the truthfulness of God's story as manifested in the life of Jesus. As worshiping community, it is evidence of the presence of God's kingdom in the world.[104] Its existence is necessary as the medium through which salvation is offered to the world. "The Christian faith recognizes that we are violent, fearful, frightened creatures who cannot reason or will our way out of our mortality."[105] Thus, without the church, the world has no alternative to its violence; it has no narrative, it has no history.[106]

## AFTER CHRISTENDOM: THE CHURCH AS RESIDENT ALIEN

As Hauerwas contemplates the church in modernity, he argues that theology cannot be done "as if our social and political considerations are an afterthought"; rather, "our understanding of salvation is shaped by the social status of the church."[107] For Hauerwas, this social status is symbolized by the event that occurred on a Sunday evening in 1963, in Greenville, South Carolina: the Fox Theater, in defiance of the state's blue laws, opened on Sunday for the first time.[108] No more can Christians assume that American values will be incorporated into an accommodating Christian frame of influence. Rather than attempting to transform culture and (instead) being transformed by culture, Christians must now become a part of an alien people who make a difference because "they see something that cannot otherwise be seen without Christ" and they "use the language of faith to describe the world right."[109] But to do so, Christians must give up any presumption of or desire for Constantinian power.

While Hauerwas would not accept the argument that religion is necessary to sustain social cohesion, his view of the church's options at this point in history is similar to that of Peter Berger. According to Berger, in the modern world of industrial capitalism, the economy was the first area of society to be liberated from religious influence. Subsequently, this process of secularization has expanded into other areas of society, including the state. The result of secularization is that religion "cannot any longer fulfill the classical task of religion, that of constructing a common world within which all of social life receives ultimate meaning binding on everybody."[110] The problem for religion, then, is how to continue in a culture that no longer simply accepts religious definitions of reality as true.

Berger sets out two alternatives. (1) Religion can accommodate itself to culture in order to be relevant and to market itself. The danger of this strategy is that the church begins to look more and more like any other social institution. On the other hand, (2) religion can resist the modern world. The project here is to create "a viable plausibility structure for reality-definitions that are not confirmed by the larger society."[111] Berger associates the latter with Karl Barth and the development of neoorthodoxy. Neoorthodoxy, according to Berger, has two necessary traits: (1) the assertion of the "objectivity" of the tradition, an objectivity that is basically independent of current social attitudes or of discoveries in historical scholarship, and (2) an emphasis on the essential corporate nature of the tradition, the church.[112] According to Berger, the necessity of the latter follows from the insistence on the former: "Put crudely, if one is to believe what neo-orthodoxy wants one to believe, in the contemporary situation, then one must be rather careful to huddle closely and continuously with one's fellow believers."[113]

Hauerwas accuses the modern church of the first alternative: accommodation, of losing its very self in its misguided effort to be effective in liberal society. As Christians attempt to participate in this society's public moral discourse, he argues, they are required to take on the liberal assumptions upon which it is based. Thus, Christians lose the resources inherent in being a Christian that would allow them to evaluate and to resist the secular world.[114] Christians in this age are unable to resist the questions identified and the answers given by the secular world. We have lost even the knowledge that there are things worth resisting.[115] According to Hauerwas, Christians no longer know how to describe the family, what it should be, and how it is "our most basic moral institution." Christians no longer know why anyone should have children.[116] Christians are unsure of what to say about sexual ethics; they do not know how to explain why we choose to live by some standards and not others.[117] Christians do not know how to think about euthanasia or suicide.[118]

For a corrective response, Hauerwas turned, in *Against the Nations*, to the intratextual method of George Lindbeck.[119] Lindbeck argues that each religion is a product of a unique cultural-linguistic community. He denies that there is a universal human religious experience that is being variously described by the different religious traditions. Rather, religious experiences themselves are essentially different because people are themselves specifically and uniquely constituted by their particular communities. Thus, Hauerwas states, "by our becoming members of a particular community, formed by Christian convictions, an experience not otherwise available is made possible."[120] The consequence of this is that different religions are fundamentally different, producing fundamentally different accounts of what it means to be human. In order to be a Christian, one's experience of the world must be interpreted through the unique vision of

Christianity. Specifically, according to Lindbeck's intratextual method, reality is redescribed according to the definitions provided by Scripture. "It is the text, so to speak, which absorbs the world, rather than the world the text."[121] Thus, religions can only be understood from the inside. Within the religious cultural-linguistic community, one learns the practices called rationality and imagination. Rationality and imagination, for Christians, are formed by the practices required by the gospel; that is, the reason and imagination of Christians are the products of living according to the convictions of Christian faith. To allow oneself to be determined by any other authorities, according to Hauerwas, is to lose the ability to see the world accurately.[122]

In his more recent book *Unleashing the Scripture*, Hauerwas turns to the work of Stanley Fish in literary criticism.[123] According to Fish, authority is not the authority of the text itself because there is no "real meaning" in the text. Hauerwas thus faults both "literalist fundamentalism" and "biblical criticism" for the assumption that the text has an objective meaning which can be discovered either by an objective reader or by an objective biblical scholar. A "text" appears only within an interpretive act. Therefore, all readings are done within interpretative strategies that arise from the community of which the reader is a part. Again, the emphasis shifts from the individual reader (and writer) to the community that has shaped the way the reader will read. I believe this more recent move distances Hauerwas somewhat from Yoder and McClendon. For example, Yoder writes:

> There have always been radio waves bringing messages to us from distant stars. Only the development of radio technology has empowered us to receive those signals. The Bible was always a liberation storybook: now we are ready to read it that way. Tomorrow some other question will provoke another "reaching back" for yet another level of meaning that was always there.[124]

However, by shifting the focus from the truth in Scripture to the truthfulness of the interpretive community, Hauerwas is making the point that the reading of Scripture, whether by fundamentalists or by biblical critics, is a political act "involving questions of power and authority."[125] Reading Scripture correctly is no more a question of being objective than is right reason. Therefore, not "everyone" should read Scripture. Because it is the church which creates the meaning of Scripture, only those who have subjected themselves to the discipline of the church and to the exercise of living as God's people should have access to Scripture.[126] It is the church that has the authority to create the meaning of Scripture in response to current challenges through a renarration of the text that Hauerwas calls allegory. The purpose is not a search for the right meaning in the text but for guidance in right living now for us as Christians. The interpretation of Scripture, indeed, the rich, saving vitality of Scripture, appears only within the life of the faithful community.

Finally, for Hauerwas, the authority to interpret and preach Scripture lies within "the Church" and with "spiritual masters."[127] It is unclear exactly who Hauerwas means by this, but in his opposition to having the Bible in the hands of individual Christians he seems to be turning to duly ordained clergy within the church. Hauerwas quotes with approval the "Dogmatic Constitution on Divine Revelation" of Vatican II: "The task of authentically interpreting the word of God, whether written or handed on, has been entrusted exclusively to the living teaching office of the Church."[128] Those with authority within the church may be informed by academic scholars in historical and literary criticism, but it is the authoritative church and its account of tradition which embodies the same Spirit that is sought through Scripture.

Hauerwas's sympathy for the authority of clergy, duly trained, separates him from the suspicion with which John Howard Yoder would view such offices:

> That theology should only be taught by theologians, that catechesis and confession must be reserved to the duly ordained, and that decisions about the exercise of power need primarily to be made by the people who legitimately hold that power, are elements of the previously prevailing moral wisdom which it is not merely permissible but imperative to doubt.[129]

It also separates him from James McClendon's emphasis on "a neverending congregational *conversation*" (emphasis in the original) for keeping the church faithful. McClendon writes: "So it is here that the often abused notion of 'decision' comes into its own, not as the private willful optings of moral individuals, but as the guiding limits set from time to time by the brothers and sisters in the course of their ongoing conversation."[130]

However, neither Yoder, McClendon, nor Hauerwas question the power relations that actually exist within church communities and the effective silencing of voices that might challenge the views they assume. Essentially, the authority-of-clergy vs. the authority-of-community debate among them conceals the reality that authority in either case lies within the hands of (predominately white) male clerical or (predominately white) male communal leadership. The obvious problematic consequence for women and for men of color is that an authentic understanding of scripture requires submission to the authority and discipline of a (white) male dominated institutional church, its self-defined traditions, its seminaries, and its professional disciplines. Nonetheless, Hauerwas, Yoder, and McClendon argue that only by this authority and under this discipline, Christians learn to "see" their world. Without this authority, we do not "see" as Christians.

## The Problem with Justice

How, then, can such a Christian, formed in this unique Christian community, join with secular society in working for justice? For Hauerwas, the question is not whether there should be justice, but whose justice it will be, since the very meaning of justice is dependent upon the context of a particular community's tradition. The problem is that when Christians attempt to affect the justice of secular, social institutions, they "allow their imaginations to be captured by the concepts of justice determined by the presupposition of liberal societies": that is, the distinctions between fact and value, public and private.[131] Furthermore, with no shared sense of what is good, liberal societies lead individuals to believe that any of their needs (wants) are justifiable claims.[132] The very experience of limits is called an injustice. We have created, says Hauerwas, a "cult of victimization." Hauerwas writes: "I attribute this development to liberal egalitarianism, which creates the presumption that any limit is arbitrary and thus unjust. As a result, we are all victims."[133]

Hauerwas finds Christian liberation movements to be examples of this accommodation to liberal expectations. He criticizes Gustavo Gutierrez for making liberation the primary metaphor for Christian salvation. Citing Gutierrez's description of liberation as a process toward a new society in which the human will be "free from all servitude" and "artisan of his own destiny," Hauerwas accuses Gutierrez of capitulating to liberalism's valuing of individual autonomy and to its understanding of freedom as freedom from suffering and servitude.[134] Hauerwas asks whether this is, in fact, consistent with the Christian gospel:

For the salvation promised in the good news is not a life free from suffering, free from servitude, but rather a life that freely suffers, that freely serves, because suffering and service is the hallmark of the Kingdom established by Jesus. . . . Freedom literally comes by having our self-absorption challenged by the needs of another.[135]

It is not that Hauerwas denies the political significance of the gospel, but, rather, that he argues that its political significance cannot be expressed in the language of justice. Hauerwas argues that there is "no clear connection between the scriptural account of the kingdom of God and the moral ideals advocated in its name," especially such ideals as love and justice.[136] While he would not deny that love and justice characterize God's kingdom, he argues that there are no scriptural bases for giving specific content to such ideals. Thus, when Christians do begin to specify such content, they must draw the content from other than biblical sources and, therefore, they display the prior commitments and strategies to which they are giving authority.[137]

Specifically, Hauerwas contends "that the current emphasis on justice as the primary norm guiding the social witness of Christians is in fact a mistake."[138] It is an accommodation to a liberal agenda in which there can be no appeal to the kind of people we should be or to the goods we should hold in common. In liberal societies it is to be expected that justice, now reduced to rules of procedure needed to protect the individual pursuit of self-interest, must become a major public concern. But Christians cannot participate in such concerns uniquely as Christians. To participate in the secular formation of justice, Christians must yield to the descriptions of justice which any "good" person might know. Furthermore, Hauerwas argues, any form of social justice must finally depend upon coercion. There is no commonly agreed upon Christian theory of justice. But even if there were, Hauerwas asserts, "the just person must envisage the possibility of using coercion if he or she is to be just and to do justice."[139] How else could one call for a theocratic theory of justice in a pluralistic and secular state?

Ultimately, according to Hauerwas, what causes Christians to believe that they must change secular society is the fear of being marginalized, of being without influence, and of being out of control. It is a will to power which betrays the Christian skills of patience and faith in God's providence. It is a will to power which leads to violence. He quotes John Howard Yoder:

The real temptation of good people like us is not the crude and the crass and the carnal, as those traits were defined in popular puritanism. The really refined temptation with which Jesus himself was tried was not crude sensuality but that of egocentric altruism; of being oneself the incarnation of a good and righteous cause for which others may rightly be made to suffer; of stating in the form of a duty to others one's self-justification.[140]

Thus, the desire for justice within modern Christian ethics is more profoundly a desire for power, and power must always be sustained by resorting to violence.[141] For Hauerwas, there is great similarity between Lyndon B. Johnson's civil rights work and his leadership into Vietnam: "We really do want to run the world, to set things right, to spread democracy and freedom everywhere."[142] The church in liberal society, by accepting the agenda of justice, freedom of religion, and the language of rights, is simply accommodating itself to the tenets of liberalism. "The power of our imagination, and thus our reason, is blunted because we have let the Gospel be identified with utopian fantasies rather than face the Christian realism of the demand to live peaceably."[143]

The Christian attempt to create social systems of justice supports the growing intrusive and coercive power of the state. The loss to both church and society is the salvation which can only be known through a community living faithfully to God. The result is the domestication of the church. Hauerwas concludes that Christians have forgotten that "genuine justice depends on more profound moral convictions than our secular polity can politically acknowledge" and that in order to develop such skills "the church and Christians must be uninvolved in the politics of our society and involved in the polity that is the church."[144]

In this shift in emphasis, Hauerwas attempts an alternative position between those of his fellow pacifists, McClendon and Yoder. For example, McClendon argues that the call to evangelize and to provide a public Christian witness of the Way necessitates Christians' involvement in social witness. His interpretation of the "principalities and powers" as social forces which impact the social morality of Christians requires a Christian engagement with the world. He warns, however, that those who undertake such activities should be wary lest they lose the distinctive Christian character of their witness.[145]

On the other hand, Yoder's influence on Hauerwas is clear. Yoder writes that "the primary social structure through which the gospel works to change other structures is that of the Christian community."[146] Yoder argues that the church in any society is a minority community that cultivates an alternative consciousness. The public role of the Christian community is the practice of subordination to all governments and submission to none. It exercises the strengths of a servant, not those of the dominant. Thus, there are tasks and exercises of power appropriate to government which Christians cannot do. And there may be times when Christians must refuse to obey government. But the basic call of discipleship, for Yoder, is the renunciation of "participation in the interplay of egoisms which this world calls 'vengeance' or 'justice.' "[147] To the extent that this requires a "sectarian" withdrawal from the world, Hauerwas would dissent, but, then, so would Yoder. Yoder would note that the "sectarian" charge is one often made from the perspective of the dominant.

Hauerwas strives for a middle ground, in a sense, by disavowing both the active social witness project of McClendon and the minority church status of Yoder. Hauerwas would rather believe that the church can be faithful without having to become a faithful minority. Rather, in this time "after Christendom," Christians should learn the posture of the peasant—learning to survive under the power of the master without desiring to become the master.[148] Presumably, Hauerwas believes that Christians can continue to actively participate in many secular institutions as long as the church is primary for our formation and as long as we evaluate all other institutions through the church's narrative and discipline.[149]

The consequence of Hauerwas's critique of Christian involvement in social justice activities leads neither to Christian withdrawal from the world into a Christian ghetto (sectarianism) nor to the attempt to impose a Christian theocracy upon the secular world (Constantinianism). Rather, he says, the political significance of the gospel is the creation, in the midst of society, of a community faithful to Jesus and to the nonviolent God who is known through Jesus. This is a society that is an alternative to all other societies that cannot know God. We become a part of a history that is not available to others.[150] And for Christians, justice is not a virtue that applies first to social systems. It is instead a description of the kind of people Christians are. Hauerwas concludes his article "Should Christians Talk So Much About Justice?" with this description of justice: "Christians do not need such accounts of justice to know that the ill need care and the hungry need food. By learning to share their lives in the church, Christians have learned that justice often demands no more than the most common acts of care."[151] It is only when the church neglects its mission to *be* a social ethic that it needs a theory of social justice.

## HOW THE PERSONAL IS POLITICAL[152]

In Hauerwas's theology, nonviolence expands into nonresistance. Hauerwas quotes Yoder, who states that what was new in Christ was the incarnation of a "willingness to sacrifice, in the interest of non-resistant love, all other forms of human solidarity, including the legitimate national interests of the chosen people."[153]

Thus, nonresistance is the way God, who has already determined the outcome of history, deals with the world and the way Christ was in the world; it is also, therefore, the way Christians should be in the world. "Christians are necessarily committed to the ethic of non-re-sistance."[154] Nonresistance is the crucial mark of the truthfulness and power of the unique Christian story, as it displays Christian confidence that God controls history and that the success of God's truth requires no turn to coercion or violence on the part of God's people. Hauerwas favorably quotes Michael Novak's description of the Christian's God:

> The God of Christianity and Judaism permits his people to wander in history in a wilderness. The sufferings, loneliness, anguish, and misery he permits them to share are fathomless. The Jewish-Christian God is no *deus ex machina*, no Pollyanna, no goody-two-shoes. . . . He exacts enormous and wearying responsibilities. The God we turn to on Christmas is not a God made in our measure, nor is he a function of our needs, personal or social. . . . He transcends our purposes and needs. . . . The God of Jews and Christians obliges us to struggle and to suffer, even when there is no hope.[155]

Freely suffering and freely serving are the hallmarks of the Kingdom. Christians are, therefore, most profoundly people of patience, hope and courage. Christians "have learned to be patient in the face of injustice," "must often endure injustice," and understand their inactivity as "the way of repentance."[156] For Hauerwas, the renunciation of violence requires the surrender of control over one's life, the giving up of illusions of power and security and order, the renunciation of possessions and all things to which we look to control our lives or the lives of others. Instead, we learn to live daily, out of control, open to the risk of the stranger and the adventure Jesus offers.[157]

What then do Christians do about the problems of the world, about hunger and injustice and oppression? Hauerwas's response is that any attempt to solve these problems involves one in the use of power and the violence that must sustain any power. Christians are instead supposed "to do one thing that might help lead myself and others to God's peace," the one thing that alters ourselves and removes us from the world of violence: be a member of a church, learn the discipline of waiting, be at rest with oneself, take the time to love and be loved, be a friend.[158] Take the time to reclaim the significance of the trivial, that is, those peaceful things that can be encountered anywhere: the birth of a child, taking a walk, reading, maintaining universities, having and caring for children. We can "pledge fidelity to another person for a lifetime, bring children into an inhospitable world, pray for reconciliation with enemies, live lives of truthfulness and honesty."[159] In this way Christians claim life from the powers of violence and destruction.[160] In this way Christians build up units of loyalty that transcend nation or class and become "God's international."[161]

In this world of violence and despair, and in the context of liberalism's emphasis on self-interested individualism, marriage becomes a profoundly political and subversive act. Contrary to liberal thought, marriage is not about personal, emotional self-fulfillment: "we always marry the wrong person. . . . Or even if we first marry the right person, just give it a while and he or she will change."[162] In marriage we learn to love and care for this stranger. The vocation of marriage bears the benefit of the gift of children, for, according to Hauerwas, marriage is not intelligible apart from having children.[163] Children also enter our life as strangers we have not chosen, as strangers who will change our life, demand our time and energies, and root us in the reality of our history. Thus, according to Hauerwas:

> One of the most morally substantive things any of us ever has the opportunity to do is to have children. A child represents our willingness to go on in the face of difficulties, suffering, and the ambiguity of modern life and is thus our claim that we have something worthwhile to pass on. The refusal to have children can be an act of ultimate despair that masks the deepest kind of self-hate and disgust. Fear and rejection of parenthood, the tendency to view the family as nothing more than companionable marriage, and the understanding of marriage as one of a series of non-

binding commitments, are but the indications that our society has a growing distrust of our ability to deal with the future.[164]

The willingness to marry and have children is a sign of the faith of Christians that God has not abandoned this world, even if there is little evidence to the contrary. Confidence in God causes Christians to bring new life into the world, to "act as an officer of the community to initiate the child into the practices of that community."[165]

Thus, marriage and the family are two of the central institutions of the political stance of the church. In doing the hard work of sticking out a marriage without reflecting much on whether one is fulfilled, Christians witness to the hard work of discipleship.[166] In our commitment to exclusive, monogamous relations, Christians witness to God's exclusive faithfulness to Israel and the church.[167] Christian marriage only makes sense and can only be sustained through the recognition that it serves a purpose larger than the happiness of individuals by contributing to a people and to their mission in the world. It is a vocation for the building up of the church. To choose to take the time to love one person rather than many and to care for these children rather than the many more in need is to exercise the patience, and the sense of the tragic, of human limitedness that Christians know to be the source of their true freedom.[168] Hauerwas concludes that marriage, having children, and the sexual ethic that supports these practices are central to the political mission of the church.[169] The personal, the trivial, are the politics of the church.

## THEMES: RELATING EXPERIENCE AND THEORY

I have presented my reading of Hauerwas's description of his experience of being shaped and formed by the stories which define his community. From his experience themes emerged out of which he describes and acts upon the world. He appropriates a postliberal concept of human subjectivity in which the creation of the human subject requires the internalization of a social identity. For Hauerwas this identity is defined in opposition to others. This results in a world that is dangerously fragmented and violent. The attempt of liberal political theory to avoid violence by separating values from facts and the private from the public results in a chaos which threatens the social order and the moral agency of persons. In response to his description of the human condition and our contemporary context,

Hauerwas's fundamental task as a Christian ethicist is the proclamation of and participation in what he claims to be a community unified in the truth of nonviolence.

These themes, human fragmentation, the subsequent threat of violence, and the turn to a community of people unified under the authority of shared values, are ones through which other contemporary secular theorists explain the particularity of modern western experience. They are, in other words, not specific to the Christian story, but themes that constitute part of our contemporary cultural discourse. As Alan Dawe points out, these are themes which relate to this particular historical context. The collapse of medievalism, with its closed and static society, its unity of public and private life, and its undifferentiated labor, gave way to an open, mobile society in which change, movement, and differentiation were required for successful endeavors in a public world of work separated from the privacy of family and religious beliefs. Under these conditions, the modern concept of "individual" became possible and necessary: the individual as a separate person with inalienable rights that exist prior to any social roles the person might obtain. With this concept of individualism, and the social mobility it enables and justifies, also came the particular modern experience of dualism. On the one hand, the liberal experience of self is one of a separate, active, choosing, planning agent who makes decisions which affect his or her own life. On the other hand, the experience of self is one of being determined and defined by, and essentially powerless before, forces beyond our control.[170] Trying to understand the human and human society in this specifically modern historical context has given rise to two basic issues: (1) the problem of understanding the relationship between the individual and society, and, subsequently, (2) the dilemma of creating a social structure, a community, within which this new individual can flourish.

Using themes similar to Hauerwas's, some social theorists respond to these issues by emphasizing the basic formlessness of the human individual, who, for both personal and social survival, must be formed and constrained into appropriate understandings and behavior by the social system. Without such constraints, human agency, fleeing its own inner emptiness, creates anarchy and chaos. For example, in *The Division of Labor in Society*, Emile Durkheim characterizes the industrial scene as a hostile struggle, filled with business crises and the unregulated activity of self-interest. He understands this chaos to be the result of the loosening of the social bonds of a past social order before the bonds of a new order are fully in place. For Durkheim, the solution is the establishment of a new social morality in which social power controls the chaos of individual desires:

> The only power that can serve to moderate individual egoism is that of the group; the only one that can serve to moderate the egoism of groups is that of another group that embraces them all.[171]

The basic problem from this perspective is that of assuring social order. As we have seen, this order, in the view of Peter Berger, is always precarious. The social world, as a human construct, is "a small clearing of lucidity in a formless, dark, always ominous jungle."[172] The human, even as a social being, is constantly threatened by the danger of personal isolation, or social disintegration, and the consequent submersion of the individual "in a world of disorder, senselessness and madness."[173] So humans cling to finite systems of meaning, now cast into sacred canopies, terrorized by the constant threat of their collapse. Thus, Berger believes that the emphasis of modern, liberal society on the primacy of the individual over social roles confronts people with the temporality and fragility of social institutions and throws them back upon their own subjectivity in order to find and sustain meaning.[174] However, because humans are essentially social beings, "stable identities can only emerge in reciprocity with stable social contexts."[175] Thus, modern culture itself is responsible for creating the conditions for the terror of meaninglessness.

Similarly, Clifford Geertz can imagine the human unshaped by culture: "Man's behavior would be virtually ungovernable, a mere chaos of pointless acts and exploding emotions, his experience virtually shapeless."[176] Geertz imagines "a kind of formless monster with neither sense of direction nor power of self-control, a chaos of spasmodic impulses and vague emotions."[177] To be able to imagine "man" naked, not dressed by culture, is, for Geertz and Berger, to glimpse a human subterranean world of disorder, chaos, and meaninglessness; an interior nakedness that functions continuously as a fundamental threat to individual well-being and to human society.

Similarly, Daniel Bell identifies the problem of modern society as the lack of Geertz's notion of religion; that is, the lack of a prior acceptance of authority (a "society without fathers") through which experience is given order. Instead, modern society, according to Bell, is characterized by an insatiable appetite "to engage any and every style it comes upon. Such freedom comes from the fact that the axial principle of modern culture is the expression and remaking of the 'self' in order to achieve self-realization and self-fulfillment."[178]

For Bell, the modern crisis is one of belief—specifically the lack of belief. It is the lack of a structure of "ultimate meanings" which give a past and future to human character, work, and culture. Instead, hedonism, pleasure as a way of life, and the rising expectations of limitless entitlements for everyone in the population have created a crisis for which there is no end. Each capitulation to equality breeds more demand for greater equalities. A refusal to accept limits has replaced a sense of *civitas*; that is, the willingness to make sacrifices for the public good.[179] Bell's response to society, like Hauerwas's response to the church, is to advocate a return to the recognition of the existential tragedies that confront humans—death and finitude, limitations and suffering—and to a historical sense of continuity, all of which only religion can restore:

> Human culture is a creation of man, the construction of a world to maintain *continuity*, to maintain the "un-animal" life. . . . But if the sacred is destroyed, then we are left with the shambles of appetite and self-interest and the destruction of the moral circle which engirds mankind.[180]

Hauerwas, then, joins contemporary theorists such as Peter Berger and Daniel Bell to identify liberal culture as the source of society's ills precisely because it releases people from the bonds of traditions and values and gives rise to moral chaos. Hal Foster names this view of the problem a "postmodernism of reaction."[181]

To point out that Hauerwas's theological anthropology shares the themes of such secular theorists is neither to prove nor to discredit it. It is only to make the point that Christian ethics, in any form it takes, is intelligible only because it participates in the sense-making paradigms of its particular historical and cultural context. It participates in contemporary themes. The "Christian tradition" we read and articulate is always a faith being constructed out of the ideas, concepts, issues, hopes, oppositions, and values which constitute meaning-making in our particular historicity. We are always historically and culturally particular Christians, given eyes and voice by the historical context we embody. That context is also always political: it arises out of the interests of our particular social location. We are never simply free to be "Christians."

## SUMMARY

Hauerwas's theological ethics begins out of his "Texan episte-mology" with a rejection of the liberal epistemological project: there is no ahistorical human reason. The only basis for human communication and cooperation is the "background" of a commu-nity of shared language, habits, customs, and meanings in which human character is formed and one's actions become intelligible to oneself and others.

However, the strong sense of identity formed within particular communities creates an equally strong aversion to the "other." Hauerwas appeals to a story from the Christian and Jewish Scrip-tures to describe what he contends is this universal human dilemma. Within each person lies a *fear of finitude* and a resulting *will-to-power*. Fleeing the truthfulness of human finitude, people cling to limited human loyalties as though they were absolute. Thus, the necessary result of all human sociality, indeed, of our loves, is fear of the "other" who presents alternative loyalties that dangerously expose the limitedness of oneself or one's group. *Violence,* born of the fear of the truth of this human condition, is the universal human problem. Today, Christians specifically exemplify this fear as our attempts to create social justice reveal our desire to grasp the means of power by which to control the outcome of history. We choose faith in ourselves over faith in the God who has already determined the outcome of history.

However, beginning with Abraham, God chose to reveal the *non-violent* nature of divine love through the story of Israel. With Jesus, the power of God's nonviolent love is revealed in the creation of a community whose nonviolent character witnesses to this ultimate, divine reality. Through the Christian narrative we are formed with the ability to face honestly our own finitude. Accepting that life is a gift and that history is firmly under the hand of God, we accept our *powerlessness.* We learn to live *out-of-control*; to *submit* our lives to the *risk* of faith in this God; to live with a sense of the *tragic*. In a violent and unfaithful world, marriage and having children are central pro-phetic acts of our peaceable living. *The personal is our profoundly political witness.*

In the summary above, I have underlined certain key terms in Hauerwas's theological ethics. One task of a liberative ethics is to identify the contemporary community for whom such terms, with the specific content given them, "ring true." For whom is the problem that Hauerwas identifies a problem? For whom does his solution appear as "gospel"? Hauerwas himself seems to assume the universal applicability of his description of the "human" condition, human society, and the Christian narrative. The question of the social location of Hauerwas's community will be taken up in chapter 4. But first I must locate myself and my own story.

# CHAPTER 3

# TOWARD AN EMANCIPATORY EPISTEMOLOGY[1]

To accept the radical historicity of human subjectivity, that is, to accept the cultural construction of meaning, does not necessarily lead us to an emphasis on the threat of chaos and the need for the imposition of a strong social, or ecclesial, order. Other social theorists emphasize the interdependence of self- and society-creating actions and interactions.[2] These theorists understand society to be the product of our positive human capacity to create meaning together and to act upon such meaning. Rather than imagining the threat of an unshaped and formless monster who must be given a civil form, they argue that humans simply do not exist apart from social interaction.

On the one hand, this refers to the obvious historical fact that humans are always born into a social context. Humans are always born into established systems of meaning and patterns of relationship. Contrary to the opinions of Berger and Geertz, there is no culturally unformed human lurking at the margins of society or in the depths of the soul. What humans lack in instinct is acquired (for better or worse) through always-present social relations. What neither Berger nor Geertz recognize are the mothers from whose bodies each human being emerges.

On the other hand, the emphasis on the interrelatedness of self- and society-creating actions also refers to the psychological observation that human consciousness and self-consciousness are products of human interaction. Contrary to Freud, intersubjective psychological theory asserts that from early infancy such interaction is one of mutual recognition; that is, in the response that the other gives in recognition of my being, I not only receive myself, but I also perceive the other in whose action of recognition I can identify someone separate from me but like me. Contrary to both Hegel and Freud, the works of developmental psychologist Piaget and of child analyst

Margaret Mahler show a human subject who at birth is active, stimulus-seeking, and needful of relating, not to an object, but to another independent subject. Intersubjective theory describes human capacities as developing in the dynamic interaction of mutual but separate selves.[3]

Therefore, apparent cultural limits to action, what Freire calls "limit-situations," must be recognized as lodging not in an eternal, "natural" order of society, not even in a necessary sacred canopy, but in humanly created structures.[4] The "way things are" is the way humans have chosen to organize our embodied life. The ethical emphasis shifts, then, from forming the character of the individual to transforming the character of community. From this perspective, it is essential for humans to consciously recognize the human construction of culture. Injustice, embedded to the point of invisibility in social structures and assumptions, is the basic problem of society, not chaos and violence in themselves. The basic problem is the reification of such injustice into sacred canopies (or master narratives) so that they seem impervious to, even outside of, human control. Karl Marx's analysis of the condition of laborers in a capitalist system is an example of the problem of a reified social order seen from this perspective:

> The estrangement of the worker in his object is expressed according to the laws of political economy in the following way: the more the worker produces, the less he has to consume; the more value he creates, the more worthless he becomes; the more his product is shaped, the more misshapen the worker; the more civilized his object, the more barbarous the worker; the more powerful the work, the more powerless the worker; the more intelligent the work, the duller the worker and the more he becomes a slave of nature.[5]

In this view, the primary concern for social theory is how humans, alienated from themselves and from the products of their activity, can regain control over their social products. The solution requires "critical thinking." Again, from Freire, critical thinking is:

> thinking which discerns an indivisible solidarity between the world and men and admits of no dichotomy between them—thinking which perceives reality as process, as transformation, rather than as a static entity—thinking which does not separate itself from action, but constantly immerses itself in temporality without fear of the risks involved.[6]

63

Through critical thinking, we become aware of the world and our activity upon it. We become aware of ourselves and others as the source of decision making. We become aware of our own creative presence in relationship with the world and others; we become aware that through our action upon the world we create a finite and changing realm of culture and history. All traditions and social codes must be questioned to reveal their political loyalties and to resist false universalizing. Such views are characterized by Hal Foster as a "postmodernism of resistance."[7] What is threatening is not the consciousness of the temporality of the social order and its meanings, but the loss of such consciousness. What is threatening is the possibility of being submerged in a world that is given to one and that can only be received passively as the "really real," "God's will," or, more cynically, as the way things always have been and always will be.

In chapter 2, I described how the experience of a strong, dominant narrative, passed down from father to son, shaped Stanley Hauerwas, by his own admission, as a Texan with a Texan epistemology. I showed how Hauerwas's ethics of character is grounded in this experience of a violent tradition which shapes, forms, and empowers the white males born within it. It has given him his theory of knowledge, guided his understanding of "the Christian narrative," and resulted in his ethics of character. As we have seen, Hauerwas describes the Christian narrative as a unified tradition of nonviolence which carries within it the gift of human unity for a world divided by limited stories and fragments of past moralities. In response to the violence of the many, Hauerwas offers the peace of unity found in the only true story of the divine and human relationship. I have also shown how these theological themes (the fear of finitude, the sin of striving for power, and the grace of salvation through an all-encompassing community) parallel some secular approaches to understanding the modern, Western experience of self. Hauerwas has illustrated for us the dialectical movement between stories and experiences, experiences and stories. Stories, such as being a Texan or (better yet) being a Christian, interpret our experiences while our experiences reinterpret these stories. What Hauerwas has not noticed is that his story is overwhelmingly male. Fathers tell sons what it means to be (male) Texans. A white male author tells his story of Texas. The stories these men tell root men like themselves in what they see as the deep meanings of life.

But many women tell of very different experiences. As women tell our stories, we reveal our struggles within the hegemony of the dominant discourses which prescribe definitions of women in the culture of the United States. In some cases women tell stories of the destructive power of false definitions which break, isolate, silence, and paralyze them. In other cases, women's struggles to resist false definitions create communities of resistance which are empowering to them. Our stories reveal women's encounters with multiple, imposed definitions of "woman" (a multiplicity intertwined with differences such as race, class, and sexual orientation). Our stories also reveal women's experiences of conflictual meanings within our individual lives (the difference, for example, between the meaning of wife and "date," woman and minister, mother and wage laborer). I claim that these pluralities of experiences of ourselves cause women to see different problems, to raise different issues, to ask and not ask different questions, and, especially, to experience community differently.

## EXPERIENCING WOMEN

Women's stories of women are only beginning to be told publicly. In the absence of women's stories, publicly told by women and heard by all, women have struggled to give voice to their own experience of experience.[8] Thus, for women, it is possible to grow up in a community receiving a self that is, somehow, not your self. Somehow it is possible to be named and called, shaped and formed, given values, molded by virtues, and instructed in roles, sometimes even by loving role models; to be given a place and a character that, somehow, is not yours. Some women know the experience of watching our self being the self that we know is not our self. We can identify with the fictional character of Martha Quest in the series *Children of Violence*, by Doris Lessing. We have watched ourselves play a role designed for people like us. We have watched ourselves glimpse opportunities that might have broken the pattern, and watched ourselves turn back into our role. We have watched ourselves drift along with the story we were given: women's roles, women's work, marriage, children. And we have lived with a constant sense of internal, infernal fragmentation: the watcher, that Lessing describes, and the self that plays the roles, living in the same woman.[9] Our home has been fragmentation.

Other women know the experience of living half-asleep, grateful for whatever touch reaches through our stupors to cause a feeling, any feeling, that lets us know we can still feel. Betty Friedan began her classic *The Feminine Mystique*, with her description of the white, suburban housewife's "problem" that, within this velvet prison, could be no problem. Surrounded in the 1950s with the securities of home, healthy children, and faithful husband, and busy with the work of housekeeping, child raising, and providing emotional support, the vague sense of unease could only be described as "nothing, really."[10]

Within the racist culture of the U.S., women of color especially know the hard, intentional, daily work of carving out a "living space" where self-affirming definitions and strategies for survival are created and shared and passed on, in spite of, and in defense against, the stories of those who would silence their stories.[11] Katie Cannon describes the dehumanizing roles imposed upon black women in the tradition of American slavery: brood sow, work-ox, property.[12] bell hooks analyzes the continuing imposition of broken characterizations upon freed black women: the shrill, nagging Sapphires, the sexual Jezebels, and the passively loyal, overweight mammies.[13] Mary Helen Washington describes sleepwalking: going through the motions of teaching and earning a Master's Degree, "without ever feeling truly connected to or passionately involved with my work" until she read her first book written by a black woman, "and I realized that I had not been able to commit myself to my work because in the literature I had been taught and in the world I was expected to negotiate, my face did not exist."[14]

Sandra Albury, a student at Temple University, writes: "Being that I am a Black woman in America, I was taught conformity at a very early age—to be like them (whites). I lost a part of me, a part I'm not sure I know."[15]

Audre Lorde asks: "What are the tyrannies you swallow day by day and attempt to make your own, until you will sicken and die of them, still in silence?"[16]

From Sojourner Truth's "ain't I a woman"[17] to Valerie Saiving's "I am a student of theology; I am also a woman,"[18] women in the U.S. (like other subjugated groups) have struggled to articulate our experiences of being rendered an object of dominant (white, male) gaze. Internalization of this gaze is the way women learn to see ourselves. As John Berger says, women's internalized (male) watcher turns a woman into an object of her own watching.[19] In this way we are made invisible to ourselves. We shape and control ourselves through the description of "woman" given to us through the dominant discourse of the community of which we are a part. Paradoxically, a public gaze instills personal invisibility. Thus, we have to face our own fear of becoming visible to ourselves, our fear of seeing and acting, of revealing ourselves to ourselves and to society.[20]

The struggle is at both an individual and social level, involving women in a process Paulo Freire called "conscientization": learning to see that one has been shaped by social, economic, and political contradictions, and learning to act to transform these contradictions.[21] In her introduction to *Talking Back,* bell hooks describes the struggle of coming to speak about herself, Gloria Jean Watkins. She speaks of her family's criticism of her youthful outspokenness; the sense she was taught that black folk don't make their business public. After a long time her conclusion was that "openness is about how to be well and telling the truth is about how to put the broken bits and pieces of the heart back together again." Yet, this is not about her personal well-being only. Making Gloria Jean's story public is also a part of the political struggle of her people. The wounds caused by white oppression must be publicly named if black people in the U.S. are to name themselves.[22]

Through women's struggles to give voice to our differing experiences of ourselves, the personal reveals the political. Womanists and feminists are learning that we must claim visibility, but on our own terms, if we are to uncover the contradictions in ourselves and in our society. The cultural contradictions which have served to mystify ourselves to our selves do not exist only as ideas. They live embodied in social institutions and the cultural norms, practices, roles, and virtues of our communities; communities that accept as their own the stories which illustrate for us who we are as this people, as this culture. Suspicion of the cultural construction of our selves as "women" (a category always more specifically defined by race, class, and sexual orientation) is lived, then, as suspicion of specific embodiments and the interests they empower, that is, of these career options, of those religious teachings and rituals, of that family custom, of this form love takes. In the experience of some women, it was often those who loved us most who insisted that we be what we were not. So, women must also learn to examine what is closest to us, our own experiences, our own loyalties, especially our own loves, to understand how dominant social loyalties, including racism, sexism, heterosexism, and class position, become enfleshed in our own particular stories; and how dominant social norms are maintained (or resisted) through us. Some white Christian feminists, in our struggles to understand the shaping of our own subjectivity, have found that we, too, have been mired in a cultural and religious context of sexism, racism, class privilege, and heterosexism. We have found that no Christian narrative comes to us untainted by the distortions of this community's participation in the development and maintenance of sexist ideologies, class elitism, and racial hatred. Annually, our Christmases anoint us blessed with images of a clean, well-dressed, white, and virginal Mary cradling her blue-eyed, well-fed Jesus.[23]

To become visible to ourselves and others, we have had to learn that life is multivocal; that all lives are intricately interrelated; that the power to affect and to be affected is a part of all relationships; and that, through the personal ways we live and the alliances we make, we have the power to affect the social reality that affects us; and we must use it. The process of finding our own voices, of insisting upon participating in the defining of our selves and of our society, is not a turn toward the unconnected, autonomous individualism of liberal societies. It is instead a quest for an ever broader community in which the dangerous memory of suffering and resistance nourishes the subversive hope for justice. Dangerous memory survives in the stories of marginal groups that remember a history of struggle against domination, in small and large acts of resistance. Through such memory the present is revealed not as the inevitable result of historical progress, but as the current site of ongoing struggle. This is the "beloved community": "the matrix within which life is celebrated, love is worshipped, and partial victories over injustice lay the groundwork for further acts of criticism and courageous defiance."[24] What follows, then, is part of the dangerous memory of my people—white, middle-class, Christian, mostly heterosexual, American, feminists—and how some of us have come to realize that we are (only) white, middle-class, Christian, heterosexual, American, and feminist.

## REMEMBERING OUR PAST

In her autobiography, Elizabeth Cady Stanton recounts her struggle, and failure, to earn the kind of love from her father that he, in unrelenting grief, could only feel for his son now dead. Befriended by the local pastor, Stanton strove to conquer the male world of Latin, Greek, and mathematics by studying with the pastor's class of boys. Finally winning the coveted prize in Greek, Stanton ran down the hill, rushed breathless into his office, laid the new Greek Testament, which was my prize, on his table and exclaimed: "There, I got it!" . . . Then, while I stood looking and waiting for him to say something which would show that he recognized the equality of the daughter with the son, he kissed me on the forehead and exclaimed, with a sigh, "Ah, you should have been a boy!"[25]

Stanton spent the rest of her life working to debunk the "cult of true womanhood," prevalent in the nineteenth century, which defined the role of white, middle-class women as one bound to home and children, shaped by piety and chasteness, and honored for its humble submissiveness to men.[26] Out of Stanton's personal experience of not fitting the prescribed definition of "feminine," she seized upon another prevailing discourse to explain her experience. The central theme of her thinking was rooted in liberal political theory: all "men" are created equal and endowed with the same innate capacity for reason. In the myth of generic language, "man" means, of course, human being. Therefore, Stanton argued, since women are human beings, they have the same capacity for reason as men and should be treated as citizens entitled to the same political rights and protections against tyranny as males.[27] In her white, middle-class context, Stanton saw the struggle to claim full personhood and moral agency for women as a political struggle for suffrage and full legal rights. Stanton exemplifies one strand of white, middle-class, feminist resistance in the nineteenth century: she appropriated liberal theory and added women.[28] Thus, her liberal argument, that women and men are equal in rational capacities and subsequent rights, could be heard, understood, and, due to all that was at stake, angrily contested and rejected.

## A Feminist Critique of Liberal Theory

As we have seen, liberalism, as a theory of human nature and of the contractual origin of society, rests on the theoretical assumption of a natural, ontological equality of isolated, rational individuals. In the history of the United States, liberalism is usually celebrated as a legitimation and a defense of individual human freedom. Liberal feminists in the nineteenth century saw in it the potential to defeat the patriarchal right of fathers and to create a nonpatriarchal civil society in which presumably all adults would enjoy the same civil liberties. In 1792 the Englishwoman Mary Wollstonecraft wrote in her classic liberal feminist treatise *A Vindication of the Rights of Women*:

> Consider, sir, dispassionately these observations—for a glimpse of this truth seemed to open before you when you observed "that to see one half of the human race excluded by the other from all participation of government was a political phenomenon that, according to abstract principles, it was impossible to explain." If so, on what does your constitution rest? . . . Consider . . . when men contend for their freedom and struggle to be allowed to judge for themselves . . . it be not inconsistent and unjust to subjugate women . . . ? Who made man the exclusive judge, if woman partake with him the gift of reason?[29]

Thus, basic tenets of liberalism, specifically the belief in the fundamental equality and rationality of all humans, and the valuing of individual freedom as a constitutive aspect of any concept of the common good, have been tenets helpful to the development of feminism in the U.S.

However, even as eighteenth-century liberal theorists claimed that individuals were free and equal in the original state of nature and that free individuals contracted together to create a society for the betterment of each, they participated in a society in which social roles were obviously unequal: that of master/mistress and servant, master/mistress and slave, or master and mistress. If women of the eighteenth century had gained the right to manage and dispose of property as they saw fit, not to mention the right to hold legal title to property, they would have changed drastically the institutional structure of marriage, in particular, as well as those of education, politics, and economics, with which marriage is interrelated. All of these interacting social institutions rested upon the assumption that the public interests of the household resided in, and would be represented legally by, the person of the male head.

> The unity of the eighteenth-century family—enshrined in the ideology of the time and revived in the 1970s by family historians—was based on the legal fiction of "coverture." . . . Hume and others justified coverture by reference to the "enlarged affections" and unity of the family. . . . But we must realize that questions of distributive justice were not considered important in the context of this type of family because not only the wife's property but her body, children, and her legal rights belonged to her husband.[30]

In fact, the social contract theory extended civil liberties to more men (but not "all"), while keeping all women legally subordinate to men. Liberal society was based on the separation of white male (public) and white female (domestic) spheres and white women's resulting dependence on and subordination to white men. It was based on racism in which all people of color were excluded from full rights of citizenship and most were denied access to any personal liberties. It was based on heterosexism in which all social institutions and values are based on the assumption of heterosexual relations and family structures. Finally, liberal society was based upon radical new divisions within social institutions: home was separated from work, economics from politics, private from public, and personal from political. Nineteenth-century liberal feminism did not challenge these divisions. Its demand for women's equality challenged women's exclusion from male spheres and male political rights, but it did not question the new social divisions necessitated by liberal capitalism, nor the theoretical assumptions these social arrangements embodied.

*Equal As Men Is Not Equal*

By the latter half of the twentieth century, it has become clear that the legal attainment of full citizenship rights for women has not resulted in concrete experiences of equality in the institutions of society: workplaces, educational institutions, the legal system, political life, religious institutions, and, for most women, home. Zillah Eisenstein's critique of liberal feminism focuses on the unequal results of women's entry into the workplace of corporate capitalism as well as on liberal feminism's failure to challenge the sexual division of labor in the domestic sphere.[31] Within the workplace a sexual division of labor continues to confine most women to the female ghetto of poorly paid work, little job security, poor working conditions, and little chance of advancement. For example, the dramatic increase of white women (especially married white women) in the labor force between 1960 and 1980 was fueled by the stagnation of the 1970s in which the real income of white males fell and their unemployment rate rose. Two-thirds of this growth in white women's employment was in the service sector of the economy. Service work pays less than manufacturing, sales, or clerical work. Furthermore, 45 percent of women's service jobs are part-time work and 45 percent of women's service work requires weekend work.[32] In 1990 the median weekly earnings of white

71

women (in full-time, year-round work) were 71 percent of those of white men. As a percentage of the median weekly earnings of white men (full-time, year-round work), black women's median weekly earnings were 62 percent and Hispanic women's median weekly earnings were 54 percent. In all three racial-ethnic groups, the wage gap between women and men of the same racial-ethnic group narrowed. However, about 40 percent of these gains were the result of the drop in men's earnings.[33] Other studies show that as the proportion of women (or of any minority racial or ethnic group) increases in a particular occupation, the wage level decreases.[34] Racial-ethnic and gender segregation of jobs continues to be the rule despite the successes of some white women and some people of color. The point is not the simplistic response that ideas and habits change slowly. More important is the recognition that the everyday processes and activities of social institutions in the U.S. assume the norm of white male middle-class participation. Social institutions embody injustice by doing business as usual.

Sharon Welch points out other areas in which women's turn to liberal political theory results in the tenets of liberalism being turned against women. That is, the argument that women are the same as men, as Wollstonecraft and Stanton argued, does not challenge the material conditions of a society that is designed around a political and economic world of males and a domestic world of females. The practical effect of pretending that material differences (differences of roles, social options, social power, economic well-being, personal safety, responsibilities, and expectations, for example) do not exist has been the devastation of women's well-being in such gender-blind laws as no-fault divorce, and in child custody cases.[35] Some studies show that young mothers' standards of living fell an average of 73 percent after a divorce, while men's standards of living after divorce rose 42 percent.[36]

The issues of prostitution and surrogate motherhood are similarly surrounded with ambiguities for women due to these assumptions of liberal theory: (1) that individuals own their own labor power, their bodies and its capacities, as one would own any property, and (2) that society is constituted by contractual relations freely entered into between equal individuals. Thus, liberal theory assumes that a woman can (freely) contract out the sexual or reproductive use of her body, as one of her property possessions, in the same manner as men can (freely) contract out their labor power for wages.[37] No distinction is made on the basis of sex or gender; no distinction is made on the basis of social location and the power inherent in that location. The commodification of bodies and babies can be legitimated when the use of women's bodies and of women's reproductive labor cannot be distinguished from the use of men's bodies or from women's or men's productive labor. Thus, the attempt of some feminists to use liberal political theory in the solution of issues facing women in the last half of the twentieth century has led to contradictions and paradoxes for which the assumptions of liberal theory are inadequate.[38]

As a theory of abstract equality, liberalism was helpful, even necessary, within the social and political contexts of the United States in the eighteenth and nineteenth centuries, contexts that defined women as "other." However, it shows its limitations when viewed through the experiences of women after legal equality has been gained. The goal of liberal political theory was, after all, liberty from legal (governmental) constraint. It was an argument made from the perspective of, and on behalf of, the newly emerging white, male bourgeois. It was not an egalitarian vision of social justice. The twentieth century version of liberal society, composed of single, isolated, equal and sex-neutral individuals who choose if and when to enter into contractual relations, has revealed itself to be congenial to a new form of patriarchy and to be basically antisocial. As Beverly Harrison concludes, it "flies in the face of most women's experience. . . . Women know, especially through childbearing and childrearing, that our social interrelations are basic even to our biological survival and are not now, nor have they ever been, entirely optional."[39] An abstract principle of ontological equality among "all men" serves only to obscure the concrete differences in social roles, social options, and social power which exist when some of the (socially defined) "men" are (socially defined) "women."

*Equal As White Women Is Not Equal*

However, perhaps the most demanding critique of liberal theory has come about through womanists' criticisms of white feminists. "By and large within the women's movement today, white women focus upon their oppression as women and ignore differences of race, sexual preference, class and age. There is a pretense to a homogeneity

73

of experience covered by the word *sisterhood* that does not in fact exist."[40]

Ignoring difference, nineteenth-century white female suffragists were able to equate their own oppression as white women with that of black men and women. Unable to see the difference between the concrete effects that political disenfranchisement had on middle-class white women and the effects the disenfranchisement of black males had on the black community, and in the context of divide-and-conquer political tactics of white males, white suffragists angrily joined the racist chorus against the passage of the fifteenth amendment, which extended the vote to black men only.[41] Ignoring difference, twentieth-century white middle-class women were able to equate their experiences of oppression in suburbia with that of black women and poor white women. They assumed that their organizing around the right to work for wages outside the home would be joyfully supported by all women struggling for equality.[42] The myth that despite the particulars of our historical contexts we are all really the same has been exposed as a tool of domination in whomever's hand it rests.[43]

By returning to particular memories of suffering and resistance, the ambiguities of a discourse are exposed. It has the power both to liberate and to oppress, to enlighten and to mystify. Susan Thistlethwaite identifies four characteristics of liberal theory which function to blind white feminists to their own participation in the oppression of black women and men. First, liberal theory's faith in human reason denies (and renders invisible) the effects of feelings, habits, beliefs and practices that compose social systems. For example, Thistlethwaite notes that the experience of slavery, and especially of the sexual exploitation of black women within slavery, is central to the writings of black women in both the nineteenth and twentieth centuries. However, the experience of owning slaves, especially the experience of owning black women who are sexually exploited by husbands, brothers, and sons, plays no role in white women's literature. Faith in human reason and the appeal to reason in oneself and others allows white women to label white men's sexual abuse of black women as aberrant behavior. As irrational behavior, it can be isolated from the total social construct of which it is, in actuality, a part. Emphasizing reason allows white women, such as the Grimke sisters, to avoid analysis of our own relations with white men, our relationships with black women, and how the intersection of these relationships make us complicit in the myth of black women's carnality and white women's purity. Faith in reason allows us to avoid facing the racist (and classist) underpinnings of the myth of (white) women's purity, as well as white racist feelings about miscegenation and the children produced.[44]

Second, Thistlethwaite argues that the liberal belief in the abstraction of an ontological equality functions to obscure actual, material differences. Before and after slavery, middle-class white women would draw parallels between their own condition of disenfranchisement and the conditions of blacks. Blind to the daily lived differences in well-being and security that existed between them and black women and men, white female suffragists worked to defeat the fifteenth amendment, which would allow " 'Sambo' [to] walk into the kingdom first."[45] In vain Frederick Douglass appealed to the 1869 convention of the Equal Rights Association:

> When women, because they are women, are dragged from their homes and hung upon lamp-posts; when their children are torn from their arms and their brains dashed upon the pavement; when they are objects of insult and outrage at every turn; when they are in danger of having their homes burnt down over their heads; when their children are not allowed to enter schools; then they will have [the same] urgency to obtain the ballot.[46]

In a related point, Thistlethwaite argues that the individualism of liberal theory (the view of the human as an isolated individual who participates in society by contract) makes the development of social criticism impossible. It is a short mental step from the abstraction of the "natural equality" of individuals to the abstraction of "equal opportunity," and the assumption that actual, social differences are the effects of individual, rational (or irrational) choice. The embeddedness within customary practices (business as usual) of privileges for the members of dominant groups and burdens for members of other groups cannot be "seen." The social imposition of group identity cannot be seen. Thistlethwaite notes that by the end of the nineteenth century white middle-class suffragists had drawn apart from both white labor leaders and black activists and had adopted arguments for women's suffrage that allied them with middle-class white men against the "rule of illiteracy, whether of home-grown or foreign-born production."[47]

Finally, Thistlethwaite argues that the doctrine of natural rights, emphasizing freedom of choice for individuals, functions to preclude the development of real social solidarity between different groups.[48]

Thus, middle-class white women at the Seneca Falls Convention in 1848 interpreted natural rights to mean women's property rights and equality in marriage and divorce laws; that is, the expansion of white middle-class choices. The convention ignored the needs of most white working-class women and all black slaves. Angela Davis chronicles the persistent reluctance of white middle-class feminists to take up the struggle for the rights of domestic workers (mostly female and black).[49] Obscuring differences of class and race by appeals to freedom of choice, when choice is defined by middle-class white women, functions to mask the need for strategies of solidarity necessary to combat the mutually reinforcing, interwoven, and divisive tactics of racism, sexism and class privilege.

Thistlethwaite's analysis shows clearly how the assumptions of liberal political theory function to reinforce white feminists' inability to see "others." They (we) could not see the concrete experiences of black women and men in slavery; nor could they (we) understand the motivations, choices, and behaviors of blacks, both slave and free. Unable to recognize the real differences that race and class make, white feminists were (are) unable to see their (our) own complicity, first, in the system of slavery and, later, in other tactics of social marginalization and exploitation. Consequently, the early promise in the nineteenth century of bonding between abolitionists and suffragists was soon broken after the defeat of legal slavery.

Paula Giddings sums up the response of many twentieth-century black women to the emergence of the contemporary (white) women's movement in the 1960s.

> As far as many Blacks were concerned, the emergence of the women's movement couldn't have been more untimely or irrelevant.... [Betty] Friedan's observation that "I never knew a woman, when I was growing up, who used her mind, played her own part in the world, and also loved, and had children" seemed to come from another planet.[50]

The history of white feminists' experience with liberal political theory warns us of the dangers of appropriating universal, abstract principles, uncorrected by the material realities of social location. Essentially, liberal political theory created a story of the abstract, universal individual unencumbered by the particularities of race, gender, sexual orientation, or class. This individual contracted with other such individuals to create a society in which each, by continuing to pursue their own interests, would contribute to a greater good for the whole. Predictably, the image of this individual was the self-image of the men engaged in the creation of the myth: affluent, white, male heads of households. The sameness that they labeled "man" was in fact the sameness of gender, sexual orientation, race, and class which they enjoyed among themselves. Similarly, this unexamined assumption of sameness has allowed white feminists to assume a bonding with all women, and to use the privileged position of our race and class to speak for all women. Audre Lorde's righteous anger continues to expose the hypocrisy of any sisterhood gained without the pain of acknowledging our different social locations and our participation in relations of domination.

> If white American feminist theory need not deal with the differences between us, and the resulting difference in our oppressions, then how do you deal with the fact that the women who clean your houses and tend your children while you attend conferences on feminist theory are, for the most part, poor women and women of Color? What is the theory behind racist feminism?[51]

For almost two centuries, liberal political theory provided a theoretical basis for all women and for men of color to claim political rights originally limited to white men of property. Hauerwas, Berger, and Bell claim that the crisis of liberalism at the end of the twentieth century is a crisis of its democratic excesses. Contrary to that claim, for those groups marginalized in U.S. society, the crisis of liberalism is a crisis caused by the revelation of the limits to equality upon which liberal capitalist patriarchy depends. It is not that liberalism provided no story, or too many stories, but that it provided only one: one that assumed the beliefs, values, behaviors, and social position of white, middle-class, heterosexual males. The emphasis on individualism, autonomy, progress, and the distinction between domestic and public served the interests of this social location. Their denial of difference has masked the reality of different social locations and differences in power. The myth of sameness has masked the violence that results when all "others" are defined and evaluated within the story told by the dominant. The fiction that we all experience life in the same way in this society, regardless of our race, sexual orientation, class, or gender, hides actual relationships of domination and exploitation in which those who are devalued are blamed for their condition. The failure of liberal political theory is a failure of white, male, liberal, capitalist patriarchy. From the perspective of the "other," Taylor's description of the "postmodern trilemma" seems right. The formation of character requires communities of tradition. The experience of injustice requires the valuing of differences. Both require resistance to social structures of domination. The dilemma is that our attention to any one of the three invites a neglect of the importance of the other two, with harmful consequences.[52]

## A Feminist Critique of the Search for Origins

In the latter half of the twentieth century, as developments in sociology and anthropology contributed to a turn away from the Enlightenment view of a universal human nature and toward an assertion of the radical historicity of human existence, feminists also began to use the tools of sociology and anthropology to expose cultural descriptions of gender as products of human construction. Gayle Rubin described the concept of a "sex-gender system" through which a culture assigns gendered characteristics to males and females that have little to do with biological sex differences.[53] Nancy Chodorow provides this summary description of the sex-gender system:

> The sex-gender system includes ways in which biological sex becomes cultural gender, a sexual division of labor, social relations for the production of gender and of gender-organized social worlds, rules and regulations for sexual object choice, and concepts of childhood. The sex-gender system is, like a society's mode of production, a fundamental determining and constituting element of society, socially constructed, and subject to historical change and development.[54]

As this description makes clear, the sex-gender system participates in the production of a cultural context which, through the process of internalization, produces genderized self-identities. Individuals, through their embodiment of a culture's norms and practices, continue to recreate the sex-gender system.

Anthropological studies of sex-gender systems originally resulted in two primary observations. First, the assumptions of Western cultures regarding the "natural" traits of men and women have been contradicted by the extraordinary amount of diversity found within our own and other cultures. Second, there is a nearly universal asymmetry within cultural sex-gender systems: that is, almost universally, sex-gender systems seem to grant to the roles and activities of men, to that which is labeled "masculine," more value and importance than is given to that which is labeled "feminine."[55] From these observations, a great variety of theories were developed by feminists in an attempt to explain the origin of this asymmetry in which, despite the tremendous variation in gender roles and characteristics, the "feminine" is not only different but also inferior to the "masculine."[56]

However, in a later article, "Moral/Analytic Dilemmas Posed by the Intersection of Feminism and Social Science," Michelle Zimbalist Rosaldo warns against the unexamined assumptions that underlie any search for "origins."[57] She makes two important points that I would like to emphasize. First, to search for the origin of asymmetric gender assumes some "always" of human life, a continuous something, which is able to transcend historical change and which must, therefore, be unchanging in its roots. In other words, the search for the origin of sexism (or violence or injustice) is a search for some universal aspect of human existence which underlies cultural particularity. It is a return to the liberal faith in universals. Second, Rosaldo argues that the search for origins fails to help us analyze the choices we make today and, specifically, fails to identify the sexist bias of unexamined assumptions functioning within social science itself.

Two concepts within social science (and other Western practices, including religion, I would argue) that support sexist theorizing, according to Rosaldo, are (1) a predilection toward individualism which assumes that social forms follow from what individuals need to do based on the natural demands of the physical, such as reproduction; and (2) the tendency in Western culture to think in binary and dualistic terms: individual and society, nature and culture, feeling and reason, unconscious and conscious, woman and man. Western dualistic assumptions become a part of the Western observer's observations. For example, if women are observed to do the cooking, the Western observer tends to assume that the observed culture (1) distinguishes between domestic and public, (2) considers cooking a domestic task, (3) values domestic tasks less than other tasks, and, therefore, (4) values women less than men.[58] Rosaldo concludes that a search for origins tends to focus us on a time (historically or psychologically) before our present, conscious time, and on universal needs (biological or psychological) of individuals, which are assumed to explain why things are the way they are. It is worthwhile to quote at length her objection to these assumptions:

> No fact of nature in and of itself decides for human actors where that bit of nature leads; similarly, no aspect of unconscious life determines how in any given social form one's dispositions shape and are shaped by their social context. Society does not make our minds, nor does the unconscious make society. Rather, human beings, shaped by histories and relationships they only partly understand, interpret what they desire and see in terms provided by their social world and negotiated with the associates, friends, enemies, and kin with whom they share their lives.[59]

In other words, the investigation of cultural definitions of gender by feminists led Rosaldo and others to the conclusion that women and men are both the products of and actors in the production of social relationships which are specific to our distinct and changing societies. Specifically, gender distinctions are socially created meanings that are not fixed but are in a constant state of flux. And, as my recounting of part of the story of my people has shown, the production of persons as middle-class white women or as middle-class black women or as poor white or black women, or as Hispanic women, or as white, or black, or Hispanic lesbian women, is (and has been) a site of struggle, a site of domination, and a site of resistance. The social construction of meaning is an ongoing political process.

## THE PERSONAL IS POLITICAL

From women's experiences of being falsely defined by the dominant discourses of society, from the critique of liberal theory developed above, and in the shift from searching for universal origins of sexism to an analysis of the current politics in the construction of social meaning, suspicion can now be cast upon liberalism's division of society into a "public" and a "private" sphere. The feminist claim from the sixties that "the personal is political" expressed the realization that the configurations of the "private" sphere, more accurately called the domestic sphere (sexuality, reproduction, gender, family life, child care, domestic labor), were integrally related to social systems of meaning and to the institutions of the "public" (political-economic) sphere that needed and supported these meanings. In order to understand and respond to the sex-gender system in which women in the United States find themselves today, a feminist ethics of liberation must analyze the system of power relations that exists within "capitalist patriarchy." This phrase, coined by Zillah Eisenstein, intends to emphasize the particular form of patriarchy that exists in a "mutually reinforcing dialectical relationship" with the class system within capitalism and the particular form of capitalism that exists in a mutually reinforcing dialectical relationship within a patriarchal sex-gender system.[60] Certainly patriarchy, as a male hierarchical ordering of society, existed before capitalism and, theoretically, capitalism, as a system of capital-wage labor, could exist without being patriarchal. However, a liberating critique must analyze the ways in which these two systems intertwine and mutually support each other.

In the modern United States, as we have seen above, women are oppressed as wage-laborers, but women are also oppressed by the specific roles they are given in the sexual hierarchy: child care, domestic labor, consumer, guardian of relational virtues. We have seen how the ideology of femininity as domesticity is used to limit equal access to work and pay. Limited access to sufficient work reinforces patriarchy by making women economically dependent on someone else's income (such as a better paid male laborer or the state welfare system shaped by male legislators). In the intersection of capitalism and patriarchy, women's designation as domestic becomes a liability for finding work in the economic sphere adequate to pay her a living wage. Limits in the labor market restrict challenges to male hierarchy in the workplace and to the maintenance of heterosexual, patriarchal marriage. Race, class, and gender converge to maintain white patriarchal capitalism. In the 1980s, for example, the ratio of black women's and Latinas' wages to white women's wages actually fell.[61] However, the unemployment rates for black men are two and a half times that of white women. Thus, to escape poverty it would be better for a black woman to change her race than to change her gender.[62] The social construction of race, class, and gender sustains white, capitalist patriarchy.

Feminist theorists have pointed out, as noted above, that liberal political theory presented a fiction of human equality which obscured from vision those groups removed from equal participation in the political economy by definitions of natural inequality. The creation of that invisibility for women was the function of the ideology of the domestic sphere.[63] The problem is not that liberalism created a separation of "public" and "private," as Hauerwas claims, but that it created a myth of separation which served the politics of a developing white, patriarchal capitalism. Eisenstein identifies the development of capitalist patriarchy beginning from the mid–eighteenth century in England and the mid–nineteenth century in the United States.[64] Capitalism, requiring the elimination of workers' access to the means of production, required the separation of the family from production.[65] Thus, the public/private division concretely refers to the separation of the family from market production. This was necessary to create a wage labor force. And it was necessary for the breaking of political or kinship bonds that traditionally often linked the owners of the means of production.[66] According to Norton, "the triumph of industrial capitalism registered a moment of world historical defeat for the institution of the family."[67]

Accompanying this division within the bourgeois world of the mid–nineteenth century was the ideology of the Cult of True Womanhood. This newly "nonproductive" woman watched over the new, prolonged childhood and adolescence of middle-class sons and daughters, limited her fertility (and her sexual desires), cared for the home that symbolized her husband's affluence, and founded, administered, and served philanthropic societies for the relief of the poor and the orphaned, for the abolition of slavery, and for the redemption of "fallen women."[68] This myth, of course, made invisible within the dominant discourse the reality of the productive work of black women slaves as well as that of poor white women who labored in urban factories. It also ignored or romanticized the labor in domestic labor: the reproduction of new laborers and their successful socialization for wage-labor employment in a society shaped by racism, classism, and sexism; the provision for the emotional and physical needs of adult males; the purchase, preparation, and consumption of the products of the marketplace; the reproduction of patriarchy; and, in women's volunteer time, the bandaging of the social wounds created by a class society. In other words, within a capitalist patriarchal economy, the myth of a domestic/public division of spheres creates a sexual division of labor that serves specific, necessary social functions:

> It stabilizes the society through the family while it organizes a realm of work, domestic labor, for which there is no pay (housewives), or limited pay (paid houseworkers), or unequal pay (in the paid labor force). This last category shows the ultimate effect on women of the sexual division

82

of labor within the class structure. Their position as a paid worker is defined in terms of being a woman, which is a direct reflection of the hierarchical sexual divisions in a society organized around the profit motive.[69]

In the last half of the twentieth century, in a post-industrial society, the capitalist market reaches ever further into every aspect of life to commodify it. Succinctly described by Harry Braverman:

> The population no longer relies upon social organization in the form of family, friends, neighbours, community, elders, children, but with few exceptions must go to market and only to market, not only for food, clothing, and shelter, but also for recreation, amusement, security, for the care of the young, the old, the sick, the handicapped. In time not only the material and service needs but even the emotional pattern of life are channeled through the market.[70]

As Juliet Mitchell notes, "The woman's task is to hold on to the family while its separate atoms explode in different directions."[71]

Today, a pretense of separation between the domestic and the public spheres of life continues to make invisible the specific ways in which the shapes, functions, and "crises" of the family are conditioned by the needs of a patriarchal, racist, capitalist system of production. Today, this ideology ignores the fact that the needs of the productive system in the United States, together with the racism, sexism, and class bias of this culture, produce a variety of kinds of families struggling to survive and flourish. To quote again from Norton: "When push comes to shove it is the health of the private sector—the capitalist system of production, distribution, exchange, and capital accumulation—that must take priority over the intimate domain of private life, that is, families with their few remaining reproductive functions."[72]

However, this move into advanced capitalism has begun to strain the relationship between capitalism and patriarchy. As more women enter the labor force, their potential for economic independence increases as does their threat to patriarchal control. With the decline in men's real wages, women's wages become necessary to the survival of the middle-class family. Still, the desire for cheap labor has not removed the sexual division of labor. For the most part, women's advancement in the work place has been a result of "trickle down" rather than real integration: white women move into white men's jobs and women of color move into female jobs traditionally held by white women. But, Eisenstein suggests, "the justification for women's double day and unequal wages is less well-protected today."[73]

Ultimately, *the* family does not exist. What does exist is a series of social relations performing a variety of social functions which may become reified and called "the family." To understand its "crisis" today and to respond with justice, that is, with a faithfulness to human relationships that are constitutive of the well-being of women, their children, men, and human society,[74] requires an understanding of how the personal becomes political. We need to understand how the family, in its reproductive and socializing functions, contributes to the reproduction of relations of domination within contemporary society, including its sexism, its heterosexism, its racism, and its class bias.[75] And we need to understand how the family can become a site of resistance and justice. Release from unexamined idealizations of a separate "haven" of enlarged affections is crucial to the task; but so also is the transformation of the "heartless world."[76] Whether Hauerwas's ethics of character and the politics of his church will help in this task will be discussed in the next chapter.

## MOVING FROM EXPERIENCE TO THEORY

Experience raises troubling questions. Why have many women found oppressive the stories given us by loving families and faithful churches? Is there a self improperly resisting formation (evidence of sin)? Is there a self resisting wrongful formation (evidence of grace)? And . . . who gets to say? One thing I am trying to understand is the ordinary, loving, and morally justified presence of oppression within our most intimate communities—church and family, communities where we presumably have some influence, whether or not we have "Constantinian" power. Hauerwas's critique of the liberal church does not explain the continuous presence (and defense) of sexism, class privilege, racism, and homophobia within Christian community.

On the other hand, reflection upon experience raises a troubling awareness of the intricately interlocking forms of domination that function in our society and of women's differing ways of complicity with and resistance to them. The social construction of my self is a participation in the social construction of inequalities. Who I am (white, woman, middle-class, Christian, heterosexual, academic, and so on) is a socially constructed identity (not "reality") which exists as a webbing of "other-denying" relationships within a larger system of control and domination. I am white, not of color. I am heterosexual, not lesbian. I am middle-class, not poor. Experience troubles me with the realization that as I legitimately work for my own well-being, or that of others—even of everyone—my best view is partial and politically motivated. I cannot strip off these social identities and reach a piece of naked humanity within me from which to see "purely." Furthermore, the interlocking relationships of race, class, gender, and sexual orientation in modern U.S. culture make all actions and theories ambiguous. The opportunities I have because of the past struggles of middle-class white feminists came at the expense of poor women and men and of women and men of color. Given my "locatedness," can I (should I) learn to learn from those whose different stories reveal my participation in systemic distortions? And can I (should I) figure out how to work with others in political solidarity? Or, as Hauerwas argues, is every turn to social activism doomed to be a practice of self-interested coercion and a loss of Christian identity?

In an attempt to struggle with these questions, I am proposing a Christian ethics which is feminist, liberationist, and uses discourse analysis as a way to analyze the production and maintenance of socially coded positions within contemporary American society, a society that includes the church and, I argue, a church that is embedded in society. We need to understand how we become socially encoded and where the possibility of social (and ecclesial) transformation lies. I turn now to what Chris Weedon proposes as a "feminist poststructuralism" for a way of understanding ourselves as socially constructed.[77] Like Weedon, I believe that a feminist appropriation of poststructuralism which emphasizes discourse analysis has the potential to explain white middle-class women's experiences of the relationship between individuals and community and between power and knowledge. Ultimately my goal is to expose the interdependence of truth and justice and to contribute to the feminist project of embodying the character of emancipatory communities.

## Relating Individuals and Community

There is a long history within the study of language of attempting to understand the relationship between language, knowledge, and reality. Hauerwas's turn to a narrative theology and ethics participates in some of the results of this history. We both agree that a "fact" is not "something real out there" which we can know without interpretation. We both agree that language is not a neutral instrument but an interpretative system. We both agree that each individual comes to know herself and her world through the interpretation given to her in the language available to her. We both agree that humans are linguistic, historical, social beings and not the autonomous selves of classical liberal theory.[78] As David Tracy says: "I belong to my language far more than it belongs to me, and through that language I find myself participating in this particular history and society."[79]

"Poststructuralism" arose out of Saussure's insights into language as a system in which meaning arises out of the differences between signs. The point is that there is no necessary relationship between a signifier and what it signifies; the two are arbitrarily related and, together, constitute a sign. For example, there is no necessary connection between the signifier "d-o-g" and that which it signifies. Thus, the meaning of a sign is a function of how it differs from the other signs in the language system: "g-o-d, d-a-w-g." So, there cannot be a sign that simply presents a single, unified meaning (what it signifies) free from the presentation also of what it is not. There is nothing in the signifier "mother" that gives it its meaning, but the meaning of the sign arises out of its difference from the signs "virgin" or "whore" or "father." This claim does not deny the "thatness" of something (the fact that the body is). What it does claim is that the "whatness" of something, its meaning(s), is socially inscribed, and that language is one of the social systems through which this encoding of meaning occurs.[80] "Thatness" has no meaning; it is not a part of our consciousness, without "whatness." Language, then, is an always present, cultural medium (an interpretation) through which the self experiences "thatness."

However, poststructuralism moves beyond Saussure's display of language as a meaning-giving system to try to explain the plurality of meanings and the changeability of meaning within a language system. For example, as Saussure has shown, the meaning of "woman" is not constructed upon some natural essence of woman. But the meaning of "woman" also is not fixed and stable within the language system. Consider the meanings of "woman" in the following statements:

Woman! You are the Devil's doorway. . . . you should always go in mourning and rags. (Tertullian)[81]

> Mother, woman:
> Walk and raise your fist,
> Affirm your desire to be free.[82]

The meaning of the sign "woman" depends upon its discursive context. In discourse, someone is trying to say something to someone about something. The meaning of the sign "woman" depends on its location in a specific discourse. Identifying the discourse requires us to move back into the social and historical context to identify and analyze the specific location of the discourse. To quote Tracy again: "And all texts, theirs and mine, are saturated with the ideologies of particular societies, the history of ambiguous effects of particular traditions, and the hidden agendas of the unconscious."[83]

Language is, then, a medium through which the self is produced, or constructed, or encoded, according to socially specific discourses. It is through language and its discursive context (and through other nonlinguistic sign systems) that consciousness is formed to be conscious of itself. Language is that which enables the self to become a self: to think, speak, interpret, intend, and give voice to meaning—meanings which are already embedded within the structure of the language. We cannot see what we cannot name. Therefore, our ability to "see" is a social ability. So, language is a tool, but it is not a neutral tool. Language is political.

The feminist ethics of liberation that I am proposing here begins, then, with the poststructuralist understanding that there is no presocial essence of the self such as fear of finitude, or love of freedom. Humans are socially constructed in all aspects, from the beginning, all the way in. Human potentiality takes form only, and always only partially, in particular, historical embodiments. This means that the development of women's personhood and consciousness, including whether and how we "see" sexual or gender identity, is a process which is constituted by our activities and the organization and meaning we are able to give to these activities from the interpretive discourses available to us.

I also use the term "discourse" in a particular way. I am not confining it to that which is linguistic. Rather, I am following McClintock Fulkerson in her sense of a "meaningful totality" which includes both the linguistic and nonlinguistic elements that produce the meaning of an event.[84] For example, when liberal feminists attempted to explain themselves in the last century, they used the language of liberal theory. However, that language expressed meanings embodied in social relationships (for example, the family, work, the church) constructed within a liberal, capitalist, patriarchal, Euro-American, male discourse (a discursive totality). As we have seen, the appropriation of liberal language for women's equality has both fit and not fit women's concrete experiences. It has both aided and hindered women's attempts to participate equally in the social construction of meaning. Women's activities always exist within (and are not prior to) a discursive system of meaning. We "understand" ourselves through already socially constructed, interpretative screens (discourses). To the extent that the discourses available are products of patriarchal interests, their usefulness for the emancipation of women is always ambiguous. That is why even a feminist appropriation of poststructuralism has to be always tentative, selected, and guarded.

This emphasis on a discursive totality also serves to deny the charge that reality is *only* language or only ideas expressed in language. (In which case, personal and social transformation would be only a matter of changing how we think about things.) In women's experiences, meanings are impressed upon us as knowledge that takes concrete form in daily social activities, institutional practices, assigned gender, race, and class characteristics, and so on. In teaching classes in human sexuality, I often ask students when they became aware that their gender identity mattered. Most women can remember specific instances in which they were suddenly confronted, often with embarrassment, even shame, with the declaration that what they were doing "girls don't do." So, for example, girls don't play softball to win, but to have fun; and, in many churches, girls don't proclaim the word of God. All of these daily practices sustain the power relations inherent in social knowledge. Similarly, the dominant understanding of the family in America as a patriarchal, nuclear family is materially embodied by law, tax structure, religious beliefs, the educational system, media, the welfare system, church practices, and other social institutions, in addition to the symbols of language.[85] The more firmly meaning is embedded in social practices and institutions, the more power and authority it can exercise simply by being "common sense," while marginalizing other "voices" as oppositional. Thus, many middle-class white women in the United

States find it very difficult to imagine the possible goodness of alternative ways of life and family distinct from the heterosexual, patriarchal, nuclear family. Many heterosexuals cannot imagine homosexual love.

However, we have also seen that the stories women tell demonstrate that our lives are the point at which a range of conflicting meanings from different discourses compete for our subjective embodiment. For example, consider the range of contemporary meanings given to the event of ending a pregnancy prior to live birth: murder, tragic necessity, right of autonomy, selfishness, responsible stewardship, violence, birth control, and so on. Each meaning arises out of a discursive totality existing within U.S. culture (and the church) in which such a meaning makes sense.[86] In the last century, the "true woman" had to fulfill the conflicting ideals of being a wife (a sexually naive sexual partner) who was passive, fragile, overly emotional, and dependent, while at the same time being a self-giving mother, nurse, and educator.[87] Many women in the wage labor force today find themselves fragmented by the conflicting roles of wage earner and primary parent (mother). Women in the work place negotiate their existence between woman-as-sex-object and woman-as-coworker.

There are three reasons, then, why I see value in a (always temporary and suspicious) feminist use of poststructuralism and discourse analysis. First, it allows us to recognize, and not to underestimate, the entrenched way things are (the stability of community meanings and customs) while exposing the temporary nature of the way things are (the threat/promise of instability). Thinking in terms of a discursive totality directs us to identify the importance of ordinary life in the formation of individual character. Women's experiences of oppression name the daily, small, trivial practices within families and schools and Sunday morning worship, as well as the more visibly contested practices within business, law, medicine, government, and so on. Thinking in terms of discourse holds together the character of individuals and the character of the communities in which they do (and learn to do) mundane things. And it shows the complexity involved in transforming either. Yet, by identifying the power of the mundane, it holds forth the promise and the necessity of such transformation.

Second, the focus on the construction of meaning within a discursive totality lets us recognize that meaning is always political. Meaning is always being produced from a particular, historically located, and interested position. Neither the "True Woman" of the last century nor the "Super Mom" of the 1980s was a description of the essence of "woman." Both were prescriptions from a particular social location. Yet, they were "real" descriptions of some women because they were embodied in the daily practices of domestic and public life. This reminds us to practice critical thinking, or a hermeneutic of suspicion. We need to analyze the material location of ideas and theories.

Third, poststructuralism and the analysis of discourse helps to explain the existence and promise of the various and conflicting discourses that circulate in our society and in our Christian tradition. As we have seen, women's experiences, and the experiences of marginalized racial groups, reveal this diversity and the power relations that produce it. For example, the very proclamation and institutionalization of certain dominant assumptions expose the possibility (perhaps even the existence) of alternative assumptions, even if such alternatives are cast in a negative light. After all, one rarely needs to proclaim the rightness of what everyone knows is right. In addition, we have seen how changing needs within powerful institutions of society, such as the economy, can contest dominant assumptions shaping other social institutions (such as the role of women in the family or the church). In contrast to Hauerwas's story of a unified (if ultimately unsatisfactory) Texan identity and his proposal for a unified Christian identity, women's stories show that we experience diversity and contradictions as part of our differing social locations within our communities. In women's dangerous memories, we have experienced community and the development of character as a process of being confronted by difference and change, and we have experienced the necessity of confronting others with our difference and our need for change. Although we are not the independent authors of our lives as liberal theory suggests, we are also not the recipients of a singular cultural-linguistic tradition as Hauerwas suggests.

More important, it has been the existence of conflicting discourses within our communities that provided the "gaps" that enabled women and other "others" to resist dominant discourses. For example, bell hooks describes how, in learning the dominant language of the culture ("white" English), she also learned the racial, sexual, and class assumptions embedded in it. She writes:

> This language that enabled me to attend graduate school, to write a dissertation, to speak at job interviews, carries the scent of oppression. Language is also a place of struggle. . . . The oppressed strug-

gle in language to recover ourselves, to reconcile, to reunite, to renew. Our words are not without meaning, they are an action, a resistance. Language is also a place of struggle.[88]

hooks exemplifies the resistance of the marginalized. Paying attention to the discursive whole, the material stuff of social and institutional racist practices as well as the language that makes such practices "common sense," allows her to analyze the power relations and the knowledges that adhere to them. Her position as a black woman within this racist culture conditioned the historically specific forms of discourse available to her. Yet it is the practices kept alive by her particular community against the discourse of the dominant race that gave her a discourse of resistance. hooks remembers the language of her childhood, of the sound of "thickly accented black Southern speech." While another language had to be learned in order to advance in the educational system of the dominant culture and to become a university teacher, it is this thick language that continues to give hooks and her black community ways to speak that "decolonize our minds."[89]

## Relating Power and Knowledge

White middle-class feminists began our struggle by demanding that we be given the same rights as males because we have the same capacity for reason. In the struggle for our own liberation, we encountered the reality of difference. On the one hand, where women embodied differing discourses (as abolitionists and suffragists) against the limiting, dominant, white, male discourse, we were empowered to resist gender oppression. On the other hand, where heterosexual, white middle-class feminists assumed we could speak for all women, we were confronted with "others" who revealed the difference that race, class, and sexual orientation make.

Certainly we have often experienced, and continue to experience, these differences as conflictual because behind these differences lie inequalities in social power that have daily ramifications for people's well-being. Yet, it is the conflict raised by difference that has the potential to be transformative. And the transformation rooted in the acknowledgment of difference is empowering. The existence of discourses other than our own allows us to name more clearly the false definitions to which we have been subjected. It also allows us to see more clearly where we continue to universalize our own experiences and use the power of our social locations to impose our "knowledge" upon others. In both cases the structures of domination and the relationship between power and knowledge become more clearly revealed. When the meanings by which we live are products of social processes, power produces knowledge. Those who hold social, political, economic, and/or religious power in a society participate in the creation of individual and social consciousness.

Contrary to Hauerwas's concern, the fear that disorder and chaos will be caused by the fragmentation of social meaning is not the fear of those who struggle for liberation. Indeed, at this time in which the voices of many "others" are claiming the power to speak and be heard, feminist theories participate in advancing "the growing uncertainty within Western intellectual circles about the appropriate grounding and methods for explaining and/or interpreting human experience."[90]

Because knowledge is always partial and historically situated, including womanist and feminist knowledge, the capacity of individuals and societies to change through their encounter with the reality of social differences is fundamental to the empowerment of marginalized groups. In the feminist, liberationist ethics I describe, confrontation with the differences that race, class, sex, and sexual orientation make in the lives of people is essential to the process of knowledge seeking and to developing more honest and mutually empowering relations between persons and groups. It is necessary to the task of ethics. As Sharon Welch writes: "We can see the foundational flaws in systems of ethics only from the outside, from the perspective of another system of defining and implementing that which is valued. . . . Pluralism is required, not for its own sake, but for the sake of enlarging our moral vision."[91]

From this perspective, the danger confronting contemporary American society cannot be stated simply as the breakdown of community and the lost of shared values. Nor can the danger confronting the contemporary American Christian church be stated simply as the loss of our traditional identity, as Hauerwas proposes. Rather, as Welch argues, our society and our church are more threatened by the assumption that one social class or one group alone has the resources to make moral judgments, whether these resources be named reason or tradition.[92] It is through a commitment to the empowerment of the concrete, marginalized "other" and to being confronted by their subjugated knowledges, produced by the differences that marginalization by race, sexual orientation, class, and gender make, that disparities in power are confronted and the "common sense" embedded in dominant discourses is challenged. When we recognize that power produces knowledge, a feminist use of poststructuralism and discourse analysis drives us to the conclusion that truth is a product of justice.

In the summary that concluded the last chapter, I emphasized the words that have significant power in Hauerwas's discourse. These are words that originally attracted me to his writings: community, nonviolence, the risk of faith, the critique of liberalism, the political significance of the personal. It took many closer readings to realize that while we spoke the same words, they are embedded in different discourses that arise out of different social locations. Our critiques of liberalism and our understandings of how and why the personal is political come from different social locations. In what follows I will indicate how other terms function in the feminist liberationist ethic I propose.

*Freedom and Solidarity*

Women's varying experiences confirm for us the reality of subjugated or marginalized discourses within our communities and, in particular, within the Christian narrative. By definition, the relationships between dominant and subjugated discourses have to do with power: the power to create defining discourses, the power to withstand definitions that subjugate, and the power to form alternative discourses of resistance.[93] As we have seen in the stories of women, the existence of such marginalized discourses has been the source of women's survival and our liberation. Using a poststructuralist theory of discourse to explain these experiences of subversive power results in an understanding of freedom as the capacity to participate in the ongoing creation of self and society, cocreating and codetermining, through our decision to embody some of the social discourses we encounter over others. Freedom involves the mutual willingness to be creative in, and to be created by, the encounter with "others."[94] In this sense, freedom involves participation in solidarity; that is, action and conversation toward action with "others," most especially those more marginalized by society than myself. Being in solidarity with others is characterized by a willingness to admit both my finitude and my power. In the liberative ethics I describe, freedom is not the liberal goal of isolation from influencing attachments. It is not the unencumbered, individualistic, freedom-to-choose of liberal theory, that requires dominating power. On the other hand, it also is not the formation of a stable, unified self in a singular, cultural-linguistic community that Hauerwas proposes. For Hauerwas, freedom is the second nature developed by total immersion into the practices, language, habits, and skills of a community; it is the power to describe and claim one's actions as one's own in the language of one's community. However, it is just this "second nature" that women have had to bring to consciousness, analyze, and resist. It has meant discovering in ourselves the unjust power relations inherent in actions from second nature. For emancipatory communities, the quest for community necessitates suspicion of second natures, the freedom to encounter and be encountered by differences, and the risk of solidarity with "others."

*Objectivity*

Beginning with our experiences of liberal theory and our recognition of culturally created definitions of gender, a feminist appropriation of poststructuralism has deepened our analysis to expose the fully social nature of all knowledge-seeking. All systems of knowledge, most especially "common sense" and "second nature," are rooted in values that support particular social loyalties. As Sandra Harding notes in *The Science Question in Feminism,* even the rules of scientific inquiry display the already existing moral norms of the inquirer.[95] Chris Weedon summarizes: "Meaning is always political. ... Not all areas of discourse are equally significant in the hierarchy of power/knowledge relations but no discursive practice is outside them."[96]

The question that is then raised is whether we are condemned to a choice between relativism or Hauerwas's disciplined community. Are we left with only the assumption that if all positions are value-ladened and self-interested, there can be no claim of "objectivity" and no way to discern greater or lesser truthfulness among positions? Does it no longer matter, as Foucault asserts, who is speaking?[97] Or are we left with Hauerwas's turn to intratextuality in which the validation of truth claims seems to be restricted to the internal sense-making of the narrative community and its masters? As we have seen, the position I have presented challenges the liberal view (as does Hauerwas) that objectivity arises from the shedding of historical contingencies and the appeal to an ahistorical, dispassionate reason. But it also challenges the postliberal emphasis of Hauerwas and Lindbeck on participation in a community of commonly accepted values and traditions; that "to be objective is to understand oneself as part of a community and one's work as part of a project and of a history."[98] Rather, feminists such as Beverly Harrison and Sharon Welch claim that objectivity is also a socially created meaning that arises from a social process of engagement in the work of social transformation. That engagement must be characterized by openness to the perspective of others, and especially to the perspective of those most disempowered and most affected by the issues. Moreover, this engagement with others must be entered with a willingness to be changed in this process.

The first step toward objectivity, then, is to acknowledge that my standpoint, my descriptions, and my method of moral thinking are inherently political; they express and defend some group's interests and my loyalty to that group. The second step is to acknowledge that social injustice means that our groups are interrelated in systems of domination and exploitation. Using poststructuralist theory and discourse analysis, a feminist ethics of liberation connects the crisis of knowledge (what is truth) and the crisis of ethics (what is good). We can then judge truth by where, and with whom, it leads us to stand. We can participate in the transformation of church and society because "we can choose between different accounts of reality on the basis of their social implications."[99] Having experienced the distortions produced by dominant narratives, this feminist ethics of liberation looks for an emancipatory epistemology, a knowledge seeking that is "for, not just about, that majority of the members of our species who have fragmented selves and oppositional consciousness."[100] As Sheila Davaney notes, some experiences "do more truth than others."[101] Choosing to encounter the marginalized "other" at their sites of empowered resistance, choosing to be open to their histories and traditions, exposes the strengths and weaknesses of my own social location. The challenge comes again from bell hooks, who describes her experience with white feminist thinkers participating in a discussion about the "other":

I was made "Other" there in that space with them. In that space in the margins, that live-in segregated world of my past and present. They did not meet me there in that space. They met me at the center. They greeted me as colonizers.

She challenges:

This is an intervention. A message from that space in the margin that is a site of creativity and power, that inclusive space where we recover ourselves, where we move in solidarity to erase the category colonized/colonizer. Marginality as site of resistance. Enter that space. Let us meet there. Enter that space. We greet you as liberators.[102]

Objectivity, then, like all meaning, is an ongoing social process, the result of a dynamic mutuality practiced in action—an "engaged reflection."[103] How "truthful" objectivity will be is fully dependent upon the justice of the social process that produces it.

## Violence and Risk

For Hauerwas, violence is the primary effect of human sinfulness. Fear of our finitude and the desire to control our lives leads us to coercive and violent behavior. Therefore, in his theology, Christian faith is focused upon the God who is in absolute control of history. A faithful response to this God is to have the faith to do nothing. Faith requires accepting the risk of giving up control of our lives, practicing patience.

However, from women's experiences of our social and fluid subjectivities, and of the diversity created by social location within communities, the problem that Christian ethics must address is injustice: the socially constructed lack of power to participate in the creation of a community's knowledge—a lack that characterizes groups marginalized within society and, also, within the church. Disempowerment and domination are maintained by discourses that deny our radical historicism and the dynamic relationship that exists between society and individuals. Liberalism imposed false ideologies with negative consequences to community, particularly white middle- and upper-class community, which both Hauerwas and I point out. However, the answer is not the secular turn to communitarianism nor the theological turn to a narrative-formed community. In women's experiences, the freedom to participate in the cocreation of either secular or religious meaning has been consistently thwarted by social roles and virtues that establish places for us within hierarchies of domination. For women, then, the understanding of violence includes the experience of the loss of power to cocreate ourself-in-relation.[104] Violence names the experience of being defined by dominant discourses that are embedded in the structures of our institutions, in the material practices of our social, political, and economic systems, as well as in the theories and stories that give them authenticity. In contrast to Hauerwas's experience of violence arising within himself in defense of his people's story, women have also experienced violence as coercion by the dominant within our community in shaping and forming us according to their worldview. It is a violence that takes women's lives, physically and spiritually. Thus, feminists and womanists have learned that it is important to ask who produced this knowledge that we are taught to speak, from which social position, and for what loyalties? We must ask who has the power to describe and define; who has the power to produce the principles or rules being brought to bear? Who authored "our tradition"? Whose sense is "common"? And, in the production of knowledge, who has not had the power to be heard, or to speak?[105]

This also requires an ethics of risk. It requires an ethics that is profoundly aware of the limits of our power and knowledge, our finitude. But it is not the risk of doing nothing. It is the risk of acting in the midst of limits and ambiguity. Sharon Welch describes a feminist ethic of risk in which the inability to control outcomes or to avoid ambiguity or to maintain some definition of moral purity requires the risk of responsible action. To stop acting is "the death of imagination, the death of caring, the death of the ability to love."[106] Imagination and the embodied expression of love depend upon ongoing participation with others in the work of creating justice. Welch argues that white feminists need to learn from womanists a "sheer holy boldness": the ways of action that acknowledge the ambiguities and the costs of all our actions and the partialness of any success.[107] We need to learn, she says, the difference between bending, and bowing and scraping. We need to learn to value that which can be done today to bring about small experiences of freedom that sow the ground with potential for future emancipatory possibilities.[108]

This ongoing work of creation is the work of salvation.[109] The motivation to participate in such work for social transformation is grounded in "a social anthropology and [image of] a self constituted by our connection with the earth and with other people."[110] The goal of such action is justice understood as "rightly ordered relationships of mutuality within the total web of our social relations"; or, the reign of God.[111] We learn our particular historical expression of sin through encountering the oppressive and exploitative social relationships of our society as we join the struggle for liberation. Sin is always a particular, concrete, historical, social reality. Therefore, justice, un-

97

derstood as the virtue that directs and empowers one to act on behalf of human well-being, is essential to salvation.[112] Such a justice is not merely procedural, but is the very substance of social relations. And, such a justice must be extended to include all women and the entirety of our social relations.[113]

The goal of this feminist ethics of liberation, informed by post-structuralist theory, is, therefore, to expose and transform the violence of marginalization and disempowerment by choosing (1) to embody those discourses, to enter that space, where the asymmetrical dualisms created by systems of domination (historically: race, class, sex, and sexual orientation) are revealed and rejected, and (2) to call into being practices of interdependence aimed toward equality of participation in the social construction of meaning. In this project, a plurality of voices, a being present to each other as "other," is an imperative to moral vision. As Welch says, "we cannot be moral alone."[114] We cannot "see" ourselves without placing ourselves in vulnerable interaction with concrete "others." Unmasking the interests of dominant discourses, especially one's own, requires meeting the "other" in the margin where individual and social transformation takes place and the power to resist is nourished.[115] This feminist ethics of liberation is, then, "a politics of knowledge seeking" in which our fragmented identities are essential sources of knowledge in communities of emancipation.[116] In other words, communities of nonviolence, for women and other "others," require justice.


## AN INITIAL RESPONSE TO HAUERWAS

In this brief account of experience and theory, I have tried to show why some white middle-class, heterosexual, Christian women have turned away from liberal political theory and from universalizing assumptions about the characteristics of humanity. In our history, these assumptions have functioned to obscure our analysis of the current, concrete context of social power relations and our participation in them.

From this reflection, I identify Hauerwas's theory of the human condition, and his correlative account of the Christian narrative, as an example of a reappropriation in postliberal motif of the liberal desire to find some ground for unassailable truth.[117] By establishing the story of the Tower of Babel as his myth of origin, Hauerwas asserts the existence of a psychological characteristic that is always present among humans: the fear of our finitude, which becomes aroused in our encounter with the other. This negative characteristic and the violence it inevitably causes transcend all particular contexts in human history. It remains the universally constant, always present danger about which, according to Hauerwas, Christian ethics must always be primarily concerned. It becomes the unchangeable ground out of which all human beliefs and behaviors are shaped, as well as evaluated, regardless of historical particularity. In other words, Hauerwas has backed away from his assertion that we are historic, socially formed beings. He has regrounded all humans in a presocial (and negative) human characteristic. It seems to me that there is a sense in which the "Fall," for Hauerwas, occurs before community, not in it. Our historicism, then, is only penultimate. It is located in our participation in particular, narrative communities and the limited stories they tell in response to this ultimate human characteristic.

The result of resisting a more complete historicism is that ethical analysis of specific, historically and socially located issues becomes skewed by allegiance to a preexisting, universal explanation. For example, sin is always, for Hauerwas, the "active and willful attempt to overreach our powers"; the need to be in control of our lives; the egocentric altruism of social activism.[118] And if active, willful attempts to impose "our" will are the universal and original sin, then submission and humility become the obviously necessary responses. Hauerwas suggests no distinction in the nature of sin based on the very different historical contexts of black Christians in a racist United States, or of white affluent men in the U.S., or of Christians in the base communities of Central America or in the black churches of South Africa, or of abused women.[119] The result of Hauerwas's assumption that all humans share equally in the same *kind* of sinfulness is the obfuscation of actual social differences: the struggle against injustice is seen by Hauerwas as motivated by the same "sin" as the imposition of injustice. In the next chapter, I will argue that this masking of differences, in the flight to an ahistorical sameness, functions to sustain the power relations of the status quo.

Despite his emphasis on community, Hauerwas continues to display a modern Western emphasis on individualism by identifying sin as a preexistent characteristic located within the individual. The violence in human relations, which Hauerwas identifies as the central problem, emanates from the fear that resides within each individual soul; a fear ignited by the encounter with an "other." By placing the root of violence within the individual, Hauerwas makes the transformation of structures (social and ecclesial) a secondary task of Christian ethics, preempted by the fundamental task of shaping individual Christian characters. In other words, his emphasis on the character of the church derives from his focus on the self-as-story. His interest is in a community that tells the right story to individuals who are distorted by fear and subject to violence. The transformation of the church into a disciplined community is the solution because the individual is the problem. Hauerwas does not identify the ongoing unjust character of the church—its practice and theological justification of relationships of domination and submission—as an essential element in its continuing acceptance of violence.

Hauerwas's description of the human condition and of the role of the church in the world reflects Western dualistic assumptions: self and other, my group and the other, church and world, resident alien and secular culture. From his worldview of violent dualisms, he yearns for a loving, nonviolent unity. His proposal of "resident alien" status for the church in society seems to assume that Christians and the church can be a part of society while not being fundamentally shaped by society. As resident aliens, we are to be firmly but nonviolently "us" in relation to "them." Womanist and feminist critiques of the church have revealed the violence to women and others that such "unity" has masked. However, it is our history in church and society that also exposes the consistent embeddedness of the church, Christians, and the Christian story in culturally particular, patriarchal views of "women." Racial-ethnic groups expose the consistent embeddedness of the Eurocentric church and its Christian narrative in racism. It is my argument, therefore, that there are no resident aliens and, indeed, cannot be.

Finally, although Hauerwas denies the existence of an ahistorical human reason, his description of a fixed Christian narrative, and the character of God and human that it alleges to represent, functions in the same universalizing manner. Thus, for example, from his identification of the centrality of the nonviolent character of God, Hauerwas can jump to the assertion that Christians have always (or should have always) opposed abortion.[120] His conclusion does not need to make note of historical context, of changing (and multiple) definitions of the term "abortion," of who is included in the term "Christians," or of the exclusion of all women, the poor, and minority races from participation in the development of church doctrine.[121] He does not need women's input in defining what is a risk and what is a gift. Fundamentally, in presenting "the Christian narrative," Hauerwas does not need to acknowledge the difference in "the proverbs, prophecies, legends, laws, and traditions" that fathers pass on to their sons and those that mothers whisper to their daughters.[122] Hauerwas seems not to recognize the reality of relationships of domination within "the Christian narrative" and its tradition, nor the multiplicity of voices, nor the silencing throughout history of many Christians' stories. I believe that in response to the differences raised by these voices today, Hauerwas's appeal to "the Christian story" reasserts a claim to unchanging truth. As I will document more clearly in the next chapter, differences of historical and social location have no significance in his description of Christian ethics, or on the particular content Hauerwas assigns to "Christian character" and "Christian community." Essentially, Hauerwas's description of "the Christian narrative" functions to deny differences in the same manner that liberal theory functioned. Who benefits and who is burdened by this denial of socially constructed differences? Who benefits and who is burdened by Hauerwas's implicit denial of the interested locatedness of his own theology? It is my contention that when we ignore social difference, we all run the risk of universalizing our own particularity and defending our truth at the expense of justice. Hauerwas flees the consequences of the knowledge seeking of a radical historicism by replacing "rational man" and ahistorical reason with "the (white, male) Christian" and "the Christian (master) narrative."

## SUMMARY

In this chapter I have recounted some of the history of white middle-class Christian feminists. I have described the process by which theoretical reflection upon our own struggles to claim the power to speak for ourselves and our confrontation with those we were at the same time silencing has caused us to suspect the tenets of liberalism and any tendency to universalize the knowledges of particular experiences. We have embraced the hermeneutics of suspicion and, with some caution, poststructuralist theory to help us explain our struggles for justice and our complicity in injustice. Most profoundly this journey has been, and continues to be, an experience of ongoing conversion: from abstract norms to concrete *others*, from orthodoxy to *orthopraxis*, from individualism to *community*, from community to *solidarities*, from certainty (in truth or action) to *risk* (in truth and action), from seeking the centers to seeking the margins. We have arrived at what Susan Thistleth-waite calls an "unstable truth-in-action."[123] This is not a place, or even a truth, but a people to hold us accountable, and to whom we hold ourselves accountable, as we continue to journey.

In the next chapter I will look again at Hauerwas's theological ethics to answer the questions raised by a feminist analysis: Does it provide for the wholeness of women and other "others" as full moral agents in the construction of ourselves, our churches, and our society? Does it clarify or obfuscate the relations of domination we have experienced in church and society? Does it provide a clarifying analysis of the fragmented world? And does it point to an adequate praxis of transformation? To whom is it accountable? For whom is it the good news?

CHAPTER **4**

# UNMASKING THE DIFFERENCES

## Nonviolence and Social Control

*The spinning process requires seeking out the sources of the ghostly gases that have seeped into the deep chambers of our minds. . . . These deceptive perceptions were/are implanted through language—the all-pervasive language of myth, conveyed overtly and subliminally through religion, "great art," literature, the dogmas of professionalism, the media, grammar.*[1]
*[Ethics], generally written from one of several (but basically the same) patriarchal perspectives, works out of hidden agendas concealed in the texture of language, buried in mythic reversals which control "logic" most powerfully because unacknowledged.*[2]

Once again Mary Daly warns women of the deadly perceptions and hidden agendas lodged in "reversals" that shape our minds through the texture of language and through the whole range of concrete, social embodiments that give material form to such perceptions. To unmask these reversals requires, as I have argued, exposing the social location from which our theological/ethical claims are made. It is, especially, to expose the consequences of such claims for people subjugated by race, class, sex, and/or sexual orientation. Unmasking the reversals reveals who "we" are when "we" speak.

In the last chapter, I described some theoretical perspectives arising out of white feminists' history of resistance against white male dominance. Specifically, I emphasized women's experiences of diverse discourses based on different social locations within communities. Reflecting upon those experiences through the use of poststructuralist theory, I have suggested that women's experiences reveal the social construction of all knowledge; but, more important, that the experiences of those marginalized by dominant discourses can be locations of liberative knowledge and the power to resist. I have contrasted these conclusions with those of Hauerwas's Texan epistemology and his ethics of character.

In this chapter, I turn to an analysis of the social roots of Hauerwas's description of the Christian and the Christian narrative. From what social location is his ethics an expression of some group's feelings, attitudes, and hopes? From what social location does his ethics sound like good news? And what are the social consequences for women and other marginalized groups of his gospel of nonviolence?

## Oneness and the Will to Power

As we have seen, Hauerwas's ethics revolves around a core theme: a universal human fear of finitude leads to fragmenting, false loyalties and to a violent defense of those loyalties. For Hauerwas, the problem of contemporary life is its moral fragmentation and the loss of identity that can only be sustained in a community of shared values. Furthermore, this problem must be resolved in the one community that bears a true story empowering people to live nonviolently in this fallen world. Thus, salvation, for Hauerwas, ultimately involves the unity of all people within the Christian narrative. Aware of Christianity's past use of violence to accomplish this end, Hauerwas emphasizes that the core characteristic of the Christian community is nonviolence. However, it is my contention that violence is intrinsic to his proposal.

Kwok Pui-lan, a Chinese Christian, describes the Asian experience of Christian missionary expansion into China in which the "Word of God" was brought to the "heathens" who lived in a deficient culture characterized by "idolatry and superstition."[3] From this position of marginality Asian Christians were confronted with a gospel of Western presuppositions and modes of thinking. For example, the very notion of a scripture that contains all of Truth in one closed (Western) canon is a characteristic, Kwok warns, of Western religious traditions. There is within the western metaphysical tradition a "logocentrism"; that is, a hope and desire to reach a fully positive meaning that does not also carry within it its dependence upon difference.[4] Christianity exhibits this in its assumption of a transcendent presence located in a sacred text that leads Westerners to search for the voice of absolute truth. Kwok argues, "if other people can only define truth according to the Western perspective, then Christianization really means westernization."[5] Her recognition of the cultural embeddedness of the truth claims of the Western Christian gospel, and her experience of how these claims have been imposed upon her culture with an imperialistic assumption of acultural, universal applicability, has led her to appreciate Foucault's exploration of the relationship between truth and power. Asian Christians, she says, must ask who owns the truth, who interprets the truth, and what constitutes the truth? Her conclusion, with specific reference to the Christian scriptures, is that truth cannot be "prepackaged" but is found in the "actual interaction between text and context in the concrete historical situation."[6] "The whole biblical text represents one form of human construction to talk about God," she writes.[7] Speaking from the context of being a Christian in the mostly other-than-Christian two-thirds world (in which most people live, affected by the exploitation of the mostly Christian one-third world), Kwok argues that this focus on the oneness of truth produces the crusading spirit in which absolute truth provides not only the answers for all people but deigns to define for them the questions as well.[8] It is this hierarchical model of truth, she warns, that leads to the coercion of all others into one sameness and homogeneity; the universalizing of the One.[9]

This identification of power with oneness lies deep within the traditional Christian image of God. Trinitarian theologies, theologies that could also have led to an emphasis on diversity and relationality as the central characteristic of divinity, were shaped in the early centuries of Christianity by an increasing emphasis upon the unity of the substance of the Godhead. From the time of Tertullian, Christian theology increasingly emphasized the power and authority of God the Father in order to counter (while copying) the claims of Rome's absolute, divine monarchy. God, the Father of Christians, the maker of heaven and earth, rules over all and rules especially over all secular rulers.[10] For Christians of the first four centuries, according to Elaine Pagels, this image of God served as a source of power for those made in "the image of God" and straining under the burden of the authority of the Roman state. These early Christians identified human equality in the human capacity to exercise the moral freedom and responsibility necessary to choose and to do good in resistance to the imperial cult.[11] However, a radical change in thought occurred that Pagels attributes to Augustine and to the theology he developed within a totally different political context. By the end of the fourth century, the emperors were Christian and Christians had come into imperial favor, wealth, and power. From this context of participation in secular power, Augustine reads the same texts from Genesis and concludes the opposite from his predecessors: the human race is incapable of ruling itself.[12] The will to rebellion lies within each human and leads to a lust for power that now distorts all human relationships.[13] The primary virtue for fallen human nature is no longer the exercise of moral freedom and responsibility, but the virtue of obedience: "our true good is free slavery."[14] Thus, as I interpret Pagels, in the age of Constantine, some Christian men gained political and economic power and yet also experienced the ambiguity and limits of their individual power. In this context of relative power, Augustine chose a theology emphasizing human guilt rather than face the possibility that human control over events, and even over the consequences of our best intentions, is limited.[15]

It is a theology, Pagels argues, that appeals to a need to imagine oneself in control even at the cost of accepting oneself as a participant in the universal human condition of sinfulness. As Christians began to participate in social power, the image of absolute power residing in the absolute oneness of God the Father was joined to a theology of human fallenness. In Augustinian theology, divine domination and human guiltiness legitimate human relationships of domination: the Righteous One stands against all others. For Augustine, Bishop of Hippo, this theology led to an increasing use of coercion both inside and outside the church and to alliances with imperial power on behalf of his orthodoxy.[16] Thistlethwaite concludes:

> God conceived as supreme ruler over all from whom other authorities take their cue is a theology of violence. Hierarchy introduces hierarchy: The absolute power of God legitimates the power of the father priest, the father of the country, the father in the family, and so on. Monotheistic monarchism has been a powerful weapon for both church and state in their efforts to legitimate the ultimate power of some over others.[17]

As we have seen in chapter 2, Hauerwas seems to accept an essentially Augustinian view of human fallenness.[18] He views all humans *a priori* as seeking to avoid the truth of their finitude by asserting control over their lives and resorting to coercion and violence against others. His remedy for this condition of chaos and violence ostensibly recoils from Augustine's resort to coercion. After all, Hauerwas argues that "we Christians" must recognize our powerlessness and do the one thing we can: participate in the one community, the Christian church, that knows the one truth of human finitude and divine, nonviolent love. Ironically, however, while purporting to eschew violence, Hauerwas legitimates the cause of the violent experiences related by Kwok Pui-lan and other non-Western Christians, the violent imposition of the one absolute truth. As Hauerwas insists: "outside the church there is no saving knowledge of God."[19]

Hauerwas is aware of the "polemical, if not violent, character of my essays"; a violence he defends as necessary to expose the sentimentalities of liberal culture.[20] The Christian church, the community of the reconciled, exists in the world as both the means and the goal of the world's salvation. While God is in control of history, the proof of that, for Hauerwas, is the existence of this faithful, nonviolent community. In his introduction to *The Peaceable Kingdom*, Hauerwas acknowledges that what he is presenting is *a* Christian ethic. Yet, he goes on to say that he also intends "to argue that the position I develop should be *any* Christian's" *(emphasis added).*[21] Therefore, the problem for Christians, writes Hauerwas, is how "we" are to survive "as disciplined communities in democratic societies" where the very values of liberty and individualism undermine the social formation necessary for Christian character.[22] In this context, the church must learn to become a disciplined and disciplining community in order to maintain its distinct identity. It is in this sense that Hauerwas sees an attractive model for Christian community in the Aristotelian polis; both are "equally antidemocratic."[23] According to Hauerwas, the church that is faithful to Jesus is not a democracy. To make a person into a Christian requires training, apprenticeship to a master, learning the "epistemological bias" of this craft.[24] Kwok Pui-lan would remind Hauerwas that "we" Christians do not all live in democratic societies, that not all Christians are being tainted by liberty and individualism, and, most important, that a theological ethics shaped by (and in response to) liberal Western society cannot be for "all" Christians.

Unaware of the imperialism of his claims, Hauerwas identifies his challenge as how to make his absolute truth (which can be known only through the witness of those persons formed by the discipline of the church) compelling to the whole world without this task itself becoming an ideology that supports patterns of domination and violence.[25] In my terms, can Hauerwas appropriate a Western, imperialistic view of God and truth and an Augustinian view of fallen humanity without resorting to Augustinian coercion? It is his contention that an absolutist, but nonviolent witness is possible because its central conviction is the nonviolence of a loving God; that is, the one nonnegotiable truth is the necessity of a nonviolent community. It is my contention that every theology and theological ethics is affected by the loyalties of one's chosen social location. Therefore, Hauerwas's claim of universality, even within the Western world, functions to mask the social origins of his ethics as well as its social consequences. It is my contention that an analysis of the social location of Hauerwas's Western, liberal "Christian" reveals a fundamental flaw in his description of the social power of his "Christians"; his contention that "we" live "after Christendom" is not accurate. Therefore, it is also my contention that his theology of a loving and nonviolent, yet all-powerful God, worshiped in an authoritative church by obedient and nonresistant Christians, is produced by the concerns of a particular social location. Specifically, it is produced by the dilemma of relative power that continues to discomfort white middle- and upper-class Christians in the U.S. who are located by virtue of race and class in positions of relative social privilege.[26] The resolution of this dilemma requires the willingness to (re)impose ecclesial institutional violence. I assert that by placing his gospel in its social location, Hauerwas's version of Christian nonviolence and nonresistance is revealed as a defense of social privilege, power, and control—especially the control of women.

## Nonviolence and the Control of Class and Race

How can a Christian theologian who argues for the utter uniqueness of Christian discourse, claiming its incomprehensibility to those who are not a part of this discourse, be understood by the wider audience he addresses? Hauerwas admits that this is a question for which his own theological assumptions can only lead to "a particularly awkward position," in which the more successful his communication the more he contradicts his own theology.[27] How can he be heard by others who do not participate in his linguistic-cultural community? If he is, as he claims, a resident alien speaking to resident aliens, would his books sell? Would he be asked to lecture? Would he teach in prestigious universities? His own presuppositions about the singularity of the Christian language-community raise the suspicion that aspects of his discourse are participating in the discourses of American culture. As Foucault points out, society does not suddenly discover, or rediscover, newly recognized greater truth. Rather, a change in politics governs the formation of what can be received as a truth statement. That is, something has shifted in the relations of power.[28] Changes in the social context prepare ears to hear a voice, such as Hauerwas's, into speaking.

With a hermeneutics of suspicion, I ask the following questions of Hauerwas's ethics of character: For whom is "fragmentation" the fundamental problem of modern society? Who experiences sin as "the overreaching" of one's power? Who benefits from labeling attempts to create social justice as masked "desire for power"? Who benefits from the assertion that doing what is "trivial" is the most faithful thing one can do? Who benefits from highlighting the procreative family as the church's most prophetic and powerful witness to the world? Who wants to be told that working for a more just society results in an unacceptable loss of Christian particularity? Who wants to hear that in accepting this "weakness," this powerlessness to transform society, this lack of control, one finds the joy of faithful, patient obedience to the absolute God who does control history? As Kwok warns, who would own these "truths"?

In order to unmask the agendas concealed in Hauerwas's language, we must first discover the social position he assumes as he speaks. As we saw above, his claim to represent a universal Christianity must be countered with an analysis of whom he means when he says "we." Whom does Hauerwas represent and address beneath his claim to universality?

Most Christians, at least in the industrialized societies of the West, are unsure how we ought to think about ourselves and/or our involvement as Christians in those same societies.[29]

We live in societies and politics formed by the assumption that there is literally nothing for which it is worth dying.[30]

We privilege our place as rich Christians who can justify our being rich because we are concerned about justice.[31]

Freedom literally comes by having our self-absorption challenged by the needs of another.[32]

We say we want justice but I suspect even more that we want power.[33]

So we must ask why it has been blacks, Native Americans, and women, and not Christians, who have been challenging the curriculum of the so-called "public schools."[34]

We simply cannot believe that the self might be formed without fear of the other.[35]

Our anxious attempts to preserve ourselves lead to violence, . . . . So the first step to peace is letting go of ourselves, our things, our world.[36]

Our lies are the correlate of our materialism.[37]
Our need to be in control is the basis for the violence of our lives.[38]
For our possessions are the source of our violence.[39]
Our sin is not merely an error in overestimating our capacities. Rather it is the active and willful attempt to overreach our powers.[40]
I only wish that Christians could be seen by the military as being as problematic as gays.[41]

"We," according to Hauerwas's descriptions, are self-absorbed, power-seeking, rich Christians who live in Western industrialized societies; "we" are neither black, nor Native American, nor women. "We" are certainly not gay. "We" live in fear of the other. "We" cause violence by our attempting to preserve our control over our lives and our material possessions. "We" sin by actively and willfully overreaching our powers.[42]

Although asserting a universal description of the human condition as revealed truthfully only in the Christian narrative,[43] by self-definition Hauerwas reveals that he speaks out of the social position and the problems, experiences, and fears of white middle- and upper-class American males. Although asserting a universal gospel of salvation, by self-definition Hauerwas reveals that he is speaking to the needs arising from the social position and experiences and fears of white middle- and upper-class American males. The social position of his Christian "we" explains his successful communication. A gospel from a position of white male privilege and power is being heard by those who share that position. A discourse that describes a fear of others, and the fear generated when one's myth of a self-reflecting, universal sameness is shaken by the claims of such others, is being heard precisely by those who are experiencing such fear. Hauerwas's unwillingness to admit the particularity and partiality of his views unfortunately serves an ideological purpose. It helps legitimate and maintain the status quo of white class-privileged male power by turning a Christian gospel of nonviolence into an ideology of domination. White middle- and upper-class women, such as myself, are also (but not equally) complicit in this system. Despite the limitations of gender, we benefit from sharing the same dominant race and class.

The Christians whom Hauerwas describes, the white middle- and upper-classes (professors, doctors, managers, CEOs, lawyers, accountants, bankers, real estate agents, ministers and priests, small business owners, and so on) are not, in the context of our personal political-economic lives, "after Christendom." We are able to maintain our real economic and political power in the world precisely at the expense of "others": poor white men and women, men and women of color, the poor of all colors, and the people of the two-thirds world, whom Hauerwas ignores when he says, "we Christians." In the United States, white male income exceeds all others. As we have already seen, the median annual income of full-time year-round white male workers far exceeds that of all other gender or racial-ethnic groups. Although by 1980 white men no longer made up a majority of the workforce when compared to all other groups combined, they continued to monopolize the most highly paid and powerful jobs.[44] According to Directorship Databank, 94.7 percent of the 7,162 directors of the 786 largest public companies in the United States are white men; 72.7 percent of them are fifty-five years old or older.[45] Together, white women and men hold the majority of the upper-tier primary jobs (92 percent in 1980) which provide higher pay, greater security and benefits, upward mobility, creativity, and decision-making opportunities.[46] While white males make up 39.2 percent of the U.S. population, they account for 82.5 percent of the Forbes 400 (people worth at least $265 million), 77 percent of congresspersons, 92 percent of state governors, almost 90 percent of daily newspaper editors, 77 percent of television news directors, and 70 percent of the tenured college professors.[47]

However, it is also true that in this age of postindustrial capitalism middle- and upper-class white men are experiencing their own fears of loss of income, social position, and control. Despite the numbers indicated above, a 1993 Newsweek poll of white males reported that 56 percent believed they were losing an advantage in terms of jobs and incomes. Sixty percent believed that white males are more frequently targets of antagonism from women and minority men. Fifty-two percent felt white males were losing their influence over U.S. culture, including style, entertainment, and the arts.[48] In fact, the shift from an industrial to a service-based economy has seen a drop in the real wages of men. Downward mobility in terms of income and occupational change is now beginning to touch more and more people whose middle-class status was always assumed to be the starting point of achieving more abundance. Structural changes in the job market place increasing pressures on the new entrants to the market as fewer middle-class jobs are being created. For the first time since the Depression, most workers can expect to earn less than their parents.[49] The biggest losers in this downward trend are white males.[50] In 1986, the Joint Economic Committee of the United States

Congress estimated that had women not entered the wage labor market in great numbers in the last two decades, real family income would have dropped eighteen percent between 1980 and 1986.[51] The impact of these economic changes and of the increasing presence of white women and women and men of color into what have been all white male prerogatives was described by Glenn Bucher:

> Because whiteness and maleness and heterosexual preference were the primary qualifications of those who shaped and controlled collective social life, each straight white male was led to believe in the potential of his own future. . . .
>
> For straight white males to see that they are on the way down the American ladder of success is no casual discovery. . . .
>
> What is more frightening is that blacks, women, and homosexuals are moving in to take places previously reserved for straight white males. With their emergence comes the prerogative to make and to write history. History is beginning to expose straight white males for what they really have been and are.[52]

In this particular social context, Hauerwas's proposals become part of the ongoing social discourse. On the one hand, this discourse acknowledges the fear that the dominant group holds toward others. It rightly identifies the fear that arises when one's social location is at risk, or even just imagined to be at risk. It names the moral chaos that occurs when the moral basis for one's privileged social identity is challenged. It rightly identifies the temptation to violent defense of one's dominant position. However, by universalizing these feelings, by claiming that these are the sins of all humans, Hauerwas's anthropology serves to obfuscate the reality of this concrete system of domination and its relationships of unequal power from which his audience benefits. Confronted by the challenges of others, white middle- and upper-class women and men may be comforted by a gospel that removes from us the ability or responsibility to respond to structural injustice.

*Reversing the Reversals*

In the chapter "How We Educate Christians in Liberal Societies," Hauerwas explores how the knowledge of the dominant culture contains the power to conceal the voices of others.[53] The teaching of American history, he acknowledges, has hidden the voices of Native Americans, blacks, and white women. While this insight becomes the source of his critique of liberal education (that there is no account of

knowledge that is not embedded in a tradition), Hauerwas's assertion of the universality of his own view allows him to exploit the
experiences of the oppressed for his own purposes without allowing
his own truth claims to be confronted by these silenced voices.[54]
Fundamentally, Hauerwas does not question his own knowledge
and its relationship to the power of his social position. It is my claim
that in the hands of those who, in fact, do have positions of social
privilege and the (relative) power that goes with them, a universally
applied gospel of nonviolence and nonresistance becomes an effective shield against responding to those "others" who would challenge this position. Violence is masked as nonviolence; coercion is
masked as nonresistance. Abstraction contributes to deception when
statements can be true and untrue at the same time. We extricate
ourselves, in Daly's phrase, by "reversing their reversals."[55] That is
the task to which I now turn.

To explore the way in which Hauerwas's theology of nonviolence and nonresistance functions as a politics of domination for
white middle- and upper-classes, I turn to Sharon Welch's analysis
of middle-class concepts of power in *A Feminist Ethic of Risk*.[56]
Welch's concern is to identify why good and well-intentioned
people participated in or acquiesced to the nuclear arms race and
why other good and well-intentioned people gave up their struggle against it. Her investigation of the views of social activists,
politicians, and defense industry personnel led her to conclude
that the problem lay in the way white middle- and upper-class
Americans understood goodness and responsible action.[57] Essentially, the experience of this social location has been an experience
of having social power within social structures that distribute this
power unequally. The white middle- and upper-classes have experienced strategizing within a political and economic system that
is responsive to their interests, that gets their needs met. To be in
this social location is to have a memory of progress and of victories
in which there were no victims.[58] From these experiences, middle-
and upper-class white people equate power with the ability to
control absolutely the outcome of their actions. Therefore, responsible action is action taken where one has the power to affect one's
intentions. Furthermore, the expectation is one of accomplishing
complete solutions, getting one's needs fully met, through this use
of power and action.[59]

Correlated with the equation of responsible action and absolute
control is a utopian expectation: that fear and insecurity can be
overcome through the establishment of a world of complete oneness

and uniformity. Like Hauerwas's vision of salvation, the utopian ideal of absolute security (and control) is achieved through the elimination of difference, of otherness. Welch argues that fear of the other, which as we have seen drives Hauerwas's theology, is grounded in this search for absolute security. In the contemporary world, fear of the other motivates the desire for control over every aspect of life; a control now exercised through infinitesimal surveillances, professional disciplines, regulations, statistics, and so on.[60] It is this absoluteness of utopian visions that creates the threat experienced in "difference." Difference, in the face of the one truth, becomes an illness, a chaos. Otherness is viewed as the "product of either ignorance or ill-will."[61]

Theologies of oneness give sacred legitimation to this white middle- and upper-class sense of power, responsibility, and utopia. As Welch notes: "A theology that valorizes absolute power through its concept of an omnipotent God is dangerous for middle-class people."[62] One result of such thinking, as Christian history clearly shows, is the too easy resort to force by which good people, obedient to the Absolute Good, serve the one Truth by eliminating the source of chaos, evil, disorder, and otherness. Thistlethwaite cites the example of Michael Novak's defense of a strategy of nuclear deterrence. Building up a stockpile of weapons of total destruction is, for Novak, a legitimate and "nonviolent" use of force. Furthermore, Novak finds no particular uniqueness in the dangers of the nuclear age in that the lessons of the Christian faith are about "the precariousness of all human life, the approaching end of history, the perennial wickedness and obdurateness of the human race, and the total sovereignty of God."[63] Is this not the temptation that Hauerwas warns against? Confidence in our knowledge of the truth can itself become the source of violence against others, or a refusal to see that our acts of good intention are, in fact, hurting others.[64]

However, in the face of the complexities of the issues of the modern world (nuclear destruction, global hunger, poverty, racism), another white middle- and upper-class possibility is the refusal to act. I believe, despite his protestations, that Hauerwas exemplifies this response in his rejection of the idea that to be moral one must do something about world hunger, injustice, or oppression: "But confronted with such mammoth challenges we feel that we can do nothing. Where is one to start? By acquiring power at the top? And we discover, even if we do start there, such power is not sufficient, since any steps to alleviate world hunger must be balanced against foreign policy objectives designed to keep the world in order."[65]

An Augustinian theology of absolute divine control and absolute human fallenness justifies, for Hauerwas, the refusal to see the social potential of the finite power-in-relation we do hold with others. It justifies the refusal to enter with others into a world of ambiguity and complexity that does not respond to the desire for absolute control that originates in the myth of one truth. In the face of problems that will not yield to the desire for total control, moral perfection, or absolute victories, nonresistance is Hauerwas's only alternative to the use of coercion.

Hauerwas has rightly identified a white middle- and upper-class fear of finitude; but, rather than addressing the particular, historically constructed ground of that fear, his theology sacralizes our compensatory longing for absolutes. Welch warns: "A theology that emphasizes the absolute power of God holds as an ideal a type of power not possible for those working for justice."[66] If one unhappy Christian solution to the experience of relative power has been the Augustinian turn to coercion, Hauerwas's equally unsatisfactory response is to deny the social power of white middle- and upper-class Christians. From this location of power and comfort (always relative, to be sure), Hauerwas pronounces the incapacity of *all* humans to work for social transformation. Faith, in his terms, is then the "risk" of doing nothing.[67] In Welch's terms, Hauerwas's labeling of all work for justice as symptomatic of a universal and sinful will-to-power is itself an expression of white middle-class cynicism and despair. To quote Juan Luis Segundo's description of such despair:

> Hope is paradoxically translated into a radically pessimistic view of the whole process of change, even when the latter is not violent, precisely because any and every change prompted by man cannot help but lose out to world-dominating sin. The kingdom of God can only be fashioned by someone who is free from sin, and that comes down to God alone.[68]

We now have a clearer picture of whom Hauerwas has in mind when he uses the term "Christians": white middle- and upper-class, with some power and possessions, who fear the other who reveals to them their limits of power and knowledge, and who fear the violence in themselves toward these others. For such Christians, faithfulness and submission to an absolute, nonviolent God, who alone is absolutely in control of history, legitimates a self-interested, middle- and upper-class pessimism and paralysis. As Soelle notes: "The cardinal virtue of authoritarian religion is obedience, the cardinal sin is resistance."[69] Authoritarian religion tends to function to support the dominant in society. Couched in the language of obedience to God, the religion of the dominant masks the politics of earthly power. Those with the benefits of work, influence, education, leisure, health care, housing, recreation, vacations, and resources are comforted in their belief that because they cannot unilaterally control and solve complex, modern issues, their finite and partial actions would be unacceptable expressions of the sinful human desire for control. We who participate in the dominant culture by virtue of our race and class protect our power by claiming to have no power. But as Margo Adair says: "Privilege is access to resources, protected by institutional control, backed up by violence."[70]

Certainly Hauerwas is addressing a legitimate concern of some contemporary Christians and a legitimate issue for Christian ethics to address: the sin of hubris, of magnifying one's own power, knowledge, and truth to universal proportions. This analysis of the "human" condition is profoundly responsive and relevant to the concrete realities of a particular social location. However, Hauerwas's ethics does not call for a renunciation of our unjust uses of power, nor is it a strategy to share power. It does not ask us to give up our institutionalized privileges, to let go of higher pay and privileged perks, or to subvert patterns of gender and race segregation in our workplaces. Rather, in the context of a social location of privilege, this theology of nonresistance serves to mask the violence of our continuing participation on the side of power in existing patterns of domination. Hauerwas writes: "Joy is thus finally a result of our being dispossessed of the illusion of security and power that is the breeding ground of our violence."[71] In this reversal, the political and economic power that white middle- and upper-class women and men have is called "illusion." Denying the "illusion" (our actual social power) is thus a joy. And the denial of actual social power, Hauerwas promises, will eliminate the breeding ground of violence. Hauerwas's ethics equates the renunciation of efforts by white privileged class folk to change the unjust structures of society that benefit us with the religious duty to trust patiently in God as a "risk" of faith. The renunciation of efforts to transform the society that privileges us is rewarded with religious joy.

Such a mystifying reversal is supported by a definition of violence as seen through middle- and upper-class eyes. While Hauerwas's proposals are passionate in their rejection of violence as a legitimate Christian action, the definition of violence seems limited to two expressions: (1) the violence of war between nation states, and (2) the violence which Hauerwas identifies as residing equally within all humans as a result of human self-interest and self-protection. As we have seen, the latter is specifically identified by Hauerwas as present in any Christian attempt to transform social structures through social justice action. But in all this talk about violence, what is not explicitly named as violence are the structural oppressions that support "our" institutionalized privileges: poverty, racism, sexism, homophobia, and political injustice. The violence embedded in our economic structures is not named. When Hauerwas does refer to global hunger or to systemic injustice, he refers to them as "tragedies." To white middle- and upper-class people, suffering that cannot be resolved by our responsible action is a tragedy. Thus, in the face of the tragedies of the world, the tragedies of starvation and of violent oppression, Christians learn that "peaceableness is a training to be patient in the face of the tragic; it is also learning to live joyfully in the face of the tragic."[72] Waiting patiently in the face of these tragedies is the "suffering" that the white middle- and upper-classes must endure as Christians. Only from the view of those oppressed, the view from below, are such "tragedies" exposed as the violence perpetrated on "others" by humanly constructed systems. Only from the view of those denied adequate education, housing, health care, employment, and nutrition due to the color of their skin, or their gender, or their residence in a nation of the two-thirds world or an abandoned center city of the U.S., can such a socially located gospel of nonviolence and nonresistance be exposed as violent.

Still, it is Hauerwas's contention that an ethics of character is not one of passivity. There are actions that can be appropriately taken. There is a politics to be practiced. What one can do are those personal acts which one does control. Acts of personal care are redefined as acts of justice.[73] Personal acts of lending and personal acts of forgiveness of debts are seen as acts of economic justice.[74] Finally, the very privileges of a secure, comfortable, white middle- and upper-class life are named as prophetic and peace-making acts:

> To take time to enjoy a walk with a friend, to read all of Trollope's novels, to maintain universities, to have and care for children, and most importantly, to worship God.[75]

117

Learning the discipline to wait, to be at rest with ourselves, to take the time to be a friend and to be loved.[76]

By applying an analysis of social location, the social source of Hauerwas's ethics of character becomes clear. The social loyalties of this theological anthropology are exposed and the material consequences revealed. The violence of continual participation in unjust social structures is called nonviolence. Participating with others in the risk of complex, often ambiguous, and limited acts toward creating and embodying social structures of justice is condemned as participation in the unfaithful and violent desire to control history. Renouncing efforts to transform the unjust power relations that benefit the white middle- and upper-classes is honored as "losing control." Choosing to act in ways that challenge such power is denounced as will-to-power.

How different these practices sound from the Christian nonviolence practices of one who chooses to confront oppression. From Martin Luther King, Jr.:

If he beats you, you develop the power to accept it without retaliating. If he doesn't beat you, fine. If he throws you in jail in the process, you go on in there and transform the jail from a dungeon of shame to a haven of freedom and human dignity. Even if he tries to kill you, you develop the quiet courage of dying if necessary without killing. . . . This is the power of nonviolence.[77]

How different also are these proposals when compared with the faith of those privileged who choose to stand with those who suffer the concrete realities of hunger, torture, brutality, imprisonment, and death. Jean Donovan, one of the four American Roman Catholic women raped and murdered in El Salvador, wrote of her involvement in social justice:

The Peace Corps left today and my heart sank low. The danger is extreme and they were right to leave. . . . Now I must assess my own position, because I am not up for suicide. Several times I have decided to leave. I almost could, except for the children . . . the poor bruised victims of adult lunacy.[78]

How different is this vision of the politics of the church from that of Archbishop Oscar Romero:

118

While it is clear that our Church has been the victim of persecution during the last three years, it is even more important to observe the reason for the persecution. It is not that just any priest or just any institution has been persecuted. It is that segment of the Church which is on the side of the poor and has come out in their defense that has been persecuted and attacked. Here once again we encounter the key to understanding the persecution of the Church: the poor.[79]

From an analysis of the social location assumed by Hauerwas's ethics and of the effects of his gospel upon a community of privilege and upon "others," the social consequences hidden in theological language are revealed. As the reversals are reversed, this gospel of nonviolence is revealed as reinforcing a fearful, white, privileged need to hold on to our position by celebrating our comforts as the joys resulting from submission to God. We see a gospel of nonresistance reinforcing a white, privileged hostility toward those who struggle against structures of oppression.[80] This is class violence masked by a theology of nonviolence rooted in a hierarchical model of truth that denies the politics of its location.

## Nonviolence and the Control of Women

The academic debates around Hauerwas's ethics of Christian character have often focused upon the question of whether his is a sectarian stance: that is, whether his theological ethics allows him to participate in a meaningful dialogue with secular society concerning its ethical issues.[81] Countering the charge that his theology leads to a sectarian ecclesiology, Hauerwas repeatedly asserts his position that Christians sharing his views would, and should, participate in the cultural, intellectual, and political life of society; that Christians, as pacifists, should involve themselves in strenuous political engagement; and that Christians only withdraw from society when society chooses to resort to violence in maintaining internal or external security. What is required of Hauerwas's Christians is that they live in the world as "resident aliens" and act politically in accord with what the church, not society, defines as "political."[82] It is Hauerwas's contention that Christians can contribute significantly to liberal societies while living uniquely Christian lives in conformity with this particular linguistic-cultural community called church. He writes that the church must be our "most determinative political loyalty."[83]

It is my contention that Hauerwas's proposal does indeed escape the sectarian charge (when that refers to a withdrawal from participating in or attempting to influence society) because (1) by focusing criticism on a political theory (liberalism) it leaves Christians to function uncritically in the economic system it supports and the work world that absorbs our time, talents, energies, and resources; (2) by its definition of what the church sees as political, it is women who become the primary focus of the church's "politics," while the work world in which white men are more highly rewarded with both money and power is left intact; and (3) as shown above, this ethics is rooted in and responds to the needs of a particular social group: straight, white, class-privileged, and, in particular, male. It is to these points that I now turn.

## What's So Alien About This Resident?

Sometimes the clearest clues to the function of an ethic are found in the things left unsaid or the problems left unexamined. By his own admission, material practices, not beliefs, are the site of character formation.[84] Yet liberalism, as a political philosophy, is the focus of Hauerwas's cultural critique, which leaves unexamined the system of economic production that is the material basis of liberal political thought. While admiring the professions of law and medicine as examples in the modern world of how the practices of particular disciplines create characters of virtue (an admiration which might not stand up under closer scrutiny), Hauerwas does not consider the everyday life of Christians in the sphere of the production and distribution of goods and services that make up social life. In a system based upon competition and self-interest, a system that requires winners and losers, his ethics does not address how Christians should function distinctly and uniquely as Christians within the work world. In a system that treats human labor power as another commodity to be bought at the lowest price, these proposals do not require of Christian employers some behavior consistent with what Christians believe. Nor do they show how Christians can function daily in public schools, work as financial loan officers, manage poultry plants, assemble cars, practice tort law, sell stocks and bonds, enforce the laws of city and state—in other words, live and work in, and depend upon for their living, institutions shaped by the norms of a capitalist society. Rasmussen gives us a litany of these realities:

Economies so totally out of sync with nature's requirements for regeneration as to quietly threaten ecocide; the destruction of indigenous cultures and peoples; the breakdown of close community and organic traditions; the disintegrative effects . . . of living out the image of mastery and control as the primary image for humanity itself; the development of weapons of apocalyptic destruction; the mountain of debt incurred; . . . the immiserization of the growing urban poor and the evacuation of many rural areas in the manner of "Appalachias"; the recognition that while different, the forms of oppression of women, many minorities, Third World, and indigenous peoples are linked and arise from forces that oppress land and nature as well; and the onset, amid abundance itself, of frazzled nerves, addiction, stress, rootlessness, chronic fatigue, and depression as serious diseases of a scattered soul and a restless, impoverished spirit.[85]

In one instance Hauerwas approaches these concerns tentatively, then backs away from giving answers: "If war preparations are wrong, then do we United Methodists want the offering of our members who work in defense industries? Should United Methodist pastors admit to the Lord's Table those who make a living from building weapons? Those are interesting, ecclesial questions . . . "[86] left unanswered. My argument is that Hauerwas's ethics ignore the all-encompassing presence of what Foucault calls the "capillary" nature of modern power: a power that operates not by opposition, but by subtle incorporation through the most trivial of habits, customs, and practices.[87] Unlike Romero and Donovan, we do not face death squads when we open soup kitchens. Unlike King, we no longer face prison when we cross the lines that used to mandate the separation of the races. But Hauerwas's criticism of American society leaves wholly untouched the entire expanse of the economic sphere that shapes the daily practices of Christian workers and their families and that continues to invade every corner of human relations in its relentless drive to commodify all human needs. It leaves untouched the daily practices that reward us while exploiting those not like us. Equally important, in doing so it leaves untouched the primary world of middle- and upper-class white men's political and economic power.[88]

If Christian ethics is to address the work world in the U.S., it will have to consider ethically how (and whether) a Christian should function in the police force, or in a defense industry during peacetime; whether a Christian lawyer should practice divorce law, try cases involving capital punishment, or represent a corporation in a hostile takeover or a move to Mexico; whether a Christian banker should foreclose on mortgages, or loan to gambling casinos, or forgive people their debts; whether Christians should pay their employees minimum wages; whether Christians, as CEOs or ball-players, should accept wages 149 times greater than the average employee, or make plans to ship production to Puerto Rico for the tax advantages. By not entering the economic life of Christian workers, Hauerwas's ethics avoids the sectarian charge. In particular, it does not withdraw Christian men from their patriarchal social/economic lives. Like the nineteenth-century bourgeois myth of the separation of public and private spheres, Hauerwas's ethics also creates a split world. The economic sphere where white middle- and upper-class men find their primary sense of identity, where their economic power is based, and where they remain in positions of authority is left through silence to its own ordering. Yet, through the highly vocal and specific authority and discipline of the church, the domestic world of sexuality and reproduction, a world that fundamentally shapes women's lives, is the location of the only real "aliens."

## The Control of the Alien

In radical contrast to the silence that leaves the economic sphere unchallenged, Hauerwas turns his full attention to what he posits as the political witness of the church: sexuality, marriage, procreation, and (negatively) abortion. This is a turn characteristic of the forms that modern power takes to control people in modern life. In my discussion of the silence of Hauerwas's ethics regarding the economic sphere, I mentioned the capillary action of modern power through the various networks of society that integrate people into systems for efficiency and control in the productive sphere. Correlated with this form of modern power is the increased attention given in the last two centuries to control over the body (most especially women's) that is the basis of all human biological needs and actions. Foucault identifies these two forms of power as the reason for the increased political attention given to human sexuality. He argues that sexuality lies at the intersection of these two forms of modern power: through the control of sexuality discipline may be exerted over the body in the sphere of production as well as in the regulation of reproduction. The control of sexuality gives access to the control of individual bodies and the social body.[89] A feminist analysis adds to this description the recognition of the difference it makes when such power is exercised in a sexist and patriarchal society. In the United States, sexuality will be controlled in accordance with the needs of a capitalist patriarchal society. More to the point, surveillances will be applied to the primary world of women, our bodies, and our sexuality.[90]

In the chapter "The Politics of the Church," Hauerwas argues that the church must recover its authority to be a disciplined and disciplining community. He criticizes the church as having adopted the liberal distinction between public and private to the extent that the church's "disciplining [of] someone in a personal crisis is simply unthinkable."[91] Hauerwas's point, made in all of his writings, is that there can be no private sphere of Christian life that would separate the Christian's personal life and body from the discipline and politics of the church. Christian moral life develops in imitation of those teachers whose authority, embedded in the historically validated intellectual and moral standards of the community, is accepted by the community.[92] This is the appropriate function of clergy.

In order to show the effect of Hauerwas's proposed colony of resident aliens upon women, I will identify those areas in which Hauerwas gives an unequivocal declaration of the authority of Christian tradition. As has been shown above, neither a substantive definition of social justice nor a critique of capitalism have been considered proper objects for the politics of the church. However, Hauerwas gives two examples of appropriate church authority in the above-mentioned chapter. In the first example he responds to the question of what the church can do regarding business ethics by replying that the church should require all its members to make public what they earn.[93] That would indeed be interesting. However, Hauerwas does not go on to suggest what the church would do with this information. Would it require specific levels of donation based on one's earnings? Would wealthier people be required to share with poorer people? Would the moral authority of the pastor exercise control over Christians' excess funds? What would a pastor do if a member refused to give such information? The use and purpose of this information is not elaborated.

In the second example the moral authority of the pastor is specific and unequivocal. In this case a parishioner's wife, having committed adultery, confessed her sin, and completed appropriate penance, has been forgiven and received back into the congregation. Her husband has gone to the pastor because he (the husband) is not ready to forgive and take his wife back into his/their home. As an appropriate example of clerical authority and the discipline appropriate to the "upbuilding of the Christian community," Hauerwas approvingly reports the pastor's reply:

> You do not have the right to reject her, for as a member of our church you too must hold out the same forgiveness that we as a church hold out. Therefore I'm not asking you to take her back, I am telling you to take her back.[94]

The authority of the church community, located in the person of the (male) pastor, is absolute in this example. This is the church functioning *as* a social ethic. That is, this is a community that lives in a way clearly distinguishable from the world; where the truth, however painful, is spoken; where one learns to desire the right things. This is the church's politics.[95] More specifically, however, note that the way Christians live out their sexuality in accordance with the ends and purposes of the church (and not how they make their living) is the "most important political task of the church in our society."[96] Thus, Hauerwas states authoritatively the content of a Christian sexual ethic. About sexual intercourse he declares: "Christians believe that all sex is marital. . . . [because Christians] fear that [nonmarital] sex would have insufficient resources to resist forms of domination that sex invites."[97]

Hauerwas's discussion of sexuality simply does not acknowledge the long Christian history of men's domination of women within marriage, approved and sanctioned in Christian practice, Christian scripture, Christian theology, Christian ethics, canon law, sermons, and the rituals of faithful Christian worship. In all his talk about violence, he never mentions the epidemic of male violence against women. He does not mention marital rape or domestic violence. Perhaps he does not realize what women fear. Vicki Noble reports the results of a survey that asked men what they most fear from women, and women what they most fear from men. "Women responded that they feared being raped and murdered, and men responded that they feared being laughed at."[98] Hauerwas does not tell us how this ethics of marriage will differ from the authoritarian, patriarchal tradition women know too well.

About monogamy, Hauerwas writes: "Our commitment to exclusive relations witnesses to God's pledge to his people, Israel and the church, that through his exclusive commitment to them, all people will be brought into his Kingdom."[99] Despite the obvious analogical problem here (one God with exclusive commitment to two peoples), what are we to make of the practices of polygamy and concubinage in the Hebrew scriptures? Or the practices of polygamy within contemporary Christian communities in various parts of the world? Or the various elaborations upon legal monogamy (mistresses, courtly love, serial monogamy) that have characterized Western Christian history? In Hauerwas's theological ethics, monogamy exists as an ahistorical, abstract principle unconnected to embodied realities.

About the purpose of marriage, Hauerwas states: "marriage must be characterized by unitive and procreative ends. . . . For the vocation of marriage in part derives its intelligibility from a couple's willingness to be open to new life. Indeed that is part of the test of the validity of their unity as one worthy to be called 'love' in the Christian sense. It must necessarily be open to creation of another."[100]

It is not clear whether this includes opposition to the use of contraceptives, a use validated by most Protestant denominations. Are there limits to this "openness" to life? One child? Three? More? The biological reality with which most women live is that we spend about forty years "open to new [biological] life"—an awesome power that we must control if we are to give life in social, nonbiological ways. Women simply cannot contribute to our world as productive workers, as intellectuals, as creative artists, if our lives and bodies are to be focused on the reproduction of biological life. And, of course, this account of sex and marriage provides no room for the unitive love of lesbian and gay couples.

About abortion: "Christians have had their minds made up about abortion from the beginning. . . . Abortion is an affront to our most basic convictions."[101] In the unequivocal tone of such statements, Hauerwas's ethics joins the silencing throughout history of women's voices and women's experiences of sexuality, marriage, procreation, and abortion.

Hauerwas posits a universal Christian sexual ethic that requires heterosexual, procreative, marital sexuality (or celibate singleness) and the condemnation of abortion. This behavior, he asserts, is the political behavior of Christians. The personal is political in that the individual is subsumed within the political purposes of the church. Thus, in the example of the adulterous wife and the unforgiving husband, no distinction is made by Hauerwas's ethics between the nature of a relationship between a community and an individual and the nature of a relationship between two individuals. The personal does not exist. As a community should forgive and welcome back a "sinner" into its life, so an individual is to forgive and welcome a "sinner" into marital intimacy. Hauerwas does not relate the wife's point of view. It is as irrelevant as the husband's. What conditions may have caused her behavior or what abuse she may receive at the hands of a man forced to take her in are irrelevant. Presumably a wife would also be required to forgive and take back her adulterous husband. Hauerwas cannot sense the real possibility of women's terror upon hearing the words, "Take her back." This is a violence that remains invisible in the politics of the church.

Feelings are transient and love easily becomes destructive, Hauerwas believes. His distrust of intimacy is revealed in this passage:

> Jealousy is the emotion required by our willingness to love another at all. Indeed, I suspect that part of the reason the church has always assumed that marriage is a reality that is prior to love is that genuine love is so capable of destruction that we need a structure to sustain us through the pain and the joy of it. At least one reason for sex being limited to marriage, though it is not a reason sufficient to support an intrinsic relation between sex and marriage, is that marriage provides the context for us to have sex, with its often compromising personal conditions, with the confidence that what the other knows about us will not be used to hurt us. For never are we more vulnerable than when we are naked and making the clumsy gestures necessary to "make love."[102]

Thus, for Hauerwas, the political purpose of marriage offers a protection against the vulnerability created by intimacy and the destructiveness of emotions. Out of this fear of emotions and intimacy, Hauerwas proposes a marriage sustained by individuals who are willing to fulfill their political roles as spouse and parent in loyalty to the political witness of the church. Carol Gilligan describes fear of intimacy and distrust of emotions as characteristic of the mainly white middle-class males she studied:

> The findings of the images of violence study suggest that men and women may perceive danger in different social situations . . . men seeing danger more often in close personal affiliation . . . and construing danger to arise from intimacy. . . . The danger men describe . . . is a danger of entrapment or betrayal, being caught in a smothering relationship or humiliated by rejection and deceit. . . . As people are brought closer together in the pictures, the images of violence in the men's stories increases.[103]

For Hauerwas's ethics of character, then, truth is endangered by feelings, and especially the feeling of compassion.[104] For example, Hauerwas writes that if a twelve-year-old girl is impregnated as a result of incest or rape, the appropriate Christian response is to provide the communal support that makes pregnancy and child-birth the only conceivable option.[105] An ethics focused on the abstraction of "the gift of life" does not ask what might be good for the twelve-year-old girl; it does not ask about the brokenness of her abused body; it does not consider the damage that pregnancy does to young bodies; it is not moved by the violence that her twelve-year-old mind and body have endured. Consider the following case reported in a Baltimore newspaper: "A Pomfret man was sentenced yesterday to six years in jail for sexually abusing a 14-year-old girl. . . . He admitted sexually abusing the Jessup girl since she was 7 and fathering the child the girl gave birth to in October 1990 at age 13."[106]

When, in Hauerwas's ethics, the personal is only the political of the church, no embodied realities of women's lives challenge the male church's authoritative pronouncement of the way Christians have "always" felt about abortion.[107] Christians are those people open to life and willing to take the risk of such openness. In terms of women's concrete reality, this translates as follows: Christian women, of any age or condition or vulnerability, are to be always open to another pregnancy, however caused. It is the community's expression of love and responsibility, according to Hauerwas's ethics, that should create the conditions in which a sexually abused twelve-year-old child is enabled to give birth to her child. In the need to defend the absolute virtue of nonviolence, as he defines it, Hauerwas's ethics consigns some of us—indeed, in this case the most vulnerable of us—to violences he may not be able to imagine. Of course, that is the issue.

In a section titled "Pastoral Counseling As Prophetic: An Example," Hauerwas again uses an example from the reproductive life of women.[108] In this case a pregnant young woman with two children was being divorced by her husband. She went to her pastor for counseling about the possibility of an abortion. The pastor sent her to a therapist to help her work out what might be best for her and her children. In the end, the woman chose to have an abortion. Hauerwas sees this as an example of the failure of prophetic ministry. He asks whether the pastor had suggested to the woman that her decision to have an abortion might be a result of her anger toward her husband; was she "seeking to kill her child as a means of attacking her husband"?[109] According to Hauerwas, the pastor failed to remind her of what it means to be a Christian; he acquiesced to the cultural assumption that to care for someone is to try to make their lives easier; and he failed to provide the community with the opportunity to be supportive. Feelings, especially compassion, threaten the service of truth. Regardless of the realities of a woman's particular situation, Christian women are those who welcome (biological) life. Despite two born children who need her care, and the almost certain economic dislocation of divorce, this woman, like all Christian women according to Hauerwas, should accept the risk of the "gift" of new life. Again, in all of this talk about violence, not a word about rape, battering, or women's realities: that we are "more in danger from men [we] know than our soldiers are from 'enemies' on the battlefield!"[110]

Although it is obvious that I disagree with Hauerwas's sexual ethics and particularly his opposition to abortion, that has not been the purpose of recounting these examples. The point has been to show the absolute certainty and vigor with which Hauerwas describes his interpretation of the Christian sexual ethic and his willingness to deal in great detail with questions of women's sexual and reproductive behavior. The point has been to expose the identity of the real resident aliens in Hauerwas's proposals by showing who is actually subject to the church's politics: a politics in which the church (a male-dominated institution) and the Christian tradition (a male account of Christianity's patriarchal history) control the sexual and reproductive lives of women while leaving the work world of men without equally explicit demands.

Hauerwas's description of the politics of the church reveals what Sharon Welch describes as the "erotics of domination." In this form of eroticism, a powerful group satisfies its own emotional needs by humbling itself to an absolute authority.[111] In this reversal, the needs of the dominant group are masked as "the will of God," to which the dominant become humbly submissive. The ruling group is now able to rule indirectly under the guise of being servants who simply carry out the commands of the absolute authority, of God and church. The actual social source of control is disguised as those who rule (that is, those whose interests are being imposed) describe themselves as "out of control," as only faithful servants. "The claim of complete obedience to a higher power justifies total control of others."[112] It is in this manner that Hauerwas's claim of submissiveness to the higher authority of the church and its clergy, which seems to be the only source of knowledge about God, legitimates the domination of women, female sexuality, and the "feminine" feelings of compassion, empathy, and connectedness. Women are the "other" who are primarily subject to the force of the church's domination. This colony of resident aliens is women and our reproductive lives. What Hauerwas's ethics do not acknowledge is that this has always been the experience of women in the church. Historically, we have been primarily defined as virgin, mother, or whore (sexual identities) by a male church in response to patriarchal needs. However unfaithful liberal society and the liberal church may be, the continuation of this violence is no solution for women, or anyone else.

In the name of a universal Christian gospel, Hauerwas's proposals present an ethics in which the substance of justice cannot be known from scripture or tradition, but an absolute stand against abortion is. Whether a Christian who works in the defense industry should be admitted to the Lord's Table is an interesting question, but whether a twelve-year-old victim of rape or incest should be supported in a choice to abort is not even a question. Marriage and women's reproduction of children are important political acts of the church, but the way Christians make their living is not. Choosing to love and care for one's own family, and resisting the temptation to respond to the needs of the global masses, is a sign of Christian patience in the face of human limits; but for a woman to choose an abortion in the face of her limits is a sign of her lack of faith in the future.[113] When the most important political witness of the church is found in marrying and having children, it is women and their reproductive lives that become the subject of church (male) surveillance. The personal lives of women become objects of political control by men. *Her* personal is *his* politics. The result of this gospel is not a life of nonviolence and nonresistance for men, but the maintenance of a domestic and religious sphere of control and coercion in which men shape the fundamental decisions facing women's lives, in God's name.

Hauerwas's vision of restoring women's "indispensable role" and "moral status" by reaffirming the political significance of the family must be rejected.[114] This obviously sexist proposal continues to perpetuate the classist and racist ideology of liberal patriarchal capitalism that associates women's moral status and indispensability with procreation, nurture, and the maintenance of the domesticating virtues while ignoring the wage work of poor women of all colors and their families. It ignores the contemporary necessity of women's work in the wage labor market as well as the value to a capitalist economy of women's unpaid domestic labor. While disagreeing with the liberal myth of the separation of public and private spheres, Hauerwas's ethics finally acquiesces to the material effects of this ideology by ignoring the concrete ways in which the demands of patriarchal capitalism have shaped and formed our "Christian" understanding of the family, gender roles, and sexual practices.

Most seriously, Hauerwas's proposals for the church simply reinforce a sexist ideology that grounds women's value in our reproductive capacities. It denies us control over our lives and bodies as we remain primarily defined by the roles of wife and mother and subject to the politics of a male-controlled tradition and institution. This narrow definition of women minimizes all women's capacities and it totally ignores the significance and moral status of the lives of lesbians. There is no space in this vision of the church for the value of lesbian, nonprocreative relationships, in which women are neither wives nor mothers. There is simply no space in this colony of resident aliens for the full moral agency of women and our participation in the construction of the meaning of our own or society's well-being— or of the Christian narrative.

## VIOLENCE, NONVIOLENCE, AND THE MEN'S MOVEMENT

Stanley Hauerwas and William Willimon begin their book, *Resident Aliens*, with the image of the church as a colony and Christians as resident aliens: "an island of one culture in the middle of another" because Christians "see something that cannot otherwise be seen without Christ."[115] In 1992 I had the opportunity to speak with several seminary students who were quite enthusiastic about Hauerwas's theological ethics. As I voiced my concerns about how his ethical system would function in the lives of women, one young man responded, "Yes, but don't you think this is something we men need to hear." That remark has set me to thinking about the cultural construction in our culture of white male, middle- and upper-class masculinity and how that might participate in the creation and welcoming of Hauerwas's image of the resident alien. It is to that cultural context that I now turn.

According to the advertising blurb on the back cover, there has been no time in history in which there have been so many men "looking for new roles, new attitudes, and new ways of being." Into that hunger, Sam Keen calls for a new brotherhood of humble and virile men.[116] Finding the popular images of adult manhood worn out, Robert Bly views with optimism the new openness with which men might envision what a man is or could be; he turns to the legend of "Iron John" in a book that sold over a half million copies in 1991.[117] Both of these authors deal with men's violence, men's brokenness, and new images of fierce and gentle men. Both of their books were national best-sellers in the early 1990s.

The new men's movement is quite diverse. There are men working on gender issues for the support of gender equality and partnership and for the end of male violence against women and men. There are others who claim to be victims of women and who work for men's rights. Somewhere in a more ambiguous, and better-selling, middle are Keen and Bly. Using their best-sellers as entrances into the self-understanding of some mostly white, middle- and upper-class men (based on the identification of those who attend their lectures and retreats), it is important to hear how these men describe their own sense of "the problem today."

Both Bly and Keen present a primary picture of men as victims. Bly uses the term "industrial domination" to describe his sense of the cause of the grief that has deepened in the lives of men since the beginning of the Industrial Revolution.[118] Today's male feels over-worked, alienated, and empty. The Industrial Revolution primarily destroyed the love relationship between fathers and sons, leaving sons in the care of dominant and possessive mothers at home. At work, "contemporary business life allows competitive relationships only, in which the major emotions are anxiety, tension, loneliness, rivalry, and fear."[119] The result is a culture in which fathers are increasingly unattractive models for their sons. Made weak and insignificant by their wage work, powerless fathers who hate their jobs are more and more the objects of ridicule. They no longer have the skills and knowledges to pass down to their sons.[120] Most important, modern men have failed to notice their own suffering.

> A man does well in his business, lives a sweet life with home and family, enjoys his weekends at Lake Tahoe, and one Sunday morning finds himself on the lawn with a loaded shotgun, and about to pull the trigger.[121]

Similarly, Keen describes the victimization of modern men. Blamed, demeaned and attacked for being the cause of all social problems, men feel as though they are engaged in a battle against an unseen enemy:

Men are angry because they resent being blamed for everything that has gone wrong since Adam ate the apple. Yes, we feel guilty because we went to useless wars. . . . we feel guilty because we created technologies that proved to be polluting. . . . we feel guilty because we were born white, middle-class, and on the fast track to power and prestige. . . . Men learned in the last decade that they were guilty by definition. It has never been clear what they were supposed to do to atone for their guilt. Change the system overnight? Call off the march toward the high-tech future? Give up power, prestige, and positions?[122]

The truth, according to Keen, is that men and women are equally victims before the SYSTEM. But, now, in the men's movement, men are beginning to feel their pain and to identify their own victimization. Whereas, according to Keen, women's biology assures them of their place and significance in the world (women "give birth to meaning out of [their] body"[123]), men live with the constant dread of not being a man, of being weak. They live with the constant pressure and tension of needing to prove themselves in war, work, and sex.

Like Bly, Keen identifies the Industrial Revolution as the point at which the powerful father was replaced by the powerful mother. Consequently, modern men spend a lifetime performing for their mothers and struggling to separate themselves from WOMAN.[124] While at work, men are engulfed by (another) womb, the corporation. Work has become the sole source of meaning for men. Yet, work is a battlefield in which men must constantly pressure themselves to produce more and faster, to win. It is a battle in which men are held captive by economic success. It is the SYSTEM that conditions men to endure pain, to be violent whenever it is necessary to kill or die to protect those he, as a man, is supposed to protect. The result is that modern working men have been "neutralized, degendered, rendered subservient to the laws of the market."[125]

Both Bly and Keen identify a truth that they believe men need to face within themselves. According to Bly, men need to learn to shutter: to learn to feel how frail human beings are, to learn to accept and love the unattractive father, to accept their wounds and their failures.[126] Similarly, Keen calls for men to face the "pain and poverty of their positions," for the powerful to "feel their impotence" and the masters to "feel their captivity."[127] Men must face their fear of loss of power and control, their fear of death and dependency, and develop a sense of the tragic. He promises that "a tragic sense of life yields more joy than warm fuzzies."[128] It is the illusion of power and control over events and self and women that men must lose: "We can never be liberated so long as we cling to the illusion that we can turn the world into paradise."[129]

Instead of the false myths of present day society, Bly argues for the reestablishment of Strong Warrior energy in service to the True King, to a purpose greater than himself, to a transcendent cause. Where there is a Sacred King, there is order, blessing, and creativity. There the anguish of the soft, modern male is replaced with pure warrior energy and the ability to work hard, doing what is necessary for a higher cause. This principle of order began to fail in the eighteenth and nineteenth centuries, according to Bly, as political kings fell. Without political kings, he argues, we cannot see the eternal King. Similarly, without male leadership for young men, male initiation rites, and male separation from possessive mothers, men cannot find their inner King. He urges the reinstatement of this three-tiered world in order to carry young men out of their youthful machismo, aggressiveness, and fantasies of domination toward commitment to the god of grief.

Similarly, having identified the central source of men's alienation as the absence of any ongoing sense of meaning in life, Keen argues that men will find fulfillment only when they surrender themselves to others and to God, in a spirit of empathy and compassion.[130] The beginning of healing is to feel oneself to be lost. From the despair of one's honest awareness of his helplessness, a man must turn to fallowness, to waiting, to silence. In that silence, in that sadness for the suffering of the world, there is the rebirth of joy, a growing sense of hope, and the deep sense of peace: "Maybe I am okay just as I am. Maybe I don't have to do anything to justify my existence. Maybe I don't have to strive anymore."[131]

Keen describes the sheer joy of being alive, of tasting, smelling, listening, and touching with greater sensitivity—of knowing life is simply a gift. He describes a sense of gentle strength that comes from self-acceptance. And he speaks of the virtues that the new heroes will have. With the virtue of wonder, men give up the illusion of control and pause to stand in awe with gratitude for life. With the virtue of a heartful mind, a man cultivates solitude, learning to listen to the dictates of his own heart and to recover the stories of his life and to heal the modern disease of lack of joy. Keen describes the virtue of enjoyment: "Bird watching, talking with children, visiting friends, preparing feasts, making love, . . . sitting quietly and doing nothing."[132] Finally, he speaks of the necessity of "our biological and spiritual destiny as the bearers, nurturers and initiators of children."[133] Children are our link with creative being, our tutors in the virtue of hope. And, it is family loyalty that is the first defense against the control of state or other institutions.

> The health, vitality, and happiness of the family is the yardstick by which a man, a woman, a society should measure success and failure. I suggest that the decline of honor in family is directly related to the continuing cold war between the sexes, the escalating climate of violence and the sense of the vacuum of meaning that haunts our time.[134]

Keen ends his book with the results of a survey he conducted through *Psychology Today* in 1989.[135] The survey was titled "What Makes an Ideal Man?" Ninety-eight percent of the over six thousand responses agreed that an ideal man believes that life is a gift that should be revered, that he should leave the world better than it was, and that he should follow the golden rule. An ideal man can feel and express his anger, but without resorting to violence. He has strong family ties, he is the breadwinner, and he is a good husband and father. He finds his primary sense of meaning in self-exploration and personal growth. Keen's conclusion is that the most startling finding of the survey is the extent to which the current ideal of manhood is apolitical. "The new ideal man may be compassionate and wise, but the sphere of his caring and action is very narrow. . . . he is more likely to be found tending his own garden and looking after his own family than he is to be involved in political action."[136] Keen points out that the survey may be skewed by its particular participants, that is, readers of *Psychology Today;* but he worries that a tyranny of inwardness may replace the larger vision of a more just society.

I believe that his worries are well-founded. It would be very inaccurate to equate the ideas of John Bly, Sam Keen, and Stanley Hauerwas. Obviously there are significant differences between them. However, I believe that this overview has also identified amazing similarities of concerns, solutions, and vocabularies. While Hauerwas assumes he is describing the human condition, Bly and Keen believe that they are describing the particular experience of the modern male. All three identify today's problem as being one of violence and chaotic change. All three root the source of violence in the illusion of power and control. All three believe that the remedy for violence begins with a recognition of men's finitude and their acceptance of a sense of the tragic. All three believe that joy and happiness require a fundamental turn away from the traditional emphasis on productive activity for men. However, none conceive this in terms of actually giving up their institutional privileges based on race, gender, and class. Bly and Hauerwas posit the need for a hierarchical, authoritarian system of order and discipline, while Keen envisions a more individually defined submission to the will of God. While Keen and Hauerwas might differ somewhat on the appropriate roles of women, both place a heavy emphasis on the centrality of home and children for men's sense of well-being, of meaning, and of hope.[137] For both, procreation is a major source of personal and social hope. Given the long history of men's control of women through their control of women's sexuality and, specifically, through their defining of women according to women's role in pro-creation, a renewed interest by men in their own progeny cannot be welcomed until these same men are ready to redress the injustices created by masculine gender privilege.

It is beyond the scope of this brief review to analyze the specific effects that Bly's and Keen's ideas might have on the lives of women.[138] It is clear, however, that without addressing the social, political, and economic causes of "industrial domination," Bly, Keen, and Hauerwas develop a primarily psychological explanation for the current crisis. Bly and Keen lay a great deal of responsibility for men's aggression upon women. Whether it is warrior strength (Bly), or fierce loving combat (Keen), or the political significance of the family (Hauerwas), none of these solutions bodes well for the full moral agency of women. Furthermore, by ignoring the concrete differences in men and women's access to social power, Bly and Keen are able to equate men's and women's sufferings and senses of powerlessness. And although Keen is aware of his position as a white middle-class man, his awareness of social location does not become part of his analysis. With frequent use of the passive voice, Bly, Keen, and Hauerwas erase the real differences between social groups and their actual relationship to social, political, and economic power.[139] Ultimately no one (everyone) is responsible for the SYSTEM/violence. All are equally victims/sinners. The good man/Christian can then deny, while maintaining, the social-economic-political power of his location.

I believe that *Iron John* and *Fire in the Belly* cast some light on the cultural context out of which white middle- and upper-class men perceive their own experiences. Powerful as a group, they feel powerless as individuals. Fearful and angry at their victimization within the SYSTEM (postindustrial capitalism), they turn from social responsibility to the family for affection, validation, and a sense of belonging. There they find changing gender roles, interpreted in our androcentric society as overwhelming women and absent, ridiculed fathers. In the midst of this fear, pain, and chaos, I believe that Hauerwas's proposals for the church are heard as providing a colony where peace and order for men are restored, the pain of the world is left to God, and men can find joy and hope tending their gardens and fathering their families.

## SUMMARY

Hauerwas rightly argues that there is no such thing as an unqualified ethic, no way to "step back" from one's particular, historical position.[140] However, his methodology fundamentally ignores his own historical particularity of sexual orientation, gender, class, and race. His description of a universal human fear of finitude, and his consequent fear of fragmentation and violence, lead him to "step back" to the abstraction of a "Christian character" and a "Christian church." Accepting the social context of language, he nonetheless presents a Christian narrative in which words, such as "life," "freedom," "family," "violence," "suffering," "sin," and "abortion," are assumed to be univocal for all Christians regardless of their social and historical location. He fails to see that these terms have no essential meaning within Christian discourses, but take on meaning as a consequence of their relationships within a historically and socially discursive whole. That Hauerwas's analysis can be so violent against violence and never mention women's experiences of violence suggests the limitations of the social location of his discourse. Rightly challenging liberal definitions of what is "natural," his ethics remains silent about the oppressive material forms these definitions took in the hands of white privileged men against people of color and white women. His ethics remains silent about the material forms that oppression continues to take in the lives of those defined by racism, homophobia, sexism, and classism. Rightly challenging the myth of the public/private split, his proposals reimpose male political control over women's bodies and reintroduce another myth of the distinct spheres of church and world. Avoiding the work world of men, this ethics of character identifies that which is distinctively Christian primarily in the reproductive lives of women: the only real aliens. Finally, openness to the stranger does not seem to include those "others" who reveal to white middle- and upper-class men the particularity of their social positions and the way in which such particularity influences theology and ethics. Continuing a myth of two distinct spheres, Hauerwas's description of the Christian narrative is unable to see that Christian character is not an ahistorical essence floating through time and space, but is constantly being formed in changing cultural contexts. And, by denying the impact of his own social location on his narrative of a Christian story, Hauerwas is unable to realize the cultural embeddedness of his proposals in the culture he shares with the readers of *Iron John, Fire in the Belly*, and *Psychology Today*. Hauerwas's ethics is unable to accept, therefore, that neither Christians nor the Christian church can be reformed without participating with "others" in a corresponding transformation of the society that shapes us Christians.

From the perspective of a feminist ethic of liberation, Hauerwas's ethics of character is flawed by its inability to see the particularity of its own social and historical location. Fleeing before the possibilities of a more radical historicity, it continues to posit an ahistorical approach to Christian social ethics. Positing a new universal theological ethics results in a defense of white male social privilege against the stirrings of subjugated voices. The error of liberal white men and liberal white women is repeated. While expressing accurately the fears, concerns, and even the sins of his social location, a universalizing methodology stunts any real challenge to the self-interest of this dominant group. When differences caused by class, sexual orientation, race, and gender are ignored, Hauerwas's gospel of nonresistance functions to contribute to the violence experienced by the marginalized and those suffering the very real pain of political and economic exploitation. Ultimately, Hauerwas's methodology is inadequate for creating the kind of Christian community among white middle- and upper-class U.S. Americans that can hear, and demand that we hear, the insistent Babel of erupting voices, voices of suffering and voices of wisdom, that are still calling from the margins.

CHAPTER 5

# THE CHARACTER OF OUR COMMUNITIES

*A feminist theology of liberation is part of an epistemic shift, a redefinition of the truth of Christian faith. The truth of Christian faith is at stake not in terms of its coherence with ontological structures and their potential modifications, but in life and death struggles, in daily operations of power/ knowledge. It is in this arena of the determination of the character of daily life that the truth of Christian faith, both its method and referent, must be determined. . . . The focus therefore of a liberating faith and of theology is not primarily the analysis of human being and its possibilities, but the creation of redeemed communities.*[1]

In response to the postpositivistic crisis in epistemology, both Welch's feminist theology of liberation and Hauerwas's ethics of character turn for verification to the evidence, in history and in community, that our truth claims do what they claim is truth. It has been my argument in the last chapter that Hauerwas's proposal for a church of resident aliens fails to accomplish his intended goal of creating a community capable of forming people able to live peaceably. By failing to follow through with the radical implications of our complete historicism, Hauerwas repeats the error of universalizing a perspective that arises out of a historically particular and socially located position. The unfortunate result is not the formation of a nonviolent people but the maintenance of social privilege for dominant white society generally, and for dominant white males particularly.

I have made an alternative epistemological claim that recognition of our fully historical consciousness and analysis of the humanly constructed discourses that compete for our embodiment lead to the conclusion that justice is integral to truth. By that I mean that once we recognize the particularity of any perspective, of any narrative or text or tradition or contemporary discourse, and once we realize the role that social power plays in privileging any one view as "truth," then we must address the social process of naming truth. It means realizing that a "truth" is always a truth-in-process, to be held with humility. Therefore, the development of truth-in-process must be accompanied by a social (secular and ecclesial) commitment to empower those with unequal access to full participation in the conversations, dialogues, and debates necessary to the social construction of knowledge.

I have also argued that in any particular cultural and historical context, Christians create Christian narratives as a part of, and in response to, existing cultural discourses. Furthermore, our particular social location constructs us and our Christianity. We are never free to be simply Christian; we are residents, but not aliens. A feminist ethics of liberation that uses the insights of poststructuralism and discourse analysis is itself primarily located among privileged white feminist academics. We are also confronted, then, with the need to hold our theories lightly. Any discourse we embody, and the theories that justify it, are ambiguous. We have the potential both to empower and to disempower marginalized voices through our theorizing and through the way we choose to live our lives. Privileged white feminists must continuously challenge ourselves to take seriously the emphasis that feminist ethics places on embodied reason; that is, the necessity to learn through embodied experiences.[2] We must literally place ourselves in the midst of concrete justice struggles and live in such a way that we participate in the building up of just communities of nonviolence. It is to the characteristics of such communities of empowerment that I now turn.

## INTEGRATING TRADITION, DIVERSITY, AND RESISTANCE

I do not make the claim that what follows is relevant to all Christians or even to all Christians in the U.S. I am attempting a smaller project. As a member of dominant white U.S. society, I want to speak to others like myself and to suggest some of the steps that we who are dominant need to take, particularly in our churches, in order to participate in the construction of what Welch calls "redeemed communities." It is a response to Hauerwas's proposal to be resident aliens. It is a response to Keen's rhetorical question: do you expect us middle-class white males just to "Give up power, prestige, and position?" But most of all it is simply a conversation with middle-

and upper-class white churches that struggle with justice issues, or would like to.

We are faced with two sources of discomfort, two challenges to our epistemological and moral equilibrium—for which we should give thanks through our grimaces. Both are included in what Foucault calls "an insurrection of subjugated knowledges." Subjugated knowledges are two kinds of knowledges: those that are present but disguised within a body of knowledge and can be revealed by intellectual criticism (the erudite knowledges), and those that are the disqualified or naive knowledges of the disempowered.[3] Both kinds of subjugated knowledges reveal the political struggles that underlie what we who are part of the dominant call knowledge or reality or truth. The knowledge that the homeless have about social safety nets, the knowledge that women have about sexism, the knowledge that gays and lesbians have about loving relationships, the knowledge that people of color have about racism challenge dominant assumptions and explanations. The knowledge that illiterate farmers in El Salvador have about economics and the political process, the knowledge that fast-food workers in the U.S. have about labor relations reveal the function of domination embedded in our institutions and the "knowledge" that validates them. These are the disqualified or naive knowledges. We, who are part of the dominant, literally cannot "see" this without learning to see the eyes with which we see. We have to "see" that we are socially located, and so is our "truth." In the first chapter, I labeled this the challenge of diversity.

The second source of our discomfort is disclosed by the erudite knowledge that intellectuals such as Stanley Hauerwas, Larry Rasmussen, Daniel Bell, Robert Bellah, and others describe so well: our sense that the pursuit of life, liberty, and happiness is slowly destroying the very relationships upon which life, liberty, and happiness depend. We who have succeeded so well in attaining the promises of material wealth through capitalism and freedom through political participation have made ourselves and our children into "autonomous creatures who, on the basis of their own wants and preferences, fashion their own world in a series of relationships they themselves make and unmake."[4] And in so doing we have lost the connections, the intimacies that yield commitments, the sense of goods-in-common that sustain community and unite self-and-other-interests. This is the knowledge that results from intellectual criticism of liberalism and, for Rasmussen, criticism of the market forces liberalism justifies. This erudite knowledge reveals a long, losing struggle, waged by families, neighborhoods, churches, and other communities that ground moral life, against the relentless atomization and commodification of all human needs and of human beings themselves. In gaining individual freedom and material wealth, we have lost the social bonds that sustain a secure and meaningful life. We who are part of the dominant, and who may participate as decision makers in institutions with social power, have to learn that *we* have lost our social grounding and that we need to reconnect with others in community building ways. This is the challenge of our own "fragmentation."

Obviously these two sources of discomfort are interconnected in our experiences. We have seen how patriarchal capitalism, despite its liberal language of equality, assumed and depended upon the maintenance of concrete social inequalities that, in turn, shape the "logic" of social institutions. However, the conflation of the two, in which the fragmentation of community affecting the dominant (but, of course, not only the dominant) becomes the interpretive screen through which all challenges to community are seen, functions to trivialize the legitimate claims of self-interest arising from the marginalized. This, I argue, is the error of Hauerwas, as well as of conservative social critics such as Bell. While we who are dominant should lament our reluctance to accept self-sacrifice for the common good and our reluctance to live lives more vulnerable to the needs of others, we protect our own privileges when we paint all people, regardless of social location, with the same brush. We are ignoring the disqualified knowledges—because we can. That is, we have the social power to protect ourselves from their challenges and we use it. Our risk of faith requires our willingness to use our social power to become vulnerable to these subjugated knowledges.

How then can we, as part of the dominant, begin to form redeemed communities characterized by both justice and nonviolence? Foucault suggests the potentially transforming power of a union of erudite knowledge and the disqualified knowledges (what he calls "genealogy"). Such a union "allows us to establish a historical knowledge of struggles and to make use of this knowledge tactically today" in order to resist the power of any unified knowledge that would "filter, hierarchise, and order" in the name of truth.[5] For middle- and upper-class white churches in the U.S. today, the direction lies, I think, in applying Foucault's concept of genealogy to the elements of Mark Kline Taylor's postmodern trilemma: tradition, diversity, and resistance to domination.[6]

## Tradition

> There is not one religious tradition or theological school existing in the world today, nor one atheistic critique of religious tradition, nor one sociopolitical arrangement nor liberating critique of such structures, nor cultures of East or West that yet does justice to the full humanity of women.[7]

When feminist theologians and ethicists turn to the church, its texts and stories, its traditions and practices, and the type of community it produces, our attention is focused on these discourses (the totality of linguistic and nonlinguistic practices) to discover what it is in them that makes a history of violence against women, and other "others," acceptable. These traditions of injustice have not simply rendered "the other" invisible. They are not simply oversights, the result of benign neglect. In the Christian narrative, the creation of inferior "others" is acceptable, even mandated, even understood as "God's will." The legitimation of relationships of domination has been the product of our best (that is, dominant) minds, minds that continue to dominate the core of Christian theology. Agreeing with Hauerwas that we are formed by the practices of our community and the skills we learn there, we must ask how this acceptable violence is rooted in the fleshy existence of this body? What material realities of Christian practices give rise to this "truth"? And what are the material realities that today reproduce these injustices and resist change? Foucault's genealogy reminds us that the kind of community we have been is a result of historical struggles to name reality: of resistances and of dominations. The analysis of contemporary Christian discourses, such as Hauerwas's, or my own, reminds us that the kind of community we are continues to be a product of struggle, resistance, and the power to dominate.

Rosemary Radford Ruether has described a history of domestic violence against women as it was civilly and ecclesially sanctioned in western Europe. She points out the consistent theological definition of women as inferior by created or fallen "nature." She describes the punishments that a husband could inflict upon his wife according to canon law, the church's identification of women with the demonic, and the subsequent death of hundreds of thousands of women by torture. And throughout this history, Ruether notes, the subjection of women's sexuality and powers of procreation to patriarchal interpretation and control remained foundational.[8] This, and women's persistent resistance to our dehumanization, as well as the contributions we have made to our traditions despite this dehumanization, are a part of our tradition—a part rarely told.

Katie Geneva Cannon has analyzed the dominant ideology that arose from the political loyalties, economic needs, and social commitments of Christian apologists for slavery. Her analysis reveals how the ideology of a social position grounds hermeneutical principles and practices. She points out that for most of the history of legal chattel slavery, "the mainline Protestant churches never legislated against slavery, seldom disciplined slaveholders, and at most gently apologized for the 'peculiar institution.' "[9] The point of her analysis is to expose the same functions of dominant discourses today to justify violence against women, opposition to homosexuality, and the exploitation of the poor. A dominant discourse identifies the "other" as different (perhaps inferior to, perhaps complementary to, the norm). The Christian narrative is then told by locating God's action in history with the actions, intentions, and goals of the dominant group. For example, the imperialism of European nations and the U.S. becomes God's way of civilizing and saving the heathen. The practices of the dominant that sustain their domination can then be labeled by them as expressions of Christian charity or Christian duty. The well-ordering of slaves becomes a religious burden for white Christian slaveowners. Finally, scriptures are selected and interpreted by the dominant to support and justify the totality of a relationship of domination. After all, the Bible says, "Slaves, be obedient to your masters." The life we are living constructs our hermeneutics. In essence, a self-justifying reality is created in which "we" learn what it means to be Christian. This, and the resistances and contributions made despite this by African American Christians and by Christians of color everywhere, are a part of our tradition. But it is a part rarely told in white churches.

Feminists point out that it is not coincidental that the myths and stories of Christian texts and tradition reflect a patriarchal and hierarchical reality of acceptable relations of domination and subordination. Many feminist and womanist scholars have pointed out the assumed naturalness of relationships of domination and subordination embedded in the most primary and powerful Christian symbols. About the Christian description of God as absolutely transcendent, absolutely powerful, absolutely in control of history and all creation, and virtually always imaged as male, Elizabeth Johnson asks:

> Is this idea of God not the reflection of patriarchal imagination, which prizes nothing more than unopposed power-over and unquestioned loyalty? Is not the transcendent, omnipotent, impassible symbol of God the quintessential embodiment of the solitary ruling male ego, above the fray, perfectly happy in himself, filled with power in the face of the obstreperousness of others? Is this not "man" according to the patriarchal ideal?[10]

Sallie McFague, and others, see a direct relationship between our model of God and our violence that threatens all of creation: "I have come to see patriarchal as well as imperialistic, triumphalist metaphors for God in an increasingly grim light: this language is not only idolatrous and irrelevant—besides being oppressive to many who do not identify with it—but it may also work against the continuation of life on our planet."[11]

The recent outpouring of rage in several denominations in response to the feminist Christian Re-Imagining Conference, held in Minneapolis in 1993, reminds feminists and womanists "that the assumption of the normalcy of (white) male superiority and dominance is deeply embedded in Christian discourses. To re-imagine the sacred in female images or to remove masculinity from the Christian symbol of the Trinity is seen as an idolatrous 'worship of a divine manifestation distinctly different.' "[12] Elizabeth Dodson Gray responds:

> But the sensuous bodily dimensions of the Godhead have never bothered male Christians when portrayed in their own male terms, as in the super-active and super-ethereal male sperm (Luke 1:35,37) which impregnated Mary to "beget" Jesus. The sperm image resonated well with male sensibilities!
>
> Likewise, the bodily dimensions of the Godhead were not considered heretical or blasphemous when, on the ceiling of the Sistine Chapel, Michelangelo portrayed the Great "I Am" Creator of the Universe as a very bodily-male patriarch with a long beard and bulging muscles.[13]

Imagining God as male seems normal to male sensibilities. A male deity reflects a long tradition of privileged men imagining God in their own physical, social, and political image. Sharon Welch puts the question sharply: "Is Christian faith itself ideological? Is it a dangerous mask for relations of domination?"[14]

*Christian Narratives as Kindred Struggles*

In the nineteenth century, paralleling the struggle for women's political equality in the secular sphere, women increasingly challenged the exclusive rights and privileges of males within the church, specifically the right to preach. Again, these were debates over the appropriate role of women. Scripture was the site of struggle. In 1868 C. Duren wrote the following:

> Man is made head of the woman. The place of woman, in the family and society, is one of subjection to man. Man was first formed, and to have dominion of the earth. Woman was formed out of man, and to be a "help meet for him" (Genesis 2:18), a help as over against him, corresponding to him, or the counterpart of him. The scriptural position of woman is one of subjection to man, both in the Jewish and Christian church.[15]

In 1862, Barbara Kellison, a member of the newly formed Disciples of Christ, published a forty-four page pamphlet in which she addressed the various objections given against women's preaching in the church:

> Objection 9th—It is not right for women to preach to men; this is all a notion, and prejudice is the cause of it, for there is more scripture to prove that women have a right to preach to men, than there is to prove they have a right to preach to women; for the Savior said to the woman: "Go, tell thy Brethren," (Matthew 28:10).[16]

Hauerwas rightly notes that the interpretation of scripture is political, involving issues of power. What he does not discuss is the role that power has played within the Christian tradition and that what we call "Christianity" is a product of the politics of domination. As Elisabeth Schüssler Fiorenza observes, in the history of women within the Christian tradition, the scriptures have been used for "the legitimation of societal and ecclesiastical patriarchy and of women's 'divinely ordained place' in it."[17] White women's experiences and the experiences of people of color of being falsely defined by Christian scriptures and traditions require that of any "Christian narrative," we ask: Who produced this story? From what social position and for what loyalties does it speak? Who had the power to define, to write, to preserve? Who authored "our tradition"? The fuller account of our tradition is an account of plurality and of conflict; of domination and of resistance to domination. Churches that participate in the dominant culture of the U.S. must tell that story, too. Let that story sharpen our skills for analyzing the cultural discourses that shape our contemporary construction of the Christian tradition and the daily practices that form our character.

Feminist resistance to Christian sexism has been diverse. Kwok Pui-lan tells of a nineteenth-century Chinese Christian woman who used a pin to cut from her Bible the Pauline teachings about the submissiveness of wives. Her name was not recorded by the missionary who records her act of resistance.[18] In 1836 Jarena Lee published *The Life and Religious Experience of Jarena Lee,* in which she argued: "If a man may preach, because the Saviour died for him, why not the woman? . . . Did not Mary *first* preach the risen Saviour, and is not the doctrine of the resurrection the very climax of Christianity. . . . Then did not Mary, a woman, preach the gospel?"[19]

In 1895, Elizabeth Cady Stanton published the first volume of *The Woman's Bible.* In her introduction she explains the need for such an enterprize, her "hermeneutics of suspicion."[20]

> From the inauguration of the movement for woman's emancipation the Bible has been used to hold her in the "divinely ordained sphere," prescribed in the Old and New Testaments. . . . The only points in which I differ from all ecclesiastical teaching is that I do not believe that any man ever saw or talked with God, I do not believe that God inspired the Mosaic code, or told the historians what they say he did about woman, for all the religions on the face of the earth degrade her, and so long as woman accepts the position that they assign her, her emancipation is impossible. . . . The canon law, the Scriptures, the creeds and codes and church discipline of the leading religions bear the impress of fallible man, and not of our ideal great first cause.[21]

Stanton's (still) radical point was that the scriptures have not just been wrongly interpreted by men, but that the biblical text is itself androcentric, that is, written by men out of their own patriarchal assumptions about women. In this way Stanton articulated a basic tenet of the historical-critical method but with a radically new application: that revelation is mediated through the historical limits and cultural particularities of its human (male) authors and their (androcentric) languages.

In the last half of the twentieth century, scripture continues to be a place of political struggle. Some Christian feminists approach scripture to find a liberating word for women, the usable tradition, the "canon within the canon," hidden under its androcentric origins. Rosemary Radford Ruether turns to the prophetic biblical traditions and their descriptions of a God who vindicates the oppressed. She turns to religions repressed by Judaism and Christianity and she turns to repressed Christian minority cultures. Her critical hermeneutical principle is the promotion of the full humanity of women and all persons. Whatever denies, distorts, or lessens this wholeness is not redemptive; it is not of God; and it must not be accepted as an authentic expression of the divine or of nature. She argues, however, that redemptive themes of justice and liberation can still be reclaimed from the patriarchal texts and traditions.[22]

On the other hand, Mary Daly, journeying beyond her earlier attempts at the revision of Christian tradition, rejects all feminists' attempts to find liberating themes or to reclaim patriarchal texts for liberating purposes. Daly understands language as the key by which women's journey of "metapatriarchal metamorphosis" is named as threatening disorder and chaos. Language, she says, legitimates the patriarchal order as the natural order of the cosmos. Therefore, Daly argues that feminist women must literally recreate the world within the consciousness and language of individual women.

> This applies to male-controlled language in all matters pertaining to gynocentric identity: the words simply do not exist. . . . Women struggling for words feel haunted by false feelings of personal inadequacy, by anger, frustration, and a kind of sadness/bereavement. For it is, after all, our "mother tongue" that has been turned against us by the tongue twisters. Learning to speak our Mothers' Tongue is exorcising the male "mothers."[23]

The point I want to emphasize is that a Christian feminist ethics of liberation must challenge our churches to expose the history of struggle, of resistance, and of domination within the elite, white, male-formations of the Christian narrative. Although Daly warns that this effort is itself a patriarchal device to de-spirit women, my presentation of a Christian feminist ethics of liberation is rooted in the stories of womanists and feminists who believe we have found a Christian story through our own and others' experiences that resists and stands in opposition to the dominant Christian narrative. Beverly Harrison describes this experience:

> The Christian story as I have come to understand it out of my experience, informed by feminist consciousness, is not the story told by the dominant tradition as I first learned it in seminary. The way I understand the Christian story is now quite different. My own theology is controversial, and by some standards it is heretical. . . . Yet coming to understand the Christian story this way—as this vision—is the reason that I am still in the Christian church.[24]

From my stand in poststructuralist theory, I would argue that a Christian feminist ethics of liberation cannot view scripture and the tradition of the Christian community from either a liberal or a postliberal point of view. Hauerwas describes the Christian church as a community shaped by a unified discourse that sustains unchanging values and behaviors. I argue that such a vision functions, and has always functioned, not to honor the skills of masters, but to mask domination by masters: the master sex, the master race, the master class. For our traditions to ground us in redeemed communities, we require a hermeneutic that appropriates the insights of a radical historicism into any account of Christian texts and narratives; one that can aid women and others in the analysis of our socially and historically fluid subjectivities; and one that uncovers the diversity, resistance, and domination within our tradition.

To support this project, I turn first to the arguments of Itumeleng J. Mosala in his book *Biblical Hermeneutics and Black Theology in South Africa.*[25] Mosala begins by analyzing black theology in South Africa. He is concerned that black theology has not become an effective tool for most oppressed black South Africans. Its use is limited primarily to a small number of educated blacks while it is ignored by most whites. He argues that the reason black theology has proven to be inadequate is because it remains rooted in a liberal, middle-class, "idealistic epistemology characteristic of white theology and Western culture."[26] Specifically, Mosala claims that when James Cone, Allan Boesak, or Bishop Tutu make universalizing propositions such as "the Bible is the Word of God," or "the Gospel is good news for all," or "the gospel rejects white imperialism," they participate in the false belief that the Bible at some level is not ideological. Their assumption, he argues, is that the oppressive use of scripture can be overcome in truer interpretations, or in distinguishing between oppressive and liberating texts, or in a more faithful application of the biblical truths. Therefore, according to Mosala, they are presuming an ahistorical truth within scripture, a truth that is above historical and cultural processes. However, the presumption that the Bible itself is above the flux of interested social interactions allows the dominant class of society to find within the Bible their own political reading of what is natural or God's will. The Bible becomes a tool of oppression when the range of conflicting discourses that might be found within specific texts is limited or made invisible.

Mosala proposes a historical-materialist method of analysis based on three assumptions: (1) that the Bible is the product and record of historical, cultural, gender, racial, and social-class struggles, (2) that the finished text is written in hegemonic codes, and (3) that biblical appropriations and interpretations are always framed by the social and cultural locations and commitments of those who do them.[27] For example, Mosala points out that the struggle between Yahweh and Baal was not simply a struggle for the hearts of people against idolatry, but was also a material struggle between the landless peasants and slaves, on the one hand, and the royal, noble, landlord and priestly classes, on the other.[28] The acceptance of the argument that the worship of Baal was simply a case of idolatry is also an acceptance of dominant interests couched in the name of Yahweh. A universalizing hermeneutic allows these social struggles to go undetected and allows ruling class interests to be uncritically appropriated as stories of faith.

Mosala argues that black theology is caught between its revolutionary racial visions and commitments and its unexamined theoretical commitment to the universalizing assumptions of middle-class discourse in a classed society.[29] He argues that black theology must rediscover its roots in and commitment to the black working-class and poor peasant cultures in opposition to a bourgeois state still practicing the culture of apartheid. Therefore, according to Mosala, the key hermeneutical factor for black South Africans is found in their own history of class struggle. It is the category of struggle for liberation. By employing this category and the social questions it raises, one avoids both co-opting the text or being co-opted by the text; and one avoids the need to ignore texts that are not liberating.

What Mosala makes clear through his historical-materialist method of exegesis is the existence of social struggle within the biblical communities that produced the texts. He points out the continuing existence of that struggle within the church communities that return to those texts. And he claims that by identifying the struggles in biblical texts as kindred struggles, the oppressed and exploited peoples of today will find inspiration for their own struggles and warnings against the methods of co-optation used by the dominant. Finally, the fact that the biblical texts are cast in the character of the dominant class shows, he warns, that the outcome is never certain and the struggle continues.[30] Mosala does not view the traditional texts as irrelevent either to the marginalized or to the dominant. But he does show that any naive appropriation of them serves to sustain the will to domination they contain. It is a will which we who benefit from a culture of domination must resist.

Similarly, suspicion must be applied to the historical process by which these writings, and not others, became "sacred" texts; that is, to the political process of canonization. As Elisabeth Schüssler Fiorenza points out, the texts selected for the canon were those acceptable to "hegemonic communities and leadership" whose authority silenced and excluded the writings of women and others.[31] Consequently, a feminist searching for tradition cannot be restricted to canonical texts but must move on to discover and critically assess those writings women might have claimed as their own "scriptures." For her, the wisdom gleaned from women's and other marginalized people's experiences in their struggle for liberation from "the paradigm of domination to one of radical equality" is the criterion for evaluating the authority claims of scriptures and the appropriateness of interpretations.[32] Thus, she argues that only those texts that break out of their "kyriarchal" (elite male domination) origins have the authority of revelation. Schüssler Fiorenza finds such revelation in the life of Jesus and in the community of equals he established. However, since canonical texts were formed, and their interpretations are formed, within kyriarchal cultures, this historical, communal experience of revelation was encoded in androcentric language and almost lost in the process of the kyriarchalization of the early church. Schüssler Fiorenza proposes that the New Testament be understood as a prototype, rather than an archetype, for a Christian community that must remain open to ongoing transformation.

> Insofar as the model proposed here locates revelation not in texts but in Christian experience and community, it can point to the actual practice of the churches which define explicitly or implicitly biblical

authority and the canon of revelation with reference to their own acknow-ledged or unacknowledged centers of ecclesial power.[33]

Her analysis of the New Testament texts reveals the remnants of the egalitarian Jesus movement within the dominant kyriarchal culture that ultimately defeated this radical vision of equality. A hermeneutic based on the struggle of the marginalized for libera-tion reveals the social struggle within the early Christian commu-nity as it attempted to avoid tension with and persecution from the Greco-Roman society by accommodating itself, more and more, to the norms of that society.[34] Uncovering this struggle for liberation allows women and others to move beyond the text to its social-historical context, discovering not only a history of domina-tion, but also the reality of women's central involvement and leadership in the early Christian movement. Thus, the hermeneu-tics of suspicion "invites readers to investigate biblical texts and traditions as one would 'search' the place and location where a crime has been committed. It approaches the canonical text as a 'cover-up' for patriarchal murder and oppression. It seeks to iden-tify the crime by carefully tracing its clues and imprints in the texts in order to prevent further hurt and violations."[35]

A hermeneutics of re-vision recognizes that these texts have also served to liberate, inspire, and empower women and others to struggle against oppression. Such a hermeneutic searches for the texts that can "nurture those who live in subjection and author-ize their struggles for liberation and transformation."[36]

What Schüssler Fiorenza makes clear through her feminist her-meneutic is the existence of this social struggle between conflicting discourses within the biblical communities that produced the New Testament texts.[37] She points out the continuing existence of that struggle today between the contemporary kyriarchal church and woman-church, each of which continue to return to those texts with their differing criteria. And she claims that by identifying both women's leadership and subordination within the biblical communities, the woman-church of today will keep alive the "memoria passionis" of these Christian foremothers who "spoke and acted in the power of the Spirit" and will reclaim with them a continuous religious-theological history and tradition of strug-gle.[38]

Hermeneutical categories taken from the life experiences of those in the margins of society, the categories of class, race, sex, and sexual orientation, reveal the social struggles within the communities of faith that produced the texts and interpretations that constitute our Christian narratives. The issue of power, related to social location, cannot be ignored in the processes that produced our texts, our traditions, our theological and our ethical teachings. These same hermeneutical categories continue to reveal the church as a community of internal social struggle for the construction of Christian practices and beliefs. An uncritical loyalty to a fictive unity called "the church" or "the text" or "the tradition" is in danger of accepting the perspectives of dominant groups as the whole of the story of faith. It is in danger of losing "dear Massa Jesus," who joined and continues to join in the struggle of the least for "resurrected, liberated existence."[39]

There can be no unproblematic appropriation of our traditions, our scriptures and our stories. We approach them as people located in a particular Christian community that gives us a way of interpreting these texts. When our location is in a community of privilege (whether by race, class, ethnicity, gender, or sexual orientation), we are in danger of missing the history of struggle and resistance to social privilege that is the history of our faith. This point is well summarized in the introductory message written by Norman K. Gottwald and Anne Wire for Itumeleng Mosala:

> The biblical world only looks placid when viewed from the composure of an established class perspective. If we are comfortable with having "arrived" at a reasonable end of our lives, biblical communities will appear to us as similarly secure and "realized" communities. If we are engaged in identifying and overcoming the splits and barriers to imperfect community, biblical communities may "open up" to us as *kindred struggle contexts.* . . . To a large extent, what the Bible is depends on who you are *(emphasis in the original).*[40]

### Christian Practices as Sites of Struggle

Mark Taylor's description of our modern trilemma requires that we hold together in our communities tradition, diversity, and resistance to domination. I have begun by recognizing that, from the view of the marginalized, diversity and resistance are our tradition. Yet, the stories we choose to tell and how we tell them and what we see in them is also a function, as Gottwald and Wire state, of the kind of community we presently are. Hauerwas is right to point out, with Stanley Fish, that "strategies of interpretation are not those of an independent agent facing an independent autonomous text, but those of an interpretive community of which the reader is but a member."[41] Rasmussen, in his description of the church as a people of the Way, raises the importance of "focal practices": those common actions that are nonetheless intrinsic to being and sustaining what is right and good for us as *this* people.[42] So, to the extent that our communities may be deformed by our participation, past and present, in social structures of domination and exploitation, we must critique our focal practices for the ways in which they may reinforce our inability to see our collusion. It is important for us to look at the most ordinary practices of our church communities.

One context to use as an example of our focal practices is that of our gathering for worship, the liturgical context in which we normally hear and pass on our traditions. Our eucharistic image of unity in diversity is a powerful one: that we come, women, men, and children, from east and west, north and south, to gather at one Table in the presence of God. Yet, for most of us, we continue to hear this potentially radical image in a very homogeneous and kyriarchal context.

For most of us, it is a ritual in which the leadership is overwhelmingly male.[43] For most of us, it is a ritual that identifies the authority of leadership in greater theological, spiritual, and moral competence. Yet, for most of us, that competence is measured specifically by knowledge of a white, male, Euro-centric tradition of theology, scripture study, and ethics.[44] To what extent, then, do our expectations, values, standards and practices shape us as communities of people characterized by an eagerness to learn the "disqualified" knowledges of our tradition?

For most of us, our liturgy depends upon the passivity and obedience of the congregants. Listening is the primary skill necessary to most of our rituals. And in most of our churches, women make up the majority of the listeners. To what extent are our practices dialogical, communal, and intended to empower the silenced voices, the suppressed questions? Delores Williams exemplifies the different theological and ethical issues raised by the identification with Hagar that resonates with many black women's lives.[45] Phyllis Trible exposes the threats to hegemonic theological and ethical interests that arise when women center the text around the experiences of the violated.[46]

Yet, for most of us the Bible is unproblematically proclaimed in our assemblies as the word of God (physically raised and verbally named) or as the basis of the preacher's proclamation of God's word (often delivered from a position elevated above the congregation).[47]

153

With many nonverbal symbols the authority of the text is central: who is allowed to touch it, to read it to the assembly, to preach it, where it is placed, how it is carried. For most of us, the text is chosen by white male clergy or by a lectionary system that has been derived from the Roman Catholic lectionary of 1969. In addition to the problem of the canon itself, an analysis of lectionary texts shows that stories about women tend to be omitted or optional. When women are included in stories, it is typically as adjuncts to central male characters. Ruth Fox points out that the 1969 Roman Catholic lectionary simply omits Romans 16:1-2, the address to Phoebe, when it assigns the reading of the rest of the chapter; the story of Simeon is read, but Anna's story is optional. The book of Ruth gets two weekday readings; but none on Sunday. Naming Miriam as a prophet is omitted altogether; naming her sin and punishment is read twice in the three-year cycle.[48] Simple practices embody kyriarchal relations.

We must also ask how our rituals reinforce the source of our fragmentation: our culture's faith in individualistic self-interest. Many of us experience beautiful and powerful baptismal services in which we recognize God's claim on this child. We lift her before the congregation and declare her to be a daughter of the covenant. It sounds communal. And some of our denominations require that it be performed only in the presence of the community. Yet, it may also be a ritual practice that reinforces our unconscious acceptance of an essentially individualized and personalized view of the covenant. We may call upon the congregation to faithfully teach this child. But we may also assume that with or without this community, with or without a just society, this child will work out her own unique relationship with the Sacred. Alternatively, Rasmussen suggests we consider how that baptismal practice might take on a very different sense of meaning and power if it were performed, for example, amid the toxic waters produced by companies in which we, or our church, hold stock. He asks, "What would the 'living waters' that flow from the throne of God (Revelation 22) mean for our collective way of life with such a baptism?"[49] The point, of course, is that even our most ancient rituals become vehicles of dominant, contemporary ideologies unless we consciously and intentionally provide a resisting context.

Similarly, there is no neutrality in our institutional business practices. Hauerwas rightly identifies money as an issue, although he did not specify why or what to do. The point that I will too briefly raise is the typical correlation between the corporate behavior of our affluent churches and the behavior of secular corporations. Wage and benefit disparities between the highest paid employee (the minister) and the lowest paid employee (the custodian or secretary) too often reflect our acceptance of marketplace assumptions. Investment strategies for savings or endowments are often based solely on self-interest without regard to the social practices of the businesses receiving our funds. Even our most ordinary institutional behaviors can be the vehicles of dominant, contemporary ideologies unless we consciously and intentionally practice resisting behaviors.

Reading our tradition as one of diversity and of resistance to domination will cast judgment upon our most mundane, taken-for-granted practices. What is the character of our gathering? To what extent are our liturgical practices committed to changing us so that our commitment to justice, to radical inclusion, to nonviolence, takes precedence over traditional hierarchical practices of exclusion? To what extent do our practices exhibit our commitment to the building up of redeemed community?[50] Beverly Harrison puts the issue succinctly: "Religious persons and institutions, like political persons and institutions, are *de*formed by participation in oppression. They are transformed by incorporating a genuinely moral resistance to oppression."[51] In order to counter the capillary nature of dominating power, that moral resistance must be practiced in the most ordinary things we do. And for those of us who participate in dominant culture, it will require constant, intentional self-critique grounded in a tradition of diversity and resistance.

## Diversity

The insight from all sides of the political spectrum, in church and society, is the increasing realization that in our liberal society community is being destroyed faster than it is being renewed. As Hauerwas and others have so convincingly argued, community is essential for self-identity and for the formation of moral character. Furthermore, where community is weak and people are thrown into a relativism that cannot make moral sense beyond claims to self-interest, and when we begin to experience a social and economic instability that threatens our well-being, we may grasp for anything that promises order. Faced with years of escalating distrust between "liberals" and "conservatives," several thousand Presbyterians at the 1994 General Assembly of the Presbyterian Church (U.S.A.) rose with spontaneous relief and elation, joined hands, and began to sing the

Doxology when a report finding a middle-ground response to the furor over the Re-Imagining Conference was adopted by a 98 percent vote.[52] A middle ground of conciliatory words seemed better than disunity. It is not just that we experience life without community as mean and harsh; we are beginning to realize that it is not survivable.

> So if we are able to live with thousands of total strangers at all, that is, live in modern society, it is only by way of what we have learned in the more circumscribed terrain of intimacy, among those who heard our borning cry, who heard our dying one, and who accompanied us on the wondrous and difficult adventure between. . . . No community, no moral life; no moral life, no society worth living in—it is as simple and basic as that.[53]

And that is not enough. As Rasmussen goes on to say, "Which conscience and convictions, formed by which Christian community in what way, with whom, where, and to what end?"[54] To cling to unity out of fear of disunity seems to lack theological or moral authenticity. Hauerwas suggests that all of our diversity can only be unified around a core commitment to nonviolence that is based in the theological proposition that nonviolence is a primary characteristic of an all-powerful deity. Using poststructuralism and discourse analysis, I have argued that there is no natural, essential, or necessary meaning to the term "nonviolence," even within the Christian tradition. As part of my internal critique of Hauerwas's ethics, I have not taken up the debate between pacifism and just war. Rather, I have argued that the meaning Hauerwas gives the term nonviolence, its causes and solutions, arises out of the discourse of a particular social location. One result is that war between nations is denounced; but daily violence against women merits no word.

Dorothee Soelle is a German, feminist, Christian, liberationist pacifist. In language similar to that of Hauerwas she writes: "in Christ, God makes Godself vulnerable; in Christ, God defines God as nonviolent."[55] She rejects any way to peace that is not peace itself. She also shares with other modern scholars a criticism of liberal society.

> It is not material pauperization but psychic emptiness that intrudes itself between Christ and the middle classes of the First World. Life without meaning, sensed by many sensitive individuals since the beginning of industrialization, is today the experience of masses of people in the First World. Nothing gives joy, nothing hurts deeply,

relationships to others are superficial and interchangeable, hopes and desires extend only as far as next year's summer vacation.[56]

Soelle describes what many of us in dominant culture experience: we have everything we need, but we still feel lacking. We are not hard, tough, competitive types; we are soft, nonviolent, care-for-our-families, hardworking types. Yet, we long for something, a spiritual fulfillment. We want, she writes, a spirituality to add to our education, profession, income, family, and friends. This is what she calls the "third way" of the middle class: securing the situation in which we live.[57] This is also the problem—for the situation in which we live, without war, is nonetheless violent. And we are a part of it. In her feminist, liberative discourse, genuine nonviolence cannot be reconciled with any form of injustice. Remembering an event that took place when Pope John Paul II visited Nicaragua, she wrote a poem addressed to Ernesto Cardinal:

The women in your country
have prepared themselves for a long time
for the visit of their holy father
when he did not speak to them
only about them
they broke in on the pope
and interrupted with peace
in the name of my raped sister
of the hope from below
So on a single day they broke
two walls
of centuries-old silence
that suffocates us from above. . . .[58]

Contrary to some of our best (that is, dominant) minds, kyriarchal right ordering is not nonviolent.[59] However, it is only the view from the margins that identifies the violence of oppression, of wrong naming, of refusing to some the power to participate in the construction of knowledge. Specifically, the social construction of the meaning of nonviolence requires the participation of those who have been marginalized by the dominant social and/or ecclesial order. Either that, or we will continue to reproduce in our families and in our churches the type of people, primarily men, who will go (or order others to go) to war.

The connections between relations of domination and violence, between constructions of masculinity and violence, and between male privilege and violence against women have been the focus of much interest in sociology and psychology, as well as in theology and ethics.[60] In the introduction to their book *Women, Violence, and Social Control*, editors Jalna Hanmer and Mary Maynard note that "it is, in the main, *men* who systematically abuse women, *men* who fight wars, *men* who revel in the sub-cultures of the gang and the hooligan . . . ." [61] They argue that male violence against women may be the one thing that all women have in common. In the same volume, David Morgan argues that the relationship between masculinity and violence, that is so much a part of our culture, is a result of the social construction of masculinities; that is "widely-held dominant and highly persuasive notions about what men are and, by implication, what women are. Such notions are rooted in, reinforce and are reinforced by the sexual division of labour, and behind this the deeper, more general, constructions of public and private, and of culture and nature."[62] Similarly, Daniel Maquire describes this distortion of male humanity as a "macho-masculinity" characterized by violence, by perceiving all relations as necessarily hierarchical, by the ability to abstract oneself from real contexts and real feelings, and by the valuing of abstract goals above the means necessary to achieve them.[63]

Analyses of violence rooted in the experiences of the marginalized tell us that if we are to become communities that form peaceable people, we will have to transform gender identities and the rule of fathers in homes, churches, and in the public sphere. We will have to develop, as Beverly Harrison argues, a wholistic and nonpatriarchal approach to sexuality.[64] We will have to undo all of the ways in which we accept the normality of domination.

Susan Thistlethwaite is an American, Christian, feminist, liberationist pacifist who sees her work in the peace movement as fully consistent with her work to end violence against women.[65] While we are accustomed to viewing militarism as violent, Thistlethwaite points out that our society has gone to great lengths to depict patriarchy, slavery, and racism as unfortunate but mostly benign social practices. She points out our unwillingness to give the name "violence" to our social systems. They are, for better or worse, simply ways of ordering society necessitated by historical contingencies. For example, it seems reasonable to argue that it was reasonable for the early Christian church to silence women and slaves in order to survive in a culturally kyriarchal society. Or, it seems reasonable to argue that southern farmers had to use slaves due to the labor-intensive nature of the growing of cotton and tobacco. Or, it seems reasonable that the culture of Native Americans was doomed in the face of the expansive waves of European immigrants. However, it is the struggles of oppressed groups against sexism, racism, classism, and heterosexism that reveal to us the violence lodged in coercion that is made reasonable by our greater social and economic power.

Thistlethwaite points out that only when white women place ourselves where we can see the intersections between racism and patriarchy will we come to admit the ambiguous social location we inhabit as both victims and beneficiaries of the violence that pervades American society. Her point is that when white women place ourselves where we must see the reality of our racism, we are forced to give up our innocence and face the violence that sustains our privileges. To live truthfully is to live with the wisdom that comes from knowing this ambiguity. To live truthfully requires that we place ourselves in the margins where we will lose our innocence.

How can we who benefit from being part of the dominant culture of the U.S. learn to see what we do not see? Soelle and Thistlethwaite illustrate the necessity, for truth and goodness, of uniting "erudite" and "naive" knowledges. Knowledges "from below" break in and reveal the violence in middle-class peace. Diversity, understood as the empowerment of disqualified knowledges, is necessary to truth and goodness. It is an epistemological and a moral necessity. The dilemma that those of us who inhabit the dominant culture face is how to place ourselves where we will be confronted by the reality of others. I am not referring to the reality of those who have been stripped bare by injustices and whose immediate survival needs solicit our charity. Such encounters often serve only to secure us in our dominance. Too often, in the soup kitchens that are increasingly essential to the physical lives of some city residents, we who are dominant feed our sense of innocence and powerlessness. I am referring instead to our response to the invitation extended by bell hooks, the invitation to enter that space of creativity and power in the margins, to enter the sites of resistance—resistance to our innocence and the social power that protects it.

*Santa Maria Madre de los Pobres*

In 1983 I was called to be the assistant pastor of a church in downtown Baltimore. It had an active Peace Committee that was primarily involved in resistance to the testing, development, and deployment of nuclear weapons. Few members of the committee or of the congregation were pacifists, but the apparently apocalyptic dimensions of nuclear war, whether intended or accidental, were enough to bring disparate views together in opposition to nuclear weapons. But, then, none of us derived our living directly from nuclear research or military contracts.

At the same time, we were becoming more and more aware of the problem of Central American refugees crossing the border into the U.S., and of the responses of the churches to care for these people. Certainly our own growing concern was stimulated by one of our members who had been born and raised in a Latin American country due to her father's international career. The committee began to look at the resources of our own parish in light of the needs of these refugees. We began to wonder if our faithful response to this misery might not require us to become a sanctuary church.

Understanding itself to be a committee of the congregation whose duty it was to facilitate the faithful witness of the congregation as a whole, and recognizing that to become a sanctuary church would require the commitment of the larger congregation, we began a year-long process of education, discussion, and debate. Every point of view we could think of was brought in to talk with the congregation, including that of an illegal refugee and that of the Immigration and Naturalization Service. Someone representing every existing response to the refugees was brought in to describe their projects and experiences. Finally, the committee compiled a list of ten possible actions, in the order of our sense of difficulty, which it presented to the congregation. The first action was to do nothing. The tenth action was to become a public sanctuary for "illegal aliens." Then we scheduled home meetings for the discussion of this list of possibilities. Finally, a congregational meeting was held for the purpose of making a decision by ballot.

We did not become a sanctuary church, public or covert. The congregation voted to join the SHARE Foundation (Salvadoran Humanitarian Aid, Research, and Education). This would involve us in a sister-parish relationship with a parish of refugees in El Salvador. I suspect that many of us thought that this relationship would reflect our church's long history of sending aid to disadvantaged people. Perhaps we thought it would be similar to the ten years of support the church had provided to one of our families who had served as medical missionaries in South Korea.

160

However, one requirement of the SHARE Foundation was that members of our congregation had to visit our sister-parish, each year, if possible, and always different members, if possible. So it happened that middle- and upper-class Christians from Baltimore, spent a time living among the refugees of Santa Maria Madre de los Pobres on the outskirts, near the railroad tracks, of San Salvador. They gave to us the best of their housing: cinder blocks on a concrete slab, with a lightbulb for electricity in each of the three small rooms, and, most lavishly, water that ran and a toilet that flushed for two hours each morning and each evening. Most of these refugees lived in huts of sticks or plastic donated by the U.S. Government, with dirt floors and no running water or electricity. And they gave to us the stories of their lives, their tragedies, their resistances, and their joys. Here no one was untouched by death, and no one was untouched by fear. Here we experienced something of what it means to live in Christian community with joy and hope in the midst of unrelenting, tragic injustice.

In this Catholic parish, on the outskirts of San Salvador, a people gathered one morning in a church of wood and corrugated steel. Indian, mestizo, and African heritages merged in bodies of all sizes and colors, and in the instruments that accompanied a joyful mass. Just as the people began to sing to the honor of their martyrs, to name all the daughters and sons, mothers and fathers, who had been killed by the military and the death squads, I looked up and saw (to my horror) that at each door of the church a soldier of the militia stood, in fatigues and combat boots, holding their M16 rifles pointed at the congregation. Three thoughts went through my mind simultaneously: (1) they're going to kill us all, it's been done before; (2) they're not going to kill us because I'm a North American and they wouldn't want the bad publicity; (3) they're going to kill us all, saunter back down the hill and never be identified. I turned, expecting to see Fr. Daniel shushing the people and toning down this exuberant praise of a liberating God. But he was singing all the louder, and the music was going all the faster, and the people were shouting "Presente! Presente!" underscoring their absolute belief that Christ, and all their recently fallen saints, were in their midst, and walking with *them*. And suddenly those soldiers looked small and foolish as they tried with M16 rifles to keep the lid on this risen congregation and its Risen Christ!

This is not a romantic memory. Within the next few years, people we met, listened to, and hugged good-bye, died violently. M16s kill. The church, clinic, and day-care center we had helped to equip were strafed and bombed by the military. The priest had to leave his parish in order to live to resist another day. There would be a new priest, and rebuilding, and new saints. There would be a lessening of death squad murders without a lessening of violence.

In this ongoing relationship, our white, affluent, U.S. parish began to struggle with new knowledges. Sometimes, when liberation theologies speak of the epistemological privilege of the poor, this is misinterpreted to mean that the poor have better answers to immediate institutional problems: that the poor can design a better mousetrap or welfare system. This is not the level of knowledge that I am addressing. The insights of subjugated knowledges are more profound. Politically, we experienced a growing awareness that the reality of the lives of these people who lived as internal refugees in their own country had no correlation to the dominant Cold War discourse that directed the policies of our country toward theirs and that influenced our U.S. Christian discourses. Economically, we learned that the reality of the lives of people we called "poor" had no correlation to our class assumptions. The "poor" were no more defective than the rich. The poor did not cause their own poverty any more than the wealthy created their own wealth. And, epistemologically, we began to recognize the correlation between power and knowledge. As good liberals we had expected to discern the facts and, by knowing the facts, discern the good. We were faced, quite simply, with a choice of commitments personified by a community of real people. The "facts" of the U.S. Embassy constructed one story. The "facts" of the lives of the people of Santa Maria constructed another. Before we could know the "facts," we had to choose the community with which we would stand. The people of Santa Maria already knew this because they already knew the priority of community.

In being with the people of Santa Maria, we also faced the ambiguity of our power. We both had, and did not have, the resources to dramatically affect people's well-being and their will to resist oppression. Their will to resist and their choice to resist did not depend upon us. Yet, we could provide enormous material resources and a commitment to be present in their lives that, simply, helped. If our first lesson was to learn to "see" differently, the second was to learn the ambiguity of anything we choose to do. The choice of what to do could not be made on the basis of effectiveness or even of moral certainty. Choosing to do anything, or choosing to do nothing, had material consequences for this community. In that context, feeding, clothing, and providing medicines, even to children, nurtured a communal spirit of political resistance. It was simply a question of commitment (or not) to these people, to their naming of their context, to their decisions about when and what to risk.

With the people of Santa Maria we faced our loss of innocence. Whether it is the always present cup of coffee, the commonness of sugar, or the expectation of the availability of fruit year-round, our U.S. abundance is not the result of an equitable exchange of goods in the global marketplace. It is not a result of a natural process toward development in which the U.S. "happens" to be preeminent. Someone pays the price for our enjoyment of cheap, imported goods. We met many who were paying the price. Losing innocence is painful; and the desire to return to a state of innocence, either by joining the resistance in El Salvador or by lamenting our powerlessness in the U.S., was strong.

Finally, we faced the ideology in our theology. We sing all the time about a god who is an almighty king with kingly power. Is it any wonder that we expect God to act like one, or that we think we see God in such expressions of power? But when five years of work was destroyed in one night of bombing and evil seemed to have sucked the spirit from even these saints, our faith faltered. We wanted to identify God with the power to control, the power to win, not with another peasant crucified. We had wanted our long struggles crowned; our work, our faith, our hope, even our money, crowned. We had wanted to claim success; to claim that when you care enough to do your very best, when your side is righteous, you win out in the end. Isn't that the message of Resurrection?

We had to go back and read the story again: a poor prophet born of the *anawim* proclaimed good news to the poor and insisted that the best perspective on the quality of social relationships, even on the whereabouts of the sacred, comes from the underside of society. He was executed in an event so insignificant that it was hardly mentioned by the chroniclers of his day. And if there is any reason to believe there is more to this story than unjust death, it has to be found in the character of the communities who give meaning to this story today.

Rita Nakashima Brock has suggested a metaphor that describes something of what the people of Santa Maria showed us.[66] Brock suggests that we image the power of Christ as the power of heart; Christ our Heart; the power of relationship; the power to feel the pains and needs of the oppressed, and to express our own heart to heart; Christ, the heart of our capacity to be intimate with our world; to know it, by heart.

This was the gospel we learned from El Salvador—that to be in Christ is to be in the heart of community touching the least of us. To be in Christ is to be in heartfelt touch with these peoples of the earth. To be in Christ is to be one in heart with these others, one in suffering and one in joy, one in life and one in death. And we touched that heart. Our hearts learned from their hearts the power of those who endure, the righteousness of their anger, the solidarity of their courage, the depth of their love, the passion of their faith. Did we not meet the Christ in them? Were we not blessed? Were our hearts not warmed? Have not our feet been set upon holy paths? We cannot return the way we came.

## Resistance

Oppression is what the slaves suffer; malaise is what happens to the slave owners whose personalities are warped and whose essential humanity is necessarily undermined by their position. Malaise and oppression are both painful, but they are not comparable. And the necessary first step in the cure for what ails the slave owner is to free the slaves.[67]

I have argued that those of us who participate in and benefit from the dominant culture of the U.S., due to race and class, are confronted with two sources of discomfort: (1) the rise of subjugated voices that I have called diversity, and (2) the destruction of community, the increased inability to see and subject ourselves to a common good, which others have labeled "fragmentation." While I have insisted that these two are separate phenomena, I have also argued that they are interconnected. Liberal theory, with its emphasis upon individual autonomy and natural rights, has contributed to both. The slogan that all people are equal in some essential way that should be recognized and sustained through social structures continues to be an important challenge to all manifestations of social inequality. At the same time, the individualism of liberal theory continues to be used as a justification for the existence of gross inequalities. As members of a dominant group, we benefit from the argument that we deserve what we have through the merit of individual effort, hard and honest work, and the values of self-discipline and postponed rewards. At the same time, we know ourselves to be threatened by the instabilities and insecurities of finding ourselves in communities (family, neighborhoods, churches, the workplace, and the larger society) where no one has a permanent commitment to the community; self-interest nuances our always voluntary membership.

With Starhawk, I am suggesting that the painful solution to our painful context lies in freeing the slaves. That is, it lies in the development of a community called church that (like God) is so committed to the well-being of humanity that we who are dominant are willing to live as though the reign of God were fully present in our society now. We are willing to live in ways that resist the suffering caused by humanly created systems. We are willing to live in ways that resist oppression and the suffering caused by poverty, by racism, by sexism, by heterosexism, and by all humanly created relationships which assume the naturalness of domination. We are willing to live in ways that will plow under the roots of our privileges.

One point needs to be emphasized: in a liberative ethic, suffering is not "the hallmark of the Kingdom established by Jesus."[68] It is not an end in itself. As Patricia McAuliffe says so clearly: "Finally, the one sort of suffering which is not oppressive is suffering to resist suffering. This is the only suffering that God blesses. Ironically, the need for this kind of suffering is implicit in the imperative to resist suffering."[69] Similarly, Beverly Harrison writes: "[Jesus] *accepted* sacrifice. But his sacrifice was *for* the cause of radical love, to make relationship and to sustain it, and, above all, to *righting* wrong relationship, which is what we call 'doing justice.' "[70]

The celebration of the goodness of life for all creation, and passing on that goodness to the next generation, is the center of our faith. But, in an unjust society and church, where the ordinary structures that sustain life also sustain unjust relationships that benefit some at the expense of others, celebrating the goodness of life for all becomes a risky, dangerous, and serious matter. Yet, such resistance, as Alice Walker has shown us, is also the secret of joy.[71] Such resistance creates and requires redeemed communities. Paradoxically, the healing of our fragmentation (our conversion to community) requires our conversion to the marginalized other, our embrace of the diversity that will de-center us.[72]

To tease out some steps for how to go about de-centering our own privileged position, I am going to turn to an article by Marvin Ellison for suggestions on how to turn the problem of privilege into a resource for liberation.[73] His first step correlates with the arguments Sharon Welch has made about the ethical necessity of our encounter with the other. Ellison writes:

165

Precisely because men's lives under patriarchal conditions are constructed on the basis of maintaining male centrality and on woman-hating . . . , men typically fail to notice, much less value, the moral wisdom of women (and of marginalized men). . . . Ironically, therefore, reclaiming our humanity as men requires us to listen to and learn from these "nobodies" who do, indeed, know much more about us and our maneuvering as social dominants, because their survival depends on this knowledge.[74]

To de-center ourselves requires that we use our resources not to maintain our distance from the other, but to move from center to margin; that is, to those places of creative resistance. The affluence of my congregation and the ability of many of its members to take time from their professions made it possible to accept the risk of living in Santa Maria. Once there, our privileged position as citizens of the U.S. (which was providing some 60 percent of El Salvador's annual budget) made it easier to risk being with the poor. Our resources made it possible to listen to how these people experienced the behaviors of U.S. companies and the U.S. government and the myths we tell to sustain the values that justify such behaviors.

There in the margins, where we listen, Ellison also calls on us to speak:

In what Stoltenberg calls revolutionary honesty, to commit ourselves to a painful, yet necessary process of "telling the truth about male power, speaking the truth to male supremacy and starting with our own lives." Privileged white men know more about the workings of male gender supremacy that we ordinarily admit.[75]

And privileged white women and men know more about the workings of racial power and class power than we usually admit even to ourselves. We might begin by a more honest telling of how we pulled ourselves up by our bootstraps. In a Business Ethics class, I often ask students to write their families' economic histories, a retelling of how the generations provisioned their lives. One point of the exercise is to show that everyone has a history of hard work and of generational sacrifices. However, the young white man who recounts with pride that his great-grandfather became a firefighter, to be followed by his grandfather and father, also needs to admit the gender and race privilege that contributed to this security, this solidly middle-class life, and the values it teaches. Our local churches need to reclaim their own institutional histories with an eye to hidden privileges of race and class. And, as I have discussed above, we need to look at the way our current practices reflect these privileges and reproduce them. Ellison calls us to a truth-telling about ourselves and the ways we defend our privileges.

Finally, Ellison, with Beverly Harrison, argues that we must not deny the power we have as members of a privileged group, we must not step back from our roles as leaders in our communities, we must not become passive. "Such privileges as access to resources and opportunities may also become useful gifts for social change and renewal. What is irresponsible is either to deny one's privileges and good fortune (that is, greater relative social power) or to avoid accountability for how and for whose benefit one uses privilege."[76]

To recognize that our power as individuals and as parishes is always a relative power, and that there are differences among us as to how much relative power we have, is not to deny the existence of our power. It means that we must go about identifying our specific links to the complex structures that make up our society. We have links to health institutions, to financial institutions, to educational institutions, to government, to private industry. Our positions of relative power give us access to other people of relative power who, as Ellison points out, may listen to people like themselves in ways they would not listen to "others." We are often people who know people who know people.

What is needed is a redeemed community that practices the right relationships we can envision and that supports us as we attempt to practice those right relations elsewhere. We can be transformed, and we can have great influence on the transformation of our society, by incarnating in our families and in our church communities a "genuinely moral resistance to oppression."[77]

I once served on a committee of a Presbytery that was assigned the task of applying theology to the question of the compensation of church employees in light of the fiscal crisis with which many local churches live. Several issues had surfaced: the inability of small churches to pay living wages to clergy, the disparity of income that often exists between lay employees and ordained employees, and the disparity of income that often exists between senior and associate pastors. Part of the committee's final report suggested that churches, and the Presbytery office staff, could immediately initiate a policy in which the highest paid employee's gross salary (full-time) would not exceed that of the lowest paid employee (full-time) by more than a ratio of four to one. For example, if a church chose to pay its full-time minister $60,000, it would pay its full-time custodian at least $15,000 (or a part-time custodian according to the percentage of full-time hours worked). We thought this was a rather mild proposal, since it did not set either minimum or maximum limits and did not speak to the additional benefits and perks that are often a part of employment, especially for the highest paid.

However, in a society in which it is reported that the average salary of a CEO is 149 times that of the average wage laborer, this proposal struck most of the larger, more affluent churches as unworkable. Churches, it was argued, must be free to pay top salaries to attract top talent, on the one hand. On the other, churches cannot afford to pay higher wages for "unskilled" work. Moreover, if we do not rely on market forces to tell us how much to pay custodians, secretaries, even Christian educators, then we get into the sticky questions of how we should determine someone's compensation. With relief we fall back on the equally sticky assumptions of liberal capitalism: that market forces are impersonal, impartial, and best express a society's sense of fairness. Or, more cynically, we simply admit that we can't buck the system.

When we find our imaginations stymied by the assumptions of our culture, or when we admit our powerlessness in the face of our culture, we who benefit from this culture have become our culture. When we find ourselves there, we must return to our practice of resistance: reestablish our connections to communities of creative resistance, learn to see our own partiality, give up our claim to innocence, tell the painful truth about ourselves, find courage by uncovering our traditions of diversity and resistance, and hold ourselves accountable to those concrete others in the margins for how we use our (always relative) social power.[78]

## CONCLUSION

It may be true that the institutional church no longer wields the type of influence in U.S. culture that it once did. It may also be true that it should not aspire to such influence if that means the exercise of coercive power over others as exemplified too often in our history. However, it is an error of liberal theory to equate social power primarily with the political sphere. And it is an error of the contemporary debate over values to equate social power primarily with culture. I am convinced that certain of "we Christians" continue to have a great deal of power in the U.S. at this time in history because we participate in the privileges that come with being a part of the dominant race and class and gender and sexual orientation of this society. We have more power in this society than we care to admit to ourselves. Moreover, we have a great deal of power, but not total power, within the institution of the church itself. Having such power and privilege is a problem. It is the source of our unacknowledged ignorance as well as of the fragmentation and malaise we lament. Because our power and privilege is only relative, it is the source of our fear and discomfort as we experience increasingly serious threats to our economic well-being and to the knowledges and values that have sustained our privileges. But because it is power and privilege, it allows us to describe reality in self-justifying ways and to retell the Christian story in self-affirming ways.

The solution is nothing less than conversion, a turning around to walk in a new direction. This is not conversion to a new truth, but to a new way of walking. That is why learning how to use the power of the dominant for the purpose of liberating others from oppression and ourselves from domination is a primary task for Christian ethics. Learning how not to dominate requires a conversion to people, to women and other "others," and to the creation of just and nonviolent communities. It is a risk of faith for men to turn and walk with the women living lives of resistance to male privilege in their homes and churches. It is a risk of faith for white privileged Christians to turn and walk with those in our cities and towns who are living lives of resistance to the oppressions created by our privileges. It is a risk to use our resources to support the ongoing resistance of those whose success will de-center us. It is a leap of faith to act like Jesus without yet knowing the joys, and the truths-in-process, and the solidarity of community that can flourish and sustain us in our risk taking, if only momentarily. And it is dangerous to risk feeling the immense, needless suffering that distorts and destroys human life; to face the ambiguities of our resistance and our complicity, our power and our powerlessness. But a Christian community that cannot enter that space is a cynical betrayal of the Jesus who could. And a Christian community that enters that space will not return by the same road.

# NOTES

## Introduction

1. "Middle-class" is a term used in the United States mostly to obscure one's actual class status. I use the term very broadly here to refer to individuals and families who reported incomes between $20,000 and $75,000 in 1989. They represent 45 percent of all tax returns for that year. Actually, there were families in the churches I served whose earned income was above $75,000. They would be a part of the top 6 percent of all tax returns filed in 1989. These figures are taken from Donald Barlett and James Steele, *America: What Went Wrong?* (Kansas City: Andrews and McMeel, 1992), xiii.

2. Sharon Ringe, "Reading from Context to Context: Contributions of a Feminist Hermeneutic to Theologies of Liberation," in *Lift Every Voice* eds. Susan Brooks Thistlethwaite and Mary Potter Engel (San Francisco: Harper & Row, 1990), 283.

3. bell hooks, *Feminist Theory: From Margin to Center* (Boston: South End Press, 1984), preface.

4. See "Appropriation and Reciprocity in Womanist/ Mujerista/ Feminist Work," *Journal of Feminist Studies in Religion* 8, no. 2 (Fall 1992): 91-122.

5. For a more complete discussion of the use of poststructuralist theory by feminists, and its limitations and dangers, see, for example, Linda Alcoff, "Cultural Feminism Versus Poststructuralism: The Identity Crisis in Feminist Theory," *Signs* 13, no. 3 (Spring 1988): 405; Sandra Harding, "The Instability of the Analytical Categories of Feminist Theory," *Signs* 13, no. 3 (Spring 1988): 646; Joan Wallach Scott, "Deconstructing Equality-Versus-Difference: or, The Uses of Post-structuralist Theory for Feminism," *Feminist Studies* 14, no. 1 (Spring 1988): 33-50; Susan Thistlethwaite, *Sex, Race, and God* (New York: Crossroad Publishing, 1989), 13-26; and Sharon Welch, *A Feminist Ethic of Risk* (Minneapolis: Fortress Press, 1990), 145-51. Given the dangers and limitations described by the above authors, not all feminists or womanists or liberationists would embrace poststructuralism. My method (see chapter 3) will differ from those feminists who use natural law theory, or those theories that posit an "essential" feminine self (Mary Daly, for example), or those that posit a feminist "standpoint" grounded in "women's" shared experience. See Sheila Greeve Davaney, "The Limits of the Appeal to Women's Experience," presentation to the Women and Religion Section of the American Academy of Religion, November, 1986; also, Mary McClintock Fulkerson, "Contesting Feminist Canons," *Journal of Feminist Studies in Religion* 7, no. 2 (Fall 1991): 53-73. There are dangers in giving up the concept of an ultimate legitimating authority. And, as Dr. Christine Gudorf has reminded me, the move to poststructuralism is much easier for those who already enjoy social privilege.

# 1. Diversity, Fragmentation, and Community

1. Helpful introductory anthologies include the following: Katie Canon, Ada Maria Isasi-Diaz, Kwok Pui-lan, Letty Russell, eds., *Inheriting Our Mothers' Gardens: Feminist Theology in Third World Perspective* (Philadelphia: The Westminster Press, 1988); Virginia Fabella and Mercy Amba Oduyoye, eds., *With Passion and Compassion: Third World Women Doing Theology* (Maryknoll: Orbis Books, 1988); Dean William Ferm, ed., *Third World Liberation Theologies: A Reader* (Maryknoll: Orbis Books, 1986); Ann Loades, ed., *Feminist Theology: A Reader* (London: SPCK, 1990); Susan Thistlethwaite and Mary Engel, eds., *Lift Every Voice: Constructing Christian Theologies from the Underside* (New York: Harper & Row, 1990).

2. For example, Diana Jean Schemo, "Poland's Church: Alienation Overtakes Devotion," *Baltimore Sun*, 28 October 1991, 1; Alan Neely, "Southern Baptists' Quiet Conflict: The 1980s Fundamentalist Drive and Its Aftermath," *Christianity and Crisis* 50 (5 March 1990): 61-65; Peter Steinfels, "Female Concept of God Is Shaking Protestants," *The New York Times*, 14 May 1994, Y7.

3. For example, Allan Bloom, *The Closing of the American Mind: How Higher Education Has Failed Democracy and Impoverished the Soul of Today's Students* (New York: Simon & Schuster, 1987); and Joan Wallach Scott, *Gender and the Politics of History* (New York: Columbia University Press, 1988).

4. See Catherine MacKinnon, *Toward a Feminist Theory of the State* (Cambridge: Harvard University Press, 1989); and Varda Burstyn, ed., *Women Against Censorship* (Vancouver: Couglas & McIntyre, 1985).

5. See Ruth Colker, *Abortion and Dialogue* (Bloomington: Indiana University Press, 1992); and Mary Ann Glendon, *Abortion and Divorce in Western Law* (Cambridge, Mass.: Harvard University Press, 1987).

6. See Christopher Lasch, *The True and Only Heaven: Progress and Its Critics* (New York: W. W. Norton, 1991); and Judith Stacey, *Brave New Families: Stories of Domestic Upheaval in Late Twentieth Century America* (New York: Basic Books, 1990).

7. Larry Rasmussen, *Moral Fragments and Moral Community* (Minneapolis: Fortress Press, 1993), 86.

8. Daniel Bell, *The Cultural Contradictions of Capitalism* (New York: Basic Books, 1976), 15-30.

9. Alasdair MacIntyre, *After Virtue: A Study in Moral Theory*, 2nd ed. (University of Notre Dame Press, 1984), 33.

10. Robert Bellah, Richard Madsen, William M. Sullivan, Ann Swidler, and Steven M. Tipton, *Habits of the Heart: Individualism and Commitment in American Life* (Berkeley: University of California Press, 1985), 271.

11. Ibid., ix.

12. Larry L. Rasmussen, *Moral Fragments and Moral Community*, 11.

13. Ibid., 21, note 1.

14. Ibid., 86-87.

15. Immanuel Kant, "What Is Enlightenment?" in *Foundations of the Metaphysics of Morals* (Indianapolis: Bobbs-Merrill Co., 1959), 85. Cited in Jane Flax, "Postmodernism and Gender Relations in Feminist Theory," *Signs* 12, no. 4 (Summer 1987): 626.

16. I am relying closely on the summary provided by Jane Flax in her article "Postmodernism and Gender Relations in Feminist Theory," *Signs* 12, no. 4 (Summer 1987): 621-43.

17. Sandra Harding, *The Science Question in Feminism* (Ithaca, N.Y.: Cornell University Press, 1986), 41-43.

18. Larry Rasmussen, *Moral Fragments*, 20.

19. For a brief account of the demise of positivism in philosophy and the effects of this on Christian theology, see Richard Lints, "The Postpositivist Choice," *Journal of the American Academy of Religion* LXI, no. 4 (Winter 1993): 655-77.

20. Sheila Greeve Davaney, ed., *Theology at the End of Modernity* (Philadelphia: Trinity Press International, 1991), 1-4.

21. See Stanley Hauerwas's discussion in *Unleashing the Scripture: Freeing the Bible from Captivity to America* (Nashville: Abingdon Press, 1993), 29-38.

22. Lints, "The Postpositivist Choice," 657.

23. George Lindbeck, *The Nature of Doctrine: Religion and Society in a Postliberal Age* (Philadelphia: Westminster Press, 1984), 30-45.

24. Linell E. Cady argues that such views are, in fact, attempts to resist the implications of historicism by making interpretive traditions decidedly ahistorical. She would, I believe, reject Lints's identification of these theologicans as "postpositivistic" in that they reassert claims to constant truths. I am sympathetic to her arguments. See Linell E. Cady, "Resisting the Postmodern Turn: Theology and Contextualization" in *Theology at the End of Modernity*.

25. John Howard Yoder, *The Priestly Kingdom* (University of Notre Dame Press, 1984), 9.

26. Ibid., 11.

27. James William McClendon, Jr., *Ethics: Systematic Theology*, vol. 1 (Nashville: Abingdon Press, 1986), 348-56.

28. Cady, "Resisting the Postmodern Turn," 89.

29. Mark Kline Taylor, *Remembering Esperanza* (Maryknoll, N.Y.: Orbis Books, 1990), chap.1.

30. Stanley Hauerwas, *Character and the Christian Life* (San Antonio: Trinity University Press, 1975; reprint, 1985).

31. Stanley Hauerwas, *Dispatches from the Front: Theological Engagements with the Secular* (Durham, N.C.: Duke University Press, 1994), 21-23.

32. For a different approach to the similarities between an ethics of character and feminist ethics, see Richard Bondi, "On Not Winking at Jesus: Points of Convergence between Feminist Ethics and an Ethics of Character," presentation to the Society of Christian Ethics, 1988.

33. See, for example, Michael Goldberg, *Theology and Narrative: A Critical Introduction* (Philadelphia: Trinity Press, 1991); James Gustafson, "The Sectarian Temptation: Reflections on Theology, the Church, and the University," *Proceedings of the Catholic Theological Society* 40 (1985): 83-94; Thomas Ogletree, "Character and Narrative: Stanley Hauerwas's Studies of the Christian Life," *Religious Studies Review* 6, no. 1 (January 1980); Douglas Ottati, "The Spirit of Reforming Protestantism," *Christian Century* (December 16, 1992); Gene Outka, "Character, Vision, and Narrative," *Religious Studies Review* 6 (April 1980): 116-18; J. Wesley Robbins, "Narrative, Morality, and Religion," *Journal of Religious Ethics* 8 (Fall 1980): 161-76.

34. See Evelyn Fox Keller, *Reflections on Gender and Science* (New Haven, Conn.: Yale University Press, 1984); Paulo Friere, *The Pedagogy of the Oppressed* (New York: Herder and Herder, 1970); and Michel Foucault, *Power/Knowledge: Selected Interviews and Other Writings 1972-1977*, ed. Colin Gordon (New York: Pantheon, 1980).

35. See Sandra Harding, *The Science Question in Feminism*.

36. Immanuel Kant, "Of the Difference of the Sublime and of the Beautiful in the Counter-relation of Both Sexes" in Martha Lee Osborne, ed., *Women in Western Thought* (New York: Random House, 1979),153-61. Jean Bethke Elshtain, ed. *The Family in Political Thought* (Amherst: University of Massachusetts Press, 1982), 157-59.

37. Carole Pateman, *The Sexual Contract* (Stanford, Calif.: Stanford University Press, 1988), 63.

38. Katie Cannon, "Slave Ideology and Biblical Interpretation," *Semeia* 47 (1989): 9-23.

39. Jane Flax, "Postmodernism and Gender," 626-27.

## 2. The Character of Hauerwas's Community

1. Stanley Hauerwas, "The Testament of Friends," *The Christian Century* (February 28, 1990): 214. Hauerwas uses this phrase "a Texan epistemology" to emphasize that his experience of

being a Texan has not only shaped his self-identity, but also his theory of knowledge. Sandra Harding notes that an epistemology, as a theory of knowledge, answers such questions as who can be a knower, what criteria mark legitimate knowledge, and what can be known. Furthermore, she notes that sociologists of knowledge see epistemologies as "strategies for justifying beliefs." Sandra Harding, ed., *Feminism and Methodology* (Bloomington: Indiana University Press, 1987), 3. It is with that warning that I proceed to analyze how Hauerwas and others, including myself, "know."

2. Hauerwas, *Christian Existence Today* (Durham, N.C.: The Labyrinth Press, 1988), 27.

3. Ibid., 28. Hauerwas believes that gender identity, like the identity of being a Texan, is a more fundamental identity than other social "roles." He believes it may be misleading to think of "male" and "female" as social roles. These sexual identities, he says, are unchosen stories we are born into and to which we must adapt. Of course, many feminists would see this quite differently.

4. Ibid., 31.

5. Ibid., 32.

6. William Humphrey, *The Ordways* (New York: Alfred Knopf, 1965), as quoted in Hauerwas, *Christian Existence*, 32-38.

7. Hauerwas, *Christian Existence*, 34.

8. Ibid., 35.

9. Ibid., 36. Hauerwas offers by way of a footnote that "the way blacks and Mexicans tell it will be quite different." However, this difference appears to function in his Texan epistemology only as the "other" who threatens one with knowledge of the limits of one's own history and identity. See *Christian Existence*, 43, note 15. Presumably, then, these "others" might raise questions about the efficacy of hard work for blacks and Mexicans in a racist society.

10. Paulo Freire, *Pedagogy of the Oppressed*, trans. Myra Bergman Ramos (New York: Continuum Publishing, 1986), 91.

11. Hauerwas, "The Testament of Friends," 214.

12. Lee Cormie, "Society, History and Meaning: Perspectives from the Social Sciences," mimeographed, 11; quoted in Judith Vaughan, *Sociality, Ethics, and Social Change* (Lanham, Md.: University Press of America, 1983), 5.

13. The term "discourse" refers to a system of meaning-making that includes both linguistic and nonlinguistic elements. See chapter 3.

14. Stanley Hauerwas, *Christian Existence Today*, 48-50. It is important to note here that despite Hauerwas's acceptance of the concept of the particularity of "religious linguistic communities," he is asserting a universal truthfulness for his description of the Christian ethical wisdom which can be derived from this Jewish myth.

15. Ibid., 49.

16. Ibid.

17. Stanley Hauerwas, *Peaceable Kingdom* (Notre Dame: University of Notre Dame Press, 1983), 47.

18. Hauerwas, *Christian Existence*, 92.

19. Hauerwas, *Dispatches from the Front* (Durham, N.C.: Duke University Press, 1994), 20.

20. Kenneth Waltz, *Man, The State, and War: A Theoretical Analysis* (New York: Columbia University Press, 1959), 168, as quoted in Hauerwas, *Against the Nations* (Minneapolis, Minn.: Winston Press, 1985), 181.

21. Hauerwas, *Against the Nations*, 176.

22. Hauerwas, "Hating Mothers as the Way to Peace," *Journal of Preachers* 11, no. 4 (1988): 18. Reprinted in Hauerwas, *Unleashing the Scripture* (Nashville: Abingdon Press, 1993), 118.

23. Hauerwas, *Against the Nations*, 183.

24. Hauerwas, *A Community of Character* (Notre Dame: University of Notre Dame Press, 1981), 157.

25. Hauerwas, "Understanding Homosexuality," *Pastoral Psychology* 24 (Spring 1976): 231-44.

26. Hauerwas, of course, is not the only theologian to develop an essentially tragic view of the human. Reinhold Niebuhr and Paul Tillich, for example, also identify anxieties arising from the human's consciousness of finitude and the resulting longing for the eternal as the existential context that leads (inevitable) to misplaced loves.

27. Hauerwas, *Peaceable Kingdom*, 114.

28. Ibid., 146.

29. Hauerwas, *Against the Nations*, 185.

30. Frederick H. Hartmann, *The Conservation of Enemies: A Study in Enmity* (Westport, Conn.: Greenwood Press, 1982), 232-33, as cited in Sharon Welch, *A Feminist Ethic of Risk* (Minneapolis, Minn.: Fortress Press, 1990), 35.

31. Peter Berger, *The Sacred Canopy* (New York: Anchor, 1969), 22.

32. Ibid., 23.

33. Ibid.

34. Hauerwas, *Christian Existence*, 38.

35. Ibid., 36-39.

36. Berger, *Sacred Canopy*, 22.

37. Hauerwas, *Christian Existence*, 49.

38. The following description of U.S. culture is a primary theme in the work of philosopher Alasdair MacIntyre, whose significant influence Hauerwas acknowledges. See especially, Alasdair MacIntyre, *After Virtue: A Study in Moral Theory* (Notre Dame, Ind.: University of Notre Dame Press, 1981), 9-10.

39. Hauerwas, *Christian Existence*, 38-39.

40. Hauerwas, *Peaceable Kingdom*, 2-5.

41. Hauerwas, *Community of Character*, 126.

42. Hauerwas, *Character and the Christian Life* (San Antonio: Trinity University Press, 1975; reprint, 1985), xviii-xxvi (page references are to reprint edition).

43. Ibid., 114. Note Hauerwas's use of the verb "impose." The human problem, for Hauerwas, is one of imposing order on a disorderly, indeed, violent, world and self.

44. Ibid., 68-71.

45. Hauerwas, *Christian Existence*, 59-60.

46. Hauerwas, *Peaceable Kingdom*, 42.

47. Ibid., 35.

48. Hauerwas, *Community of Character*, 125.

49. Hauerwas, *Peaceable Kingdom*, 36.

50. Ibid.

51. Hauerwas, *Character and the Christian Life*, xxii.

52. Hauerwas, *Peaceable Kingdom*, 96-97.

53. Hauerwas, *Character and the Christian Life*, xvi.

54. Ibid., 101.

55. Ibid., 231.

56. Hauerwas, *Peaceable Kingdom*, 35.

57. Stanley Hauerwas, Richard Bondi, and David Burrell, *Truthfulness and Tragedy* (Notre Dame: University of Notre Dame Press, 1977), 16-17. Hauerwas's discussion of the metaphor of "stepping back" is found in *Character and the Christian Life*, 124-26.

58. Hauerwas, *Character and the Christian Life*, 222.

59. Beverly Harrison, *Our Right to Choose* (Boston: Beacon Press, 1983), 94.

60. Hauerwas, *Christian Existence*, 71. See also *Dispatches from the Front*, 118-20.

61. Hauerwas, *Christian Existence*, 84.

62. Hauerwas, *Peaceable Kingdom*, 116.

63. Ibid., 116-19.

64. Asserting the need for a truthful narrative is problematic. It raises the question of the criteria needed to assess a truthful narrative. That leads us back to some kind of universal, or at least cross-narrative, agreement—a result that seems to contradict Hauerwas's emphasis on the social construction of the self. See *Truthfulness and Tragedy*, 35, for one listing of such criteria. The question has also been raised as to how a self can "see" the untruthfulness of its formative narrative in order to choose another, truer one. One of Hauerwas's criteria requires a story to provide ways of "seeing through current distortions." If the self is narratively shaped, how can it make such a determination about its own tradition? Others have discussed these issues in light of Hauerwas's work. See, for example, Gene Outka, "Character, Vision, and Narrative," *Religious Studies Review*, vol. 6, no. 2 (April 1980): 116.

65. Hauerwas, *Peaceable Kingdom*, 17.

66. William Hixson, "Liberal Legacy, Radical Critique," *Commonweal* 105/20 (October 13, 1978): 649, quoted in Hauerwas, *Community of Character*, 78-79.

67. Ibid.

68. Hauerwas, *After Christendom* (Nashville: Abingdon Press, 1991), 31, 64.

69. Ibid., 133, 135.

70. Ibid., 147.

71. Hauerwas, *Community of Character*, 27.

72. Ibid., 126; Hauerwas, *Peaceable Kingdom*, 7.

73. Hauerwas, *Peaceable Kingdom*, 5, 12.

74. Ibid., 75.

75. See Daniel Bell, *The Cultural Contradictions of Capitalism* (New York: Basic Books, 1976), 10-15.

76. I should note here, as the following chapters will make clear, that Hauerwas does not specify who he is describing. As I suggested in the first chapter, a lack of distinction between individualistic fragmentation and the challenge of diversity caused by the rise of previously silenced perspectives is very problematic.

77. George Will, *The Pursuit of Happiness and Other Sobering Thoughts* (New York: Harper & Row, 1978), 192, quoted in Hauerwas, *Community of Character*, 248.

78. Hauerwas, *Community of Character*, 79.

79. Hauerwas, *After Christendom*, 64.

80. Ibid., 66.

81. Alasdair MacIntyre, "Power and Virtue in the American Republic" (unpublished manuscript), 8-9, quoted in Hauerwas, *Community of Character*, 250.

82. Hauerwas, *After Christendom*, 66-68. See also *Dispatches from the Front*, 136-52, for Hauerwas's critique of the church's reaction to the Persian Gulf War and the use of just war theory in the discussions of that war.

83. Hauerwas, *Community of Character*, 127.

84. Hauerwas, *Christian Existence*, 31.

85. Hauerwas, *Peaceable Kingdom*, 42.

86. Ibid., 43.

87. Hauerwas, *Community of Character*, 115.

88. Hauerwas, *After Christendom*, 98.

89. Ibid.

90. Ibid., 101-105.

91. Hauerwas, *Against the Nations*, 17.

92. Hauerwas, *Community of Character*, 151.

93. Hauerwas, *Dispatches from the Front*, 26.

94. Hauerwas, *Christian Existence*, 49. This claim of divine parochialism is obviously problematic for multireligious dialogues. While Hauerwas does not want to restrict God's relationship to Jews and Christians, he does want to preserve the claim of God's unique witness which is displayed to the rest of the world through God's irrevocable covenant with the Jews and the story of Jesus. Hauerwas identifies himself as a Christian theologian. He identifies the duty of Christian theologians to be the writing of Christian discourse for Christians. See *After Christendom*, 13.

95. Hauerwas, *Against the Nations*, 154-55.

96. I suspect that Hauerwas would find a Jewish critique of this interpretation of Israel's relationship with God somewhat irrelevant since he would argue, I believe, that Christians must interpret this part of the story through the eyes given us by the story of Jesus.

97. Hauerwas, *Peaceable Kingdom*, 90.

98. Ibid., 83.

99. Ibid., 87, 89.

100. Ibid., 142-46. The social analysis that I will use in chapter 4 will argue that these images of an all-powerful God and of humans whose every assertion of power is tainted by sin are products of a particular social location and the concerns specific to that location.

101. Ibid., 91.

102. Hauerwas, *Community of Character*, 101.

103. Hauerwas, *After Christendom*, 36-37.

104. Hauerwas, *Dispatches from the Front*, 112.

105. Stanley Hauerwas and William H. Willimon, *Resident Aliens* (Nashville: Abingdon Press, 1989), 83.

106. Hauerwas, *Christian Existence*, 61.

107. Hauerwas, *After Christendom*, 19.

108. Hauerwas, *Resident Aliens*, 15. Dr. John Raines, Chair, Department of Religion, Temple University, has pointed out to me that other things were going on in Greenville in 1963; specifically, the civil rights movement in which some would say that "the church" was appropriately and effectively involved in trying to influence certain values of society.

109. Ibid., 24, 28. Hauerwas writes: "It is the eucharistic community that is the epistemological prerequisite for understanding 'how things are.' " *Dispatches from the Front*, 112.

110. Berger, *The Sacred Canopy*, 133-34.

111. Ibid., 156.

112. Ibid., 162-63.

113. Ibid., 164.

114. Hauerwas and Willimon, *Resident Aliens*, 27. See also *Dispatches from the Front*, especially the chapter, "Democratic Policing of Christianity," 91-106.

115. Ibid., 27.

116. Hauerwas, *Community of Character*, 156-57.

117. Ibid., 175-76.

118. Stanley Hauerwas, Richard Bondi, and David Burrell, *Truthfulness and Tragedy*, 101.

119. Hauerwas, *Against the Nations*, 1-9. See George Lindbeck, *The Nature of Doctrine: Religion and Theology in a Postliberal Age* (Philadelphia: Westminster, 1984).

120. Hauerwas, *Against the Nations*, 2. See *Dispatches from the Front*, 7.

121. Lindbeck, *The Nature of Doctrine*, 118, as quoted in Hauerwas, *Against the Nations*, 3.

122. Hauerwas, *Against the Nations*, 6-8. Hauerwas repeatedly asserts the uniqueness of the Christian story. It is the only story shaped by God's self-revelation. Therefore, while it is the story carried by a particular historical people, it is the only true description of reality.

123. Hauerwas, *Unleashing the Scripture*, 19-28. See Stanley Fish, *Is There a Text in This Class? The Authority of Interpretive Communities* (Cambridge, Mass.: Harvard University Press, 1980).

124. Yoder, *The Priestly Kingdom* (Notre Dame: University of Notre Dame Press, 1984), 71. McClendon speaks of the Bible as the source of the narrative by which Christians are to live our lives. The story of Jesus gives direction for the community that follows him. We are to be hearers of the Word which presents "another world" and invites us to make it our own. See McClendon, *Ethics* (Nashville: Abingdon Press, 1986), 38, 340-43.

125. Hauerwas, *Unleashing the Scripture*, 25.

126. Ibid., 9.

127. Ibid., 16.

128. Ibid., 22. Despite Hauerwas's positive presentation of the hierarchical order of the Roman Catholic Church and his positive reference to Richard Neuhaus's choice of the Roman Catholic Church due to its apostolic ordering, Hauerwas is not suggesting that Protestants all become Catholic. He is lamenting, I believe, the loss within American Protestant churches of a "practice of authority" traditionally associated with ordination. For example, see *After Christendom*, 95. This emphasis is not clearly drawn in his writings since he most often simply speaks of the authority of "the church" or of "gathered communities." Yet, he also says that his own preaching contradicts the arguments he makes because he has no such ecclesial authority. His unhappy conclusion is that we Protestants just find ourselves in this individualistic liberal exchange. The answer to the question "By what authority does Hauerwas preach?" is that he is to be jduged by his work. He does not comment on why this should not be true of others. See *Unleashing the Scripture*, 157, n. 10.

129. Yoder, *The Priestly Kingdom*, 17.

130. McClendon, *Ethics*, 223.

131. Hauerwas, *After Christendom*, 63, 68.

132. Again, Hauerwas echoes the concerns of Daniel Bell in *The Cultural Contradictions of Capitalism*, 22-25.

133. Hauerwas, *Dispatches from the Front*, 191, fn. 10.

134. Gustavo Gutierrez, *A Theology of Liberation* (Maryknoll, N.Y.: Orbis, 1972), 91, as quoted in Hauerwas, *After Christendom*, 53.

135. Hauerwas, *After Christendom*, 53.

136. Hauerwas, *Against the Nations*, 110.

137. It is interesting (and pertinent) to note that Hauerwas makes the same argument with regard to war, violence, and nonviolence. He says that there is no specific biblical test that one can point to that would justify Christian pacifism. The point, of course, is that only people participating in a community that practices nonviolence are able to understand what nonviolence is and rightly read the texts out of that perspective. So, also, it would seem that only a community that practices justice can understand what justice requires and rightly read the Christian texts. I will make more of that in the last chapter.

138. Hauerwas, "Should Christians Talk So Much About Justice," *Books and Religion* 14, 6 (May/June, 1986), 5.

139. Hauerwas, *Christian Existence*, 190.

140. John Howard Yoder, "What Would You Do If?" *Journal of Religious Ethics* 2/1 (Fall 1974): 101, quoted in Hauerwas, *Peaceable Kingdom*, 131.

141. Hauerwas, *Christian Existence*, 214. For Hauerwas's complete argument, see his article "Should Christians Talk So Much About Justice"; and "The Politics of Justice," in *After Christendom*.

142. Hauerwas, *Resident Aliens*, 159.

143. Hauerwas, *Against the Nations*, 8.

144. Hauerwas, *Community of Character*, 74.

145. McClendon, *Ethics*, 159-62, 174-77, 230-39.

146. Yoder, *The Politics of Jesus* (Grand Rapids, Mich.: William B. Eerdmans, 1972), 157.

147. Ibid., 214; and *The Priestly Kingdom*, 80-101.

148. Hauerwas, *Dispatches from the Front*, 105.

149. Hauerwas, *Christian Existence*, 15-16.

150. Hauerwas, *Against the Nations*, 58. See *Dispatches from the Front*, 106.

151. Hauerwas, "Should Christians Talk So Much About Justice?" 15.

152. This phrase was coined in the 1960s as women who were engaged in civil rights and in antiwar activities faced the sexism of men in left-wing organizations and began to make connections between the marginalization of women and political structures. I use the phrase purposefully to raise that memory. On the one hand, it shows that some feminists will agree with Hauerwas's critique of liberal theory and its pretense of separating the public from the domestic. I discuss that in the next chapter. On the other hand, it must also serve to warn us that there is a fluid, movable boundary between what is considered public and what is considered private. Where to draw the boundary between private and public is a social construction. It is also a permeable boundary, with influences moving in both directions. Thus, solutions to "public" issues shape private lives; private choices create social conditions to which public responses may be sought. For an in-depth discussion of the issues, see Jean Bethke Elshtain, *Public Man, Private Woman: Women in Social and Political Thought* (Princeton: Princeton University Press, 1981).

153. John Howard Yoder, *The Original Revolution* (Scottdale, Penn.: Herald Press, 1971), 60-61, as quoted in Hauerwas, *Against the Nations*, 195.

154. Hauerwas, *Community of Character*, 173.

155. Michael Novak, "Jonestown: Five Columns" (Washington, D.C.: American Enterprise Institute Reprint, 94, 1978), 6, as quoted in Hauerwas, *Against the Nations*, 105. In 1994 Novak was awarded the one million dollar Templeton prize.

156. Hauerwas, *Peaceable Kingdom*, 104, 106, 137.

157. Ibid., 85-91.

158. Ibid., 150.

159. Hauerwas, *Dispatches from the Front*, 19.

160. Hauerwas, *Christian Existence*, 256-65.

161. Hauerwas, *Peaceable Kingdom*, 151.

162. Hauerwas, *Community of Character*, 172.

163. Ibid., 282.

164. Ibid., 165-66.

165. Hauerwas, *Suffering Presence* (Notre Dame, Ind.: University of Notre Dame Press, 1986), 129.

166. See Hauerwas, *Dispatches from the Front*, where Hauerwas identifies a woman's unfailing loyalty to a "scoundrel" as displaying the virtues of constancy and forgiveness.

167. Hauerwas, *Community of Character*, 191.

168. Ibid., 172.

169. While Hauerwas gives very little space to the issue of singleness, he does argue that it is also a valid style of Christian life. Singleness, he says, reminds us that the future is dependent upon God's power to change lives and not upon our power to procreate. However, it should also be noted that Hauerwas's primary emphasis is displayed by the chapters he devotes to the issue of marriage and procreation and the few sentences he gives to singleness. See

*Community of Character*, 189-91; *Dispatches from the Front*, 167-68. Other than a now outdated article (see note 25 of this chapter), Hauerwas has not written about homosexuality and the church. A chapter in *Dispatches from the Front* called "Why Gays (as a Group) Are Morally Superior to Christians (as a Group)" (153-55) blithely ignores the painful issue of the exclusion of gay and lesbian persons from our churches. Hauerwas merely uses this title as a "come-on" to restate his usual refrain: Christians don't know who they are or who their enemies are (gays, and the military, do).

170. Alan Dawe, "Theories of Social Action" in Tom Bottomore and Robert Nisbet, *A History of Sociological Analysis* (New York: Basic Books, Inc., 1978), 362-78.

171. Emile Durkheim, *The Division of Labor in Society*, trans. W. D. Halls (New York: MacMillan, 1933; reprint, New York: The Free Press, 1984), 337 (page reference refers to reprint).

172. Berger, *The Sacred Canopy*, 23.

173. Ibid., 22.

174. Peter Berger, "On the Obsolescence of the Concept of Honor," *Archives of European Sociology*, XI (1970), 339; reprinted in *Revisions: Changing Perspectives in Moral Philosophy*, ed. Alasdair MacIntyre and Stanley Hauerwas (Notre Dame: University of Notre Dame Press, 1984), 178.

175. Ibid.

176. Clifford Geertz, *The Interpretation of Cultures* (New York: Basic Books, Inc., 1973), 46.

177. Ibid., 99.

178. Daniel Bell, *The Cultural Contradictions of Capitalism*, 13. The phrase "society without fathers" is taken by Bell from Alexander Mitscherlich's post–World War II analysis of the rise of fascism in Germany, *Society without the Father* (N.Y.: Harcourt, Brace, and World, 1970).

179. Ibid., 22-25.

180. Ibid., 170-71. I should note that Hauerwas does not share Bell's view that religion, *per se*, is essential to the ordering of society. See *Vision and Virtue*, 68.

181. Hal Foster, ed. *The Anti-Aesthetic: Essays on Postmodern Culture* (Port Townsend, Wash.: Bay Press, 1983), xi-xiii.

# 3. Toward an Emancipatory Epistemology

1. This term is taken from Sandra Harding's use of the phrase "emancipatory knowledge-seeking" in *The Science Question in Feminism* (Ithaca: Cornell University Press, 1986), 20.

2. For example, see C. H. Cooley, *Human Nature and the Social Order* (New York: Schocken, 1902, 1970); Paulo Freire, *Pedagogy of the Oppressed*; George Herbert Meade, *Mind, Self, and Society* (Chicago: University of Chicago Press, 1955); Karl Marx, *Karl Marx: Early Writings* trans. and ed. by T. B. Bottomore (New York: McGraw-Hill Books, 1964); David Rasmussen, "Between Autonomy and Sociality," *Cultural Hermeneutics* 1 (April 1973): 3-45. Roberto Manabeira Unger, *Knowledge and Politics* (New York: The Free Press, 1975).

3. Jessica Benjamin, *The Bonds of Love* (New York: Pantheon, 1988), 15-25. See also Judith Kegan Gardiner, "Self Psychology as Feminist Theory," *Signs* 12, no. 4 (1987): 761-80.

4. Paulo Freire, *Pedagogy of the Oppressed*, trans. Myra Bergman Ramos (New York: Continuum, 1986), 89.

5. Karl Marx, *Early Writings*, ed. Quintin Hoare, trans. Rodney Livingstone (New York: Vintage Books, 1975), 325.

6. Freire, *Pedagogy*, 81. Critical theory developed in the twentieth century in response to the concern that science and technology, once hailed as the defenders of human freedom, had become the new, omnipotent authorities with claims of unique access to truth and reality. See Max Horkheimer, *Critical Theory: Selected Essays* trans. Matthew J. O'Connell et al. (New York: Continuum, 1982). David Tracy defines critical theory as any theory that "renders explicit how

cognitive reflection can throw light on systemic distortions, whether individual or social, and through that illumination allow some emancipatory action." David Tracy, *Plurality and Ambiguity: Hermeneutics, Religion, Hope* (San Francisco: Harper & Row, 1987), 80.

7. Hal Foster, ed., *The Anti-Aesthetic: Essays on Postmodern Culture* (Port Townsend, Wash.: 1983), xii.

8. Carol Christ, "Spiritual Quest and Women's Experience," in *Womenspirit Rising*, Carol Christ and Judith Plaskow, eds. (San Francisco: Harper & Row, 1979), 228-29. There is now a large collection of works on the issue of women's voices and women's stories. Christ's *Diving Deep and Surfacing: Women Writers on Spiritual Quest* (Boston: Beacon Press, 1980) remains a classic. More recently, see also Elizabeth A. Say, *Evidence on Her Own Behalf: Women's Narrative as Theological Voice* (Savage, Md.: Rowman & Littlefield Publishers, 1990) for the role of the novel as a modern genre in which western women first gained a public voice.

9. Doris Lessing, *Martha Quest* (London: Panther Books, 1972). See Carol Christ's analysis of Lessing's character in "Spiritual Quest and Women's Experience." Also, see Judith Plaskow, *Sex, Sin, and Grace* (Lanham, Md.: University Press of America, 1980), 29-48.

10. Betty Friedan, *The Feminine Mystique* (New York: Dell Publishing Co., 1963), 19.

11. Katie G. Cannon, *Black Womanist Ethics* (Atlanta: Scholars Press, 1988), 7. White feminists' use of womanist literature is problematic. See my discussion of this issue in the Introduction.

12. Ibid., 32-41.

13. bell hooks, *Ain't I a Woman* (Boston: South End Press, 1981), 51-86.

14. Mary Helen Washington, *Black-Eyed Susans/Midnight Birds* (New York: Anchor Books, 1990), 3-4.

15. Sandra Albury, unpublished paper, 19 September 1991.

16. Audre Lorde, *Sister Outsider* (Trumansburg, N.Y.: The Crossing Press, 1984), 41.

17. hooks, *Ain't I a Woman*, 160.

18. Valerie Saiving, "The Human Situation: A Feminine View," *Womanspirit Rising*, 25.

19. John Berger, *Ways of Seeing* (London: BBC & Penguin Books, 1972), 47. Berger writes: "A woman must continually watch herself. She is almost continually accompanied by her own image of herself. From earliest childhood she has been taught and persuaded to survey herself continually." *Ways of Seeing*, 46.

20. In her presentation to the American Academy of Religion, Anne Marie Hunter discusses the "public" visibility of women that requires women to continually meet the needs and definitions of males and the "private" experience of minute scrutiny experienced by battered women. Her point is the disciplinary and distorting power of this scrutiny (public and private) that disconnects women from their own sense of self. To find our own point of view, Hunter concludes, "We must establish visibility on our own terms." Anne Marie Hunter, "Numbering the Hairs of Our Heads: Male Social Control and the All-Seeing Male God," presentation to the Woman and Religion Section, American Academy of Religion, November 23, 1991: 12 (unpublished).

21. Freire, *Pedagogy*, 95.

22. bell hooks, *Talking Back* (Boston: South End Press, 1989), 2-3. See also, Audre Lorde's essay "The Transformation of Silence into Language and Action" in *Sister Outsider*.

23. For the issue of race in Scripture, see Cain Hope Felder, ed., *Stony the Road We Trod: African American Biblical Interpretation* (Minneapolis: Fortress Press, 1991), 127-45. For a discussion of the issue of gender and women's sexuality in the birth narratives, see Jane Schaberg, *The Illegitimacy of Jesus* (New York: Crossroad, 1990). For the issue of class, see Richard Horsley, *The Liberation of Christmas: The Infancy Narratives in Social Context* (New York: Crossroad, 1989), 110-14.

24. Sharon Welch, *A Feminist Ethic of Risk* (Minneapolis: Fortress Press, 1990), 160-61. Welch notes that her use of the term "beloved community" is dependent upon the work and thought of Martin Luther King, Jr. Her book is explicitly dependent on the moral wisdom she finds in

the stories of black women and their rootedness in the power of their communities of resistance.

25. Elizabeth Cady Stanton, *Eighty Years and More, Reminiscences 1815-1897* (New York: Schocken, 1971), 32.

26. See Barbara Welter, "The Cult of True Womanhood: 1820-1860," *American Quarterly* 18, no. 2 (Summer 1966): 151-74; Carroll Smith-Rosenberg, *Disorderly Conduct* (New York: Alfred A. Knopf, 1985), 197-216; and Elizabeth Say, *Evidence on Her Own Behalf*, 11-18.

27. See Susan B. Anthony and Ida Husted Harper, *The History of Woman Suffrage* (Indianapolis: Hollenbeck Press, 1902), as cited in Susan Thistlethwaite, *Sex, Race, and God* (New York: Crossroad Publishing Co., 1989), 38.

28. Other feminists in the nineteenth century took different approaches. Some, for example, emphasized the differences between women and men and argued that (white, middle-class) women must enter the public arena because their moral perspective was necessary to correct the violent, masculine world. Thus, the "Cult of True Womanhood" was turned around to argue against women's isolation in the private sphere and to support their social crusades in the public. For a concise overview of these differences in feminist thought, see Josephine Donovan, *Feminist Theory* (New York: Frederick Ungar Publishing Co., 1985; rev. ed. New York: Continuum, 1992).

29. Mary Wollstonecraft, *A Vindication of the Rights of Women* as quoted in Rosemary Radford Ruether and Rosemary Skinner Keller, eds., *Women and Religion in America*, vol. 2, *The Colonial and Revolutionary Periods* (San Francisco: Harper & Row, 1983), 404-5.

30. Susan Moller Okin, *Justice, Gender, and the Family* (United States: Basic Books, 1989), 30.

31. Zillah R. Eisenstein, *The Radical Future of Liberal Feminism* (Boston: Northeastern University Press, 1986), 132-39.

32. Teresa L. Amott and Julie A. Matthaei, *Race, Gender, and Work* (Boston: South End Press, 1991), 135-36, 327.

33. Teresa Amott, *Caught in the Crisis* (New York: Monthly Review Press, 1993), 77-78.

34. Sara M. Evans and Barbara J. Nelson, *Wage Justice* (Chicago: University of Chicago Press, 1989), 43-46.

35. Sharon Welch, "Ideology and Social Change" in Judith Plaskow and Carol Christ, eds., *Weaving the Visions* (San Francisco: Harper & Row, 1989), 340. See also Elizabeth Fox-Genevese, *Feminism without Illusions: A Critique of Individualism* (Chapel Hill: University of North Carolina Press, 1991), 65.

36. Evans and Nelson, *Wage Justice*, 30. While different surveys yield different percentages, all show that the financial well-being of the custodial parent (mother) and children falls while that of the noncustodial parent (father) increases.

37. Carole Pateman, *The Sexual Contract* (Stanford: Stanford University Press, 1988), 216. See also Fox-Genevese, *Feminism without Illusions*, chap. 4.

38. See Carole Pateman, *The Problem of Political Obligation* (New York: John Wiley & Sons, 1979; reprint, Berkeley: University of California Press, 1985), 188-94 (page references are to reprint edition).

39. Beverly Harrison, *Making the Connections*, with an introduction by Carol Robb (Boston: Beacon Press, 1985), 51.

40. Audre Lorde, *Sister Outsider*, 116.

41. Susan Thistlethwaite, *Sex, Race, and God*, 37. See also Donovan, *Feminist Theory*, 20-21. The amendment also placed the word *male* into the U.S. Constitution for the first time.

42. Ruether, *Sexism and God-Talk* (Boston: Beacon Press, 1983), 221. For example, in 1920 32.5 percent of married black women participated in the wage labor force compared to 6.5 percent of married white women. By 1980 the gap had narrowed to 60.5 percent participation rate for married black women and 48.1 percent for married white women. Amott and Matthaei, *Race, Gender, and Work*, 303.

43. See the essay by Audre Lorde, "The Master's Tools Will Never Dismantle the Master's House," in *Sister Outsider*.

44. Thistlethwaite, *Race, Sex, and God*, 28-33.

45. Elizabeth Cady Stanton, *New York Standard* (December 26, 1865) as quoted in Thistlethwaite, *Sex, Race, and God*, 37.

46. Frederick Douglass as quoted in Elizabeth Cady Stanton, Susan B. Anthony, and Matilda, Joslyn Gage, eds., *History of Woman Suffrage*, vol. 2 (1861-1876) (Rochester, N.Y.: Charles Mann, 1887), 382; as quoted in Angela Davis, *Women, Race, and Class* (New York: Vintage Books, 1983), 82.

47. Susan B. Anthony and Ida Husted Harper, eds., *History of Woman Suffrage* 4: 216, as quoted in Thistlethwaite, *Sex, Race, and God*, 41.

48. Thistlethwaite, *Sex, Race, and God*, 39-41.

49. Davis, *Women, Race, and Class*, 90-98.

50. Paula Giddings, *When and Where I Enter: The Impact of Black Women on Race and Sex in America* (New York: Bantam, 1984), 299. See also Sara Evans's history of black and white women in the civil rights movement. Sara Evans, *Personal Politics* (New York: Vintage, 1980).

51. Lorde, *Sister Outsider*, 112.

52. Mark Kline Taylor, *Remembering Esperanza* (Maryknoll, N.Y.: Orbis Books, 1990), 31-45.

53. Gayle Rubin, "The Traffic in Women: Notes on the 'Political Economy' of Sex," in *Toward an Anthropology of Women*, ed. Rayna Reiter (New York: Monthly Review Press, 1975), 159-64.

54. Nancy Chodorow, "Mothering, Male Dominance, and Capitalism," in *Capitalist Patriarchy and the Case for Socialist Feminism*, ed. Zillah R. Eisenstein (New York: Monthly Review Press, 1979), 84.

55. Michelle Zimbalist Rosaldo, "Woman, Culture, and Society: A Theoretical Overview," in *Woman, Culture and Society*, eds. Michelle Zimbalist Rosaldo and Louise Lamphere (Stanford, Calif.: Stanford University Press, 1974), 17-19.

56. For example, Shulamith Firestone used a theory of biological differences in *The Dialectic of Sex* (New York: Bantam, 1970); Michelle Zimbalist Rosaldo suggested the cultural separation of private and public spheres in "Woman, Culture, and Society: A Theoretical Overview," Rosaldo and Lamphere, eds. *Woman, Culture, and Society* (Stanford: Stanford University Press, 1974). Nancy Chodorow suggested the universality of women's role in mothering in *The Reproduction of Mothering: Psychoanalysis and the Sociology of Gender* (Berkeley: University of California Press, 1978). Nancy Hartsock analyzed reproduction in *Money, Sex and Power: Toward a Feminist Historical Materialism* (New York: Longman, 1983). Sherry B. Ortner suggested the need of culture to conquer nature in "Is Female to Male as Nature Is to Culture?" in *Woman, Culture, and Society*.

57. Michelle Zimbalist Rosaldo, "Moral/Analytic Dilemmas Posed by the Intersection of Feminism and Social Science," in *Social Science as Moral Inquiry*, ed. Norma Haav (New York: Columbia University Press, 1983), 76-93.

58. For a discussion of the work of those feminist anthropologists who challenge the biases of Western observations concerning women's subordination, see Henrietta Moore, *Feminism and Anthropology* (Minneapolis: University of Minnesota Press, 1988). Moore points out the distorting assumptions of Western social science regarding the distinctions between public/private, culture/nature, autonomy/dependence, and society/individual, as well as Western definitions of human personhood.

59. Rosaldo, "Moral/Analytic Dilemmas," 90.

60. Zillah Eisenstein, "Developing a Theory of Capitalist Patriarchy and Socialist Feminism," in *Capitalist Patriarchy and the Case for Socialist Feminism*, 5.

61. Teresa Amott, *Caught in the Crisis*, 77.

62. Pamela K. Brubaker, "Economic Justice for Whom? Women Enter the Dialogue," in Michael Zweig, ed. *Religion and Economic Justice* (Philadelphia: Temple University Press, 1991), 110.

63. Of course, this was only invisibility in the public sphere. The demands of the Cult of True Womanhood created intense surveillance of women in the private sphere. For an analysis of male surveillance of women, see Anne Marie Hunter, "Numbering the Hairs of Our Head: Male Social Control and the All-Seeing God," presentation to the Women and Religion Section, American Academy of Religion, November, 1991.

64. Eisenstein, "Relations," 23.

65. Theodore Mills Norton, "Contemporary Critical Theory and the Family," in *The Family in Political Thought,* ed. Jean Bethke Elshtain (Amherst, Mass.: University of Massachusetts Press, 1982), 257.

66. Ibid., 258.

67. Ibid., 256.

68. Carroll Smith-Rosenberg, *Disorderly Conduct: Visions of Gender in Victorian America* (New York: Alfred Knopf, 1985), 13, 88-89, 225.

69. Eisenstein, "Developing a Theory of Capitalist Patriarchy," 30.

70. Harry Braverman, *Labor and Monopoly Capital: The Degradation of Work in the Twentieth Century* (New York: Monthly Review Press, 1974), 276, as quoted in Mosala, *Biblical Hermeneutics and Black Theology in South Africa* (Grand Rapids, Mich.: William B. Eerdmans, 1989), 47.

71. Juliet Mitchell, *Woman's Estate* (New York: Pantheon, 1971), 156-62.

72. Norton, "Contemporary Critical Theory and the Family," 261.

73. Eisenstein, "Developing a Theory," 28-29.

74. William Werpehowski, "Justice," in *The Westminster Dictionary of Christian Ethics*, eds. James Childress and John Macquarrie (Philadelphia: Westminster Press, 1986), 330.

75. Jane Flax, "The Family in Contemporary Feminist Thought: A Critical Review," in *The Family in Political Thought*, 223-24.

76. Christopher Lasch, *Haven in a Heartless World* (New York: Basic Books, 1977).

77. Chris Weedon, *Feminist Practice and Poststructuralist Theory* (Oxford: Basil Blackwell, 1987), 10. Weedon states her agenda as making "a case for recent poststructuralist developments in the theory of language, subjectivity and power for knowledge production which will serve feminist interests. . . . that poststructuralism offers a useful, productive framework for understanding the mechanisms of power in our society and the possibilities of change."

78. Note that in positing the human subject as a fully social product of a dynamic interaction of the (always, already) socially coded subject with other social discourses, this poststructuralist feminist ethic of liberation differs from those feminist theories that posit an "essential" feminine self (Mary Daly, for example) and from those that posit a feminist standpoint grounded in "women's" shared experiences as a unified social group (such as a universal experience of subjugation). For a critique of the latter, see Sheila Greeve Davaney, "The Limits of the Appeal to Women's Experience," presentation to the Women and Religion Section of the American Academy of Religion, November, 1986; and Elizabeth Spelman, *Inessential Woman* (Boston: Beacon Press, 1988), for issues of race and class.

79. David Tracy, *Plurality and Ambiguity,* 50. Tracy's book, especially chapters 3 and 4, is an excellent source for understanding this history of analyzing the relationship between language, knowledge, and reality. Another good source is Diane MacDonell, *Theories of Discourse: An Introduction* (Oxford: Basil Blackwell, 1986).

80. Mary McClintock Fulkerson, "Sexism as Original Sin: Developing a Theocentric Discourse," *Journal of the American Academy of Religion,* vol. LIX, no. 4 (Winter 1991): 654-55. With Weedon and Fulkerson, I will move away from a purely linguistic emphasis in the formation of the subject to include nonlinguistic symbol systems; for example, advertising images, architectural forms, ritual actions, institutional practices, and so on.

81. Tertullian, quoted in Joan Chittister, *Women, Ministry and the Church* (New York: Paulist Press, 1983), 6.

82. Anon., a Mozambican poem trans. Nadine Samanich-Camprubi in *Churches in Solidarity with Women* (Geneva: World Council of Churches Publications, 1988), 26.

83. Tracy, *Plurality and Ambiguity*, 62. Tracy identifies several diverse practitioners of discourse analysis: Michel Foucault, Jacques Lacan, Michel de Certeau, Julia Kristeva, Frederic Jameson, Edward Said, Emil Benveniste, and Paul Ricoeur.

84. Mary McClintock Fulkerson, "Feminist Theology and the Subjecting of the Feminist Theologian," unpublished presentation to the American Academy of Religion, November, 1993. See also Weedon, *Feminist Practice and Poststructuralist Theory*, 25, 35.

85. Weedon, *Feminist Practice and Poststructuralist Theory*, 38-40.

86. See Kristin Luker, *Abortion and the Politics of Motherhood* (Berkeley: University of California Press, 1984) for a description of the differing discourses out of which "pro-life" and "pro-choice" women activists make meaning.

87. Carroll Smith-Rosenberg, *Disorderly Conduct* (New York: Knopf, 1985), 198-99. Smith-Rosenberg argues that these contradictions, combined with the particular socialization of women in the bourgeois family, contributed to the production of the historically situated disease "hysteria." Her analysis shows "hysteria" to be consistent with a conflictual social role produced by particular historical circumstances.

88. bell hooks, *Yearning* (Boston: South End Press, 1990), 146.

89. Ibid., 146, 150.

90. Jane Flax, "Postmodernism and Gender Relations in Feminist Theory," *Signs* 12, no. 4 (Summer, 1987): 624.

91. Welch, *A Feminist Ethic of Risk*, 126. See Sharon Welch's discussion of power and discourse in *Communities of Resistance and Solidarity* (Maryknoll, N.Y.: Orbis, 1985), 15-31. Note that while both Welch and I find useful Foucault's description of the forms of modern power and his point that we can only know the limitations of a system of meaning when that system is no longer our own, there are also problematic aspects for feminists in Foucault. For feminist critiques of Foucault, see Nancy Frazer, *Unruly Practices* (Minneapolis: University of Minnesota Press, 1989); Nancy Hartsock, "Foucault on Power" in *Feminism/Postmodernism*, ed. Linda J. Nicholson (New York: Routledge, 1990).

92. *A Feminist Ethic of Risk*, 126.

93. See Michel Foucault, "Truth and Power," in *Foucault Reader*, ed. Paul Rabinow (New York: Pantheon Books, 1984), 51-75.

94. Vaughan, *Sociality, Ethics, and Social Change*, 88-91.

95. Sandra Harding, *The Science Question in Feminism* (Ithaca: Cornell University Press, 1986), 200-202. On the gendered character of views of the natural world and the rules of scientific inquiry, see also Evelyn Fox Keller, *Reflections on Gender and Science* (New Haven, Conn.: Yale University Press, 1985) and Evelyn Fox Keller, *A Feeling for the Organism* (New York: W. H. Freeman and Co., 1983); also, Carolyn Merchant, *The Death of Nature* (New York: Harper & Row, 1980). With regard to social theory, see Alvin W. Gouldner, *The Coming Crisis of Western Sociology* (New York: Basic Books, 1970), 481.

96. Weedon, *Feminist Practice and Poststructuralist Theory*, 138.

97. Michel Foucault, "What Is an Author?" in *Language, Counter-memory and Practice: Selected Essays and Interviews*, ed. and trans. Donald F. Bouchard (Ithaca, N.Y.: Cornell University Press, 1980), 138.

98. Alasdair MacIntyre, "Objectivity in Morality and Objectivity in Science," in *Morals, Science, and Society*, eds. Tris Engelhardt and Dan Callahan (New York: The Hastings Center, 1978), 36-37, quoted in Stanley Hauerwas, *Christian Existence Today* (Durham, N.C.: The Labyrinth Press, 1988), 20.

99. Weedon, *Feminist Practice and Poststructuralist Theory*, 29.

100. Harding, *The Science Question in Feminism*, 195-96.

101. Davaney, "The Limits to the Appeal to Women's Experience," quoted in Susan Thistlethwaite, *Sex, Race, and God*, 79.

102. hooks, *Yearning*, 151-52.

103. Carol S. Robb, introduction to *Making the Connections* by Beverly Harrison (Boston: Beacon Press, 1985), xv.

104. Vaughan, *Sociality, Ethics, and Social Change*, 148.

105. Welch, *A Feminist Ethic of Risk*, 150.

106. Ibid., 20.

107. Toni Cade Bambara, *The Salt Eaters* (New York: Vintage Books, 1981), 265, as quoted in Welch, *A Feminist Ethic of Risk*, 19.

108. Welch, *A Feminist Ethic of Risk*, 80.

109. Gustavo Gutierrez, *A Theology of Liberation* (Maryknoll, N.Y.: Orbis, 1973), 159.

110. Welch, *A Feminist Ethic of Risk*, 162.

111. Harrison, *Making the Connections*, 253.

112. Ada Maria Isasi-Diaz, "Solidarity: Love of Neighbor in the 1980s," in *Lift Every Voice: Constructing Christian Theologies from the Underside*, eds. Susan Brooks Thistlethwaite and Mary Potter Engel (San Francisco: Harper & Row, 1990), 34.

113. Robb, *Making the Connections*, xiv.

114. Welch, *A Feminist Ethic of Risk*, 127.

115. hooks, *Yearning*, 153.

116. Harding, *The Science Question in Feminism*, 20.

117. See Linell E. Cady, "Resisting the Postmodern Turn: Theology and Contextualization," in Sheila Greeve Davaney, ed., *Theology at the End of Modernity* (Philadelphia: Trinity Press International, 1991), 81-98. Cady analyzes how theological resistance to modernity's claims for reason now appropriates a postmodern historicism in order to reestablish a type of foundationalism.

118. Stanley Hauerwas, *Peaceable Kingdom* (Notre Dame, Ind.: University of Notre Dame Press, 1983), 31, 47; and Hauerwas, with William Willimon, *Resident Aliens* (Nashville: Abingdon Press, 1989), 36.

119. See Judith Plaskow, *Sex, Sin, and Grace* (Lanham, Md.: University Press of America, 1980) for a discussion of the inadequacies for white women of this understanding of sin as prideful aggression. See Mary Potter Engel, "Evil, Sin, and Violation of the Vulnerable," in *Lift Every Voice*, Susan Thistlethwaite and Mary Potter Engel, eds. (San Francisco: Harper & Row, 1990) for a discussion of sin in the context of abused women. See Patricia McAuliffe, *Fundamental Ethics: A Liberationist Approach* (Washington, D.C.: Georgetown University Press, 1993), 46-47, for a discussion of sin in the context of rich and poor.

120. Stanley Hauerwas, *Community of Character* (Notre Dame, Ind.: University of Notre Dame Press, 1981), 223.

121. For a full discussion of these points, see Beverly Harrison, *Our Right to Choose* (Boston: Beacon Press, 1983).

122. Harrison, *Christian Existence Today* (Durham, N.C.: The Labyrinth Press, 1988), 35.

123. Thistlethwaite, *Sex, Race, and God*, 26.

## 4. Unmasking the Differences

1. Mary Daly, *Gyn/Ecology: The Metaethics of Radical Feminism* (Boston: Beacon Press, 1978), 3.

185

2. Ibid., 12.

3. Kwok Pui-lan, "Discovering the Bible in the Non-Biblical World," in *Lift Every Voice*, eds. Susan Brooks Thistlethwaite and Mary Potter Engel (San Francisco: Harper & Row, 1990), 272.

4. David Tracy, *Plurality and Ambiguity: Hermeneutics, Religion, Hope* (San Francisco: Harper & Row, 1987), 57-58. See also my discussion of poststructuralism in chapter 3.

5. Pui-lan, "Discovering the Bible," 273. For a similarly compelling analysis of the embeddedness of Christianity in Western paradigms, from the perspective of Native Americans, see Vine Deloria, Jr. *God Is Red* (New York: Grosset and Dunlap, 1973).

6. Ibid., 274.

7. Ibid., 278.

8. Ibid., 273, 278.

9 . Ibid., 281.

10. Susan Thistlethwaite, " 'I Am Become Death': God in the Nuclear Age," in *Lift Every Voice*, 99-100.

11. Elaine Pagels, *Adam, Eve, and the Serpent* (New York: Random House, 1988), xxiii.

12. Ibid., 105.

13. Ibid., 113-14.

14. Augustine, *De Civitate Dei* 14, 15, as cited in Pagels, *Adam, Eve and the Serpent*, 120.

15. Pagels, 147.

16. Ibid., 124.

17. Susan Thistlethwaite, *Sex, Race, and God* (New York: Crossroad, 1989), 121.

18. And this represents a point at which Hauerwas can (and has been) criticized for having an extremely pessimistic theological anthropology. Whether he believes it or not, he writes as though there is no presence of grace, of the Christ, or the goodness of creation in the "world." Essentially, the world has no revelatory word to speak to the church other than to challenge the church to be faithful dispite the world's ongoing display of possible forms of unfaithfulness. While I do disagree with Hauerwas's theology of the fall, my own interest is in showing why that theology makes sense from his social location—and not from mine—and the concrete social realities that result from such a "theological" choice.

19. Stanley Hauerwas, *After Christendom?* (Nashville: Abingdon Press, 1991), 16, 36-37.

20. Hauerwas, *Dispatches from the Front*, (Durham, N.C.: Duke University Press, 1994), 25. He says, "I will not apologize for being at war with war."

21. Hauerwas, *The Peaceable Kingdom* (Notre Dame, Indiana: University of Notre Dame Press, 1983), xvi.

22. Hauerwas, *After Christendom?*, 97.

23. Ibid., 180, footnote 6.

24. Ibid., 105.

25. Ibid., 152. Hauerwas puts this comment in the context of recalling the missionary work of Bartoleme de las Casos. Therefore, it seems to me that Hauerwas continues to confuse whether he is addressing the liberal Western world or the world.

26. There is a particular blindness in the U.S. to the issue of class. And there is great disagreement among social scientists as to how to define this term. Barlett and Steele note that in Washington folk like to identify the top of the middle-class as whatever is being earned in Congress—$125,100 in 1992—or more than 97 percent of all American households! I accept Barlett's and Steele's own definition of middle-class as "those wage-earners who reported incomes between $20,000 and $50,000 on their tax returns in 1989." This is 35 percent of all tax returns. Another 10 percent of returns were filed by those making between $50,000 and $75,000—what Barlett and Steele call an upper extended middle-class. Only 6 percent of all tax returns were from individuals or families making over $75,000. Donald Barlett and James Steele, *America: What Went Wrong?* (Kansas City, Mo.: Andrews and McMeel, 1992), xiii.

27. Hauerwas, *After Christendom?*, 14.

28. Michel Foucault, "Truth and Power" in *The Foucault Reader*, ed. Paul Rabinow (New York: Pantheon Books, 1984), 57.

29. Hauerwas, *After Christendom?*, 23. I think that Hauerwas is directing his views to Christians in liberal Western societies. However, he also seems to assume that the gospel he brings to liberal societies is the same gospel that should be brought to the world. In other words, I don't think he would acknowledge that his gospel is a social construction within the liberal Western world. His use of the story *Watership Down* by Richard Adams in *A Community of Character*, 12-34, displays his conviction that a foundational, fixed narrative can exist to guide a community through history and changing contexts.

30. Ibid., 44.

31. Ibid., 47.

32. Ibid., 54.

33. Ibid., 60.

34. Ibid., 144.

35. Hauerwas, *Peaceable Kingdom*, 47.

36. Stanley Hauerwas and William Willimon, *Resident Aliens* (Nashville: Abingdon Press, 1989), 89.

37. Ibid., 131.

38. Hauerwas, *Peaceable Kingdom*, 47.

39. Ibid., 86.

40. Ibid., 31.

41. Hauerwas, *Dispatches from the Front*, 153.

42. Recent demographic statistics show that the great majority of the population of the U.S. still identifies itself as Christian. According to the Census Bureau, in 1991 81 percent of the noninstitutionalized, civilian population over 18 identified themselves as Protestant (56%) or Catholic (25%). Reports from 133 church groupings identified 55 percent of the population as members of churches (this figure includes children under the age of 18). See Bureau of the Census, *Statistical Abstract of the U.S. 1993* (Washington, D.C.: U.S. Government Printing Office, 1993), 67-69. Individual denominations often provide further demographic information. For example, surveys by the Presbyterian Panel show that most Presbyterians have middle- or upper-class incomes. The median family income for Presbyterians in 1992 was between $35,000 and $49,999, compared to a median income for the U.S. population of between $25,000 and $34,999 in 1991. Thirty-six percent of Presbyterian families reported incomes of $100,000 or more in 1992. See Presbyterian Panel, *Summary* (Louisville: Presbyterian Distribution Service, 1994).

43. Hauerwas, *Christian Existence Today* (Durham, N.C.: Labyrinth Press, 1988), 39-42.

44. Teresa L. Amott and Julie A. Matthaei, *Race, Gender, and Work* (Boston: South End Press, 1991), 315. White men hold 61 percent of the upper-tier primary jobs and white women hold 31 percent of those jobs. However, most women continue to work in female-dominated jobs that pay less than men's jobs of comparable educational and responsibility levels. See Amott and Matthaei, 341.

45. Steve Lohr, "Pulling Down the Corporate Clubhouse," *New York Times* 12 April 1992, 5 (3).

46. Amott and Matthaei, *Race, Gender, and Work*, 341.

47. David Gates, "White Male Paranoia," *Newsweek* (29 March 1993): 49.

48. Ibid., 50-51.

49. Task Force on Issues of Vocation and Problems of Work in the United States, *Challenges in the Workplace* (Louisville, Ky.: Publications Service, Presbyterian Church (U.S.A.),1989), 19.

187

50. Katherine S. Newman, *Falling From Grace: The Experience of Downward Mobility in the American Middle Class* (New York: The Free Press, 1988), 31.

51. Task Force on Issues of Vocation and Problems of Work in the United States, *Challenges in the Workplace* (Louisville, Ky.: Publications Service, Presbyterian Church (U.S.A.), 1990), 19. For other resources on the troubled middle-class, see Barbara Ehrenreich, *Fear of Falling: The Inner Life of the Middle Class* (New York: Pantheon Books, 1989); and Katherine S. Newman, *Falling From Grace.*

52. Glenn R. Bucher, "The Enemy: He Is Us" in *Straight White Male,* ed. Glenn R. Bucher (Philadelphia: Fortress Press, 1976), 13, 16.

53. Hauerwas, *After Christendom?* 133-52.

54. Similarly, Hauerwas quotes Catherine MacKinnon to make the point that the ethics of sex is a question of power, dominance, and politics. However, because he does not go on to talk about whose power, whose dominance, and whose politics, his understanding of how this is so and what to do about it would be, I believe, antithetical to MacKinnon's. His quoting of her does not lead to real conversation. See *After Christendom?* 116-17.

55. Mary Daly, *Gyn/Ecology,* 46.

56. Sharon Welch, *A Feminist Ethic of Risk* (Minneapolis, Minn.: Fortress Press, 1990).

57. Ibid., 2.

58. Ibid., 15, 103. For example, only by footnote does Hauerwas acknowledge that his way of telling what it means to be a Texan might not be the way blacks and Mexicans tell it. This recognition does not become integrated into his telling of his story. While the story of Texas requires that these other stories be told, the story of Hauerwas does not. Hauerwas, *Christian Existence Today* (Durham, N.C.: The Labyrinth Press, 1988), 43 footnote 15.

59. Welch, *A Feminist Ethic of Risk,* 23-26.

60. Ibid., 36-37. Welch makes use of Michel Foucault, *The History of Sexuality,* vol. 1, *An Introduction* (New York: Vintage Books, 1980), 135-45.

61. Ibid., 35.

62. Ibid., 111.

63. Michael Novak, *Moral Clarity in the Nuclear Age* (Nashville: Thomas Nelson, 1983), 37, 41, cited in Susan Thistlethwaite, " 'I Am Become Death': God in the Nuclear Age," in *Lift Every Voice,* 101-2.

64. Hauerwas, "Tragedy and Joy: The Spirituality of Peaceableness," in *Peaceable Kingdom,* 135-51.

65. Ibid., 149-50.

66. Welch, *A Feminist Ethic of Risk,* 113.

67. Hauerwas, *Peaceable Kingdom,* 135-51.

68. Juan Luis Segundo, S. J., *The Liberation of Theology,* trans. John Drury (Maryknoll, N.Y.: Orbis Books, 1976), 65, quoted in Welch, *A Feminist Ethic of Risk,* 107.

69. Dorothee Soelle, *The Window of Vulnerability* (Minneapolis, Minn.: Fortress Press, 1990), 87.

70. Margo Adair, "Will the Real Men's Movement Please Stand Up?" in *Women Respond to the Men's Movement,* ed. Kay Leigh Hagan (San Francisco: Harper, 1992), 58.

71. Hauerwas, *Peaceable Kingdom,* 148.

72. Ibid.

73. Stanley Hauerwas, "Should Christians Talk So Much About Justice?" *Books and Religion* 14: 6 (May-June, 1986): 15.

74. Hauerwas, *Christian Existence Today,* 74-75.

75. Ibid., 257. Universities, of course, are particularly classed, gendered, and race-specific. See Lynne Billard, "Twenty Years Later: Is There Parity for Academic Women?" *Thought and Action,* vol. X, no. 1 (Spring 1994): 115-44. John Raines points out that college is still a class

and race-specific setting. Only 19 percent of Euro-Americans graduate with a four year degree; 11 percent of African Americans; and 8 percent of Hispanic Americans. He notes further that the families of origin of college-degreed persons parallel closely the 20 percent of the population of the U.S. who get 80 percent of the wealth. John Raines, "A Classroom Is Well Named," *Cross Currents*, vol. 42, no. 2 (Summer 1992): 230. *How* Christian teachers in such universities should teach and influence institutional policies about content and methodology, as well as about hiring, promotion, wages, and so on, would seem to be an important topic in Christian ethics.

76. Hauerwas, *Peaceable Kingdom*, 150.

77. Martin Luther King, Jr. "The American Dream," an address given at Lincoln University, 6 June 1961, as quoted in James Cone, *Martin and Malcolm and America: A Dream or a Nightmare* (Maryknoll, N.Y.: Orbis Books, 1991), 77.

78. Jean Donovan quoted in *Central American Reflections: A Handbook for Religious Witness*, ed. Margaret Swedish (Washington, D.C.: Religious Task Force on Central America, undated), 69.

79. Oscar Romero, "The Political Dimension of Faith in the Option for the Poor," speech at Louvain, Belgium, February, 1980, quoted in *Central American Reflections: A Handbook for Religious Witness* (Religious Task Force on Central America: Washington, D.C., undated), 56. Archbishop Romero was assassinated in El Salvador on March 24, 1980.

80. See the two responses that Hauerwas makes to liberation theology, that is, to Gustavo Gutierrez. Stanley Hauerwas, "Some Theological Reflections on Gutierrez's Use of 'Liberation' As a Theological Concept," *Modern Theology* 3: 1 (October 1986): 67-76; and "Why Justice Is a Bad Idea for Christians," in *After Christendom?*, 50-58. I believe that Hauerwas fundamentally misreads Gutierrez by reading him against the background of North American liberal political theory which is not the context in which Latin American liberation theology is lived or written. Hauerwas does not take into account the context of "la communidad"; that is, the communal context of faithful resistance to structural oppression.

81. See James Gustafson, "The Sectarian Temptation: Reflections on Theology, the Church, and the University," *Proceedings of the Catholic Theological Society* 40 (1985): 83-94. And Hauerwas's responses: "On the Right to Be Tribal," *Christian Scholars Review*, vol. xvi, 3 (March 1987): 238-41; and "On Representing 'Something New,' " introduction to *Christian Existence Today*, 1-19.

82. Hauerwas, *Christian Existence Today*, 11-15.

83. Hauerwas, *Dispatches*, 11.

84. See, for example, Hauerwas's discussion of the virtues as skills that require practice, in *A Community of Character* (Notre Dame, Ind.: University of Notre Dame Press, 1981), 115, 131, 150. In an ethics of character, one learns the virtues by putting them into practice consistently, until they become habits.

85. Larry Rasmussen, *Moral Fragments and Moral Community* (Minneapolis: Fortress Press, 1993), 30.

86. Hauerwas and Willimon, *Resident Aliens*, 160.

87. Michel Foucault, *Power/Knowledge*, ed. and trans. Colin Gordon (New York: Pantheon Books, 1980), 92-99.

88. Hauerwas's critique of capitalism with regard to the family is that it has an "inherent drive to make all relationships contractual" which undermines the type of relationships that he believes should characterize the family. For him, the issue is that the ideas of market freedom have invaded the home. See Hauerwas, *After Christendom?*, 128, 184 n. 9.

89. Foucault, *History of Sexuality*, vol. 1, *An Introduction* (New York: Vintage Press, 1980), 145-46.

90. For a critical analysis of men's surveillance over the women they batter, and how this mirrors society's surveillance of women in general, see Anne Marie Hunter, "Numbering the

Hairs of Our Heads: Male Social Control and the All-Seeing Male God," presentation to the Women and Religion Section, American Academy of Religion, November, 1991, unpublished.

91. Hauerwas, *After Christendom?*, 95.

92. Ibid., 105. For additional discussions by Hauerwas on the authority of the church and the role of clergy, see *Christian Existence Today*, 149-65; *Community of Character*, 64-71; *Resident Aliens*, 112-43; and *Unleashing the Scripture*, 19-28.

93. Ibid., 100.

94. Ibid., 110-11.

95. Hauerwas, *Christian Existence Today*, 101-4; *Community of Character*, 187, 191.

96. Hauerwas, *Community of Character*, 189.

97. Hauerwas, *After Christendom?*, 26. For Hauerwas's discussion of premarital sex as an example of the failure to live faithfully, see *Resident Aliens*, 108-9.

98. Vicki Noble, "A Helping Hand from the Guys," in *Women Respond to the Men's Movement*, 106.

99. Hauerwas, *Community of Character*, 191.

100. Ibid., 176, 226.

101. Ibid., 223, 221.

102. Ibid., 181.

103. Carol Gilligan, *In a Different Voice* (Cambridge, Mass.: Harvard University Press, 1982), 42. See also Nancy Chodorow, *The Reproduction of Mothering* (Berkeley, Calif.: University of California Press, 1978).

104. In a discussion of Christians' need to kill compassion, Hauerwas writes: "charity is first and foremost disciplined by the witness of our God who would have us die, yea even our children die, rather than to live unworthily. Therefore, Christians are formed by a harsh and dreadful love . . . rather than . . . compassion." *Dispatches From the Front*, 166.

105. Hauerwas, *Peaceable Kingdom*, 124.

106. Jackie Powder, "Man Sentenced to 6 Years for Abuse of Girl," *The Baltimore Morning Sun*, 28 April 1992, 10(B).

107. For an excellent rebuttal to Hauerwas's historical and theological claims, as well as an analysis of how Christian theologies have functioned to support male control over female reproduction, see Beverly Harrison, *Our Right to Choose* (Boston: Beacon Press, 1983).

108. Hauerwas, *Christian Existence Today*, 162-65.

109. Ibid., 164.

110. Steven Greaves, "Letters to the Editor," *Yoga Journal*, Sept.-Oct. 1991, 16, quoted in Vicki Noble, "A Helping Hand from the Guys," 102.

111. Welch, *A Feminist Ethic of Risk*, 112.

112. Ibid.

113. Hauerwas, *Community of Character*, 172, 226-27.

114. Ibid., 170.

115. Hauerwas and Willimon, *Resident Aliens*, 12, 24.

116. Sam Keen, *Fire in the Belly: On Being a Man* (New York: Bantam Books, 1991), 154.

117. Robert Bly, *Iron John: A Book About Men* (New York: Vintage Books, 1990), ix.

118. Bly, *Iron John*, 98.

119. Ibid., 33.

120. Ibid., 96-99.

121. Ibid., 71.

122. Keen, *Fire in the Belly*, 206.

123. Ibid., 17.

124. Ibid., 14-15. Hauerwas has an entertaining way with words in his recent publications, so I wouldn't make too much of some of his provocative titles. However, one has always troubled me, "Hating Mothers as the Way to Peace" now reprinted in *Unleashing the Scripture*. Given the terrible reality of domestic violence against women (in Michigan, where I live, one woman is killed per week in domestic violence), and given the political reality that it is, in fact, fathers who have the power to declare and wage war, sending their sons off into battle, I've wondered at this title. Bly and Keen present a traditional concept of Western masculinity that requires identity with the father and separation from the mother with a concurrent devaluing of what is identified as "feminine." Feminists (male and female) have shown the relationship between this concept of masculinity and war/violence. See, for example, Chodorow, *The Reproduction of Mothering*. A feminist gender analysis might lead to a different title, "Teaching Sons to Love Mothers as a Way to Peace" and a different analysis of the relationship of intimacy and violence.

125. Keen, *Fire in the Belly*, 65.

126. Bly, *Iron John*, 85-91.

127. Keen, *Fire in the Belly*, 206.

128. Ibid., 136.

129. Ibid., 137-38.

130. Ibid., 102-3.

131. Ibid., 150.

132. Ibid., 172.

133. Ibid., 223.

134. Ibid., 224.

135. Ibid., 247-68.

136. Ibid., 265-66. In his own listing of new virtues, "moral outrage" is included.

137. For example, Keen names as "Exemplars" the women who are identified with the origins of the twentieth-century women's movement (de Beauvoir, Friedan, Steinem, Rich) because they added the words "free, equal, and powerful" to the definition of woman. See *Fire in the Belly*, 86. Whereas Hauerwas believes that "women's liberation" is a result of women's loss of their "indispensable role" due to the family's loss of status in liberal society. See *A Community of Character*, 170.

138. See Kay Leigh Hagan, *Women Respond to the Men's Movement* (San Francisco: Harper-SanFrancisco, 1992); and Marvin M. Ellison, "Holding Up Our Half of the Sky: Male Gender Privilege as Problem and Resource for Liberation Ethics," *Journal of Feminist Studies in Religion*, vol.9, no. 1-2 (Spring/Fall 1993): 95-113.

139. Hauerwas writes: "For example, the current fashion to identify with the 'oppressed,' admirable though it may be, lacks moral intelligibility. We end up in the shabby game of trying to figure out who is the most oppressed." *Dispatches from the Front*, 3.

140. Hauerwas, *Peaceable Kingdom*, chapter 2.

## 5. The Character of Our Communities

1. Sharon D. Welch, *Communities of Resistance and Solidarity: A Feminist Theology of Liberation* (Maryknoll N.Y.: Orbis, 1985), 74.

2. See, for example, Beverly Harrison, *Making the Connections*, ed. Carol Robb (Boston: Beacon Press, 1985), 12-15.

3. Michel Foucault, *Power/Knowledge: Selected Interviews and Other Writings, 1972-1977* (New York: Pantheon Books, 1980), 81-83.

4. Larry Rasmussen, *Moral Fragments and Moral Community: A Proposal for Church in Society* (Minneapolis: Fortress Press, 1993), 37.

5. Foucault, *Power/Knowledge*, 83-84.

6. Mark Kline Taylor, *Remembering Esperanza* (Maryknoll N.Y.: Orbis, 1990), 29-39.

7. Elizabeth A. Johnson, *She Who Is: The Mystery of God in Feminist Theological Discourse* (New York: Crossroad, 1992), 21-22.

8. Rosemary Radford Ruether, "The Western Religious Tradition and Violence Against Women in the Home" in *Christianity, Patriarchy, and Abuse: A Feminist Critique*, eds. Joanne Carlson Brown and Carole R. Bohn (New York: Pilgrim Press, 1989), 31-41.

9. Katie Geneva Cannon, "Slave Ideology and Biblical Interpretation," *Semeia*, vol. 47, 1989: 10.

10. Johnson, *She Who Is*, 21.

11. Sallie McFague, *Models of God: Theology for an Ecological, Nuclear Age* (Philadelphia: Fortress Press, 1987), ix. See also Rosemary Radford Ruether, *Sexism and God-Talk: Toward a Feminist Theology* (Boston: Beacon Press, 1983); Susan Thistlethwaite, "I Am Become Death," in *Lift Every Voice: Constructing Christian Theologies from the Underside* (San Francisco: Harper & Row, 1990); Mary Daly, *Gyn/Ecology: The Metaethics of Radical Feminism* (Boston: Beacon Press, 1978).

12. Peter Steinfels, "Presbyterians Try to Resolve Long Dispute," *The New York Times* 17 June 1994: A9.

13. Elizabeth Dodson Gray, "Interpreting the Furor over the Re-Imagining Conference," *Courage*, Newsletter of the Sisters of Loretto (Spring 1994), unnumbered pages.

14. Welch, *Communities of Resistance and Solidarity*, 3.

15. C. Duran, "Woman's Place in Religious Meetings," *Congregational Review* (January, 1868): 22, as quoted in Rosemary Radford Ruether and Rosemary Skinner Keller, eds. *Women and Religion in America*, vol. 1, *The Nineteenth Century* (San Francisco: Harper & Row, 1981), 223.

16. Barbara Kellison, *Rights of Women in the Church* (Dayton, Ohio: Herald and Banner Office, 1862), 19, as quoted in Ruether and Keller, *Women and Religion in America*, 1: 222.

17. Elisabeth Schüssler Fiorenza, *In Memory of Her* (New York: Crossroad, 1983), 7.

18. Kwok Pui-lan, "Racism and Ethnocentrism in Feminist Biblical Interpretation," in *Searching the Scriptures: A Feminist Introduction*, ed. Elisabeth Schüssler Fiorenza (New York: Crossroad, 1993),104.

19. Jarena Lee, "The Life and Religious Experience of Jarena Lee," in *Sisters of the Spirit: Three Black Women's Autobiographies of the Nineteenth Century*, ed. William L. Andrews (Bloomington: Indiana University Press, 1986), 36.

20. Elisabeth Schüssler Fiorenza, *Bread Not Stone* (Boston: Beacon Press, 1984), 15-18.

21. Elizabeth Cady Stanton, *The Woman's Bible* (Salem, N.H.: Ayer Company, 1895; reprint, Salem, N.H.: Ayer Company, 1988), 7-13 (page references are to reprint edition).

22. Rosemary Radford Ruether, *Sexism and God-Talk*, 18-46.

23. Mary Daly, *Gyn/Ecology: The Metaethics of Radical Feminism* (Boston: Beacon Press, 1978), 330.

24. Harrison, *Making the Connections*, 216.

25. Itumeleng J. Mosala, *Biblical Hermeneutics and Black Theology in South Africa* (Grand Rapids, Mich.: William B. Eerdmans, 1989).

26. Ibid., 5.

27. Ibid., 6, 9.

28. Ibid., 16.

29. Ibid., 39.

30. Ibid., 188.

31. Elisabeth Schüssler Fiorenza, ed., *Searching the Scriptures* (N.Y.: Crossroad, 1993), x.

32. Ibid., 18-19. See also, Elisabeth Schüssler Fiorenza, *In Memory of Her* (New York: Crossroad, 1983), 32.

33. Fiorenza, *In Memory of Her*, 43.

34. Ibid., 334.

35. Fiorenza, *Searching the Scriptures*, 11. See also, Fiorenza, *Bread Not Stone*, 15-22.

36. Ibid.

37. See also Francis Schüssler Fiorenza, "The Crisis of Hermeneutics and Christian Theology," in *Theology at the End of Modernity*, ed. Sheila Greeve Davaney (Philadelphia: Trinity Press International, 1991), 124.

38. Schüssler Fiorenza, *In Memory of Her*, 36.

39. Jacqueline Grant, "Subjectification as a Requirement for Christological Construction," in *Lift Every Voice*, eds. Susan Thistlethwaite and Mary Potter Engel (San Francisco: Harper & Row, 1990), 210-11.

40. Norman K. Gottwald and Anne Wire quoted in Mosala, *Biblical Hermeneutics*, unnumbered page.

41. Stanley Hauerwas, *Unleashing the Scripture: Freeing the Bible from Captivity to America* (Nashville: Abingdon Press, 1993), 21.

42. Rasmussen, *Moral Fragments*, 154-62.

43. 1993 statistics from the Presbyterian Church (U.S.A.) state that 86 percent of clergy are male and 52 percent of session members (elders) are male in a denomination in which only 38 percent of the membership is male. John P. Marcum, "The Demography of Presbyterians," *Monday Morning* July 1994: 14.

44. For a discussion of how "theological education" assumes a white Euro-centric tradition, see William Myers, "The Hermeneutical Dilemma of the African American Biblical Student," in *Stony the Road We Trod: African American Biblical Interpretation*, ed. Cain Hope Felder (Minneapolis: Fortress Press, 1991), 40-56.

45. Delores Williams, *Sisters in the Wilderness* (Maryknoll, N.Y.: Orbis, 1993).

46. Phyllis Trible, *Texts of Terror* (Philadelphia: Fortress Press, 1984).

47. This discussion of the liturgical context in which we hear our tradition is taken primarily from Marjorie Proctor-Smith, "Feminist Interpretation and Liturgical Proclamation," in *Searching the Scriptures*, 313-25.

48. Ruth Fox, "Strange Omission of Key Women in Lectionary," *National Catholic Reporter* 13 May 1994: 13.

49. Rasmussen, *Moral Fragments*, 159. For a feminist interpretation of the sacraments "rightly administered," see Letty Russell, *Church in the Round: Feminist Interpretation of the Church* (Louisville, Ky.: Westminster/John Knox Press, 1993), 139-48.

50. For an extensive discussion of how the image and practices of the church can change when we understand it as a community of empowerment for the marginalized, see Letty Russell, *Church in the Round*. See also Rosemary Radford Ruether, *Theology and Practice of Feminist Liturgical Communities* (San Francisco: Harper & Row, 1985).

51. Beverly Harrison, *Making the Connections*, 260.

52. Peter Steinfels, "Presbyterians Try to Resolve Long Dispute," *The New York Times* 17 June 1994: A9.

53. Rasmussen, *Moral Fragments*, 12.

54. Ibid., 14.

55. Dorothee Soelle, *The Window of Vulnerability: A Political Spirituality*, trans. Linda M. Maloney (Minneapolis: Fortress Press, 1990), xi.

56. Ibid., 14.

57. Ibid., 5.

58. Ibid., 84.

59. See Augustine, *The City of God*, Book XIX, ch. 13, trans. Henry Bettenson (New York: Penguin Books, 1984, reprint 1986), 870. Augustine argues that peace is dependent upon the "tranquillity of order" and that "order is the arrangement of things equal and unequal in a pattern which assigns to each its proper position."

60. For example, see Jessica Benjamin, *The Bonds of Love: Psychoanalysis, Feminism, and the Politics of Domination* (New York: Pantheon Books, 1988), especially "Master and Slave"; Nancy Chodorow, *The Reproduction of Mothering* (Berkeley: University of California Press, 1978); R. E. Dobash and R. Dobash, *Violence Against Wives: A Case Against Patriarchy* (New York: Free Press, 1978); James Nelson, *Embodiment: An Approach to Sexuality and Christian Theology* (Minneapolis, Minn.: Augsburg Publishing House, 1978) and *The Intimate Connection: Male Sexuality, Masculine Spirituality* (Philadelphia: Westminster Press, 1988).

61. Jalna Hanmer and Mary Maynard, *Women, Violence and Social Control* (Atlantic Highlands, N.J.: Humanities Press International, Inc., 1987), 9.

62. David H. J. Morgan, "Masculinity and Violence," in *Women, Violence, and Social Control*, 180.

63. Daniel Maguire, "The Feminization of God and Ethics," *Christianity and Crisis*, vol. 42, no. 4 (15 March 1982): 63-64, as cited in Ruether, *Sexism and God-Talk*, 179.

64. Beverly Harrison, "Misogyny and Homophobia," in *Making the Connections*, 135-51.

65. Susan Thistlethwaite, *Sex, Race, and God: Christian Feminism in Black and White* (New York: Crossroad, 1989). This discussion is taken from her chapter "A Difference in Common: Violence," 126-41.

66. Rita Nakashima Brock, *Journeys by Heart: A Christology of Erotic Power* (New York: Crossroad, 1988).

67. Starhawk, "A Men's Movement I Can Trust," in *Women Respond to the Men's Movement*, ed. Kay Leigh Hagan (San Francisco: HarperSan Francisco, 1992), 29.

68. Stanley Hauerwas, *After Christendom?* (Nashville: Abingdon Press, 1991), 53.

69. Patricia McAuliffe, *Fundamental Ethics: A Liberationist Approach* (Washington, D.C.: Georgetown University Press, 1993), 31.

70. Harrison, *Making the Connections*, 19.

71. Alice Walker, *Possessing the Secret of Joy* (London: Vintage, 1993), 264.

72. See Patricia Hill Collins, *Black Feminist Thought: Knowledge, Consciousness, and the Politics of Empowerment* (New York: Routledge, 1991), 235-37, for a description of an epistemological approach, grounded in the experiences of black women in the U.S., which calls for the necessary de-centering of the dominant as a prologue to dialogues that pivot the center. In other words, dealing with unequal access to the power to name is essential to the construction of truth.

73. Marvin Ellison, "Holding Up Our Half of the Sky: Male Gender Privilege as Problem and Resource for Liberation Ethics," *Journal of Feminist Studies in Religion*, vol. 9, nos. 1-2 (Spring/Fall 1993): 95-113.

74. Ibid., 99.

75. Ibid., 108. John Stoltenberg, "A coupla things I've been meaning to say about really confronting male power," *Changing Men* 22 (Spring-Winter, 1991): 8.

76. Ibid., 110.

77. Harrison, *Making the Connections*, 260.

78. Different opportunities will exist in different communities for the kinds of connections to communities of resistance that I have described. The city where I worked in ministry was fortunate to have a well-run, grassroots organization associated with the Industrial Areas Foundation (a descendent of the work of Saul Alinsky in Chicago). Dr. Mary McClintock Fulkerson has made me aware of the Highlander Center near Knoxville, Tennessee, which brings together grassroots activists, as well as the Empty the Shelters coalition of the homeless, local activists, and students in Atlanta, Georgia.

# BIBLIOGRAPHY

Adair, Margo. "Will the Real Men's Movement Please Stand Up?" In *Women Respond to the Men's Movement*, Kay Leigh Hagan, ed. San Francisco: Harper and Row, 1992.

Alcoff, Linda. "Cultural Feminism Versus Poststructuralism: The Identity Crisis in Feminist Theory." *Signs* 13 (Spring): 405-40, 1988.

Amott, Teresa. *Caught in the Crisis*. New York: Monthly Review Press, 1993.

Amott, Teresa, and Julie Matthaei. *Race, Gender, and Work*. Boston: Northeastern University Press, 1991.

Barlett, Donald, and James Steele. *America: What Went Wrong?* Kansas City: Andrews and McMeel, 1992.

Bell, Daniel. *The Cultural Contradictions of Capitalism*. New York: Basic Books, 1976.

Benjamin, Jessica. *The Bonds of Love*. New York: Pantheon, 1988.

Berger, John. *Ways of Seeing*. London: BBC & Penguin, 1972.

Berger, Peter. *The Sacred Canopy*. New York: Anchor, 1969.

Bloom, Allan. *The Closing of the American Mind: How Higher Education Has Failed Democracy and Impoverished the Soul of Today's Students*. New York: Simon & Schuster, 1987.

Bly, Robert. *Iron John: A Book About Men*. New York: Vintage, 1990.

Braverman, Harry. *Labor and Monopoly Capital: The Degradation of Work in the Twentieth Century*. New York: Monthly Review Press, 1974.

Brock, Rita Nakashima. *Journeys by Heart: A Christology of Erotic Power*. New York: Crossroad, 1988.

Brubaker, Pamela K. "Economic Justice for Whom? Women Enter the Dialogue." In *Religion and Economic Justice*. Michael Zweig, ed. Philadelphia: Temple University Press, 1991.

Bucher, Glenn, ed. *Straight White Male*. Philadelphia: Fortress Press, 1976.

Burstyn, Varda, ed. *Women Against Censorship*. Vancouver: Couglas & McIntyre, 1985.

Cannon, Katie. *Black Womanist Ethics*. Atlanta: Scholars Press, 1988.

——. "Slave Ideology and Biblical Interpretation." *Semeia*, vol. 47 (1989): 9-23.

Cannon, Katie, Isasi-Diaz, Ada Maria, Kwok Pui-lan, Letty Russell, eds. *Inheriting Our Mothers' Gardens: Feminist Theology in Third World Perspective*. Philadelphia: Westminster Press, 1988.

Chittister, Joan. *Women, Ministry and the Church*. New York: Paulist Press, 1983.

Chodorow, Nancy. *The Reproduction of Mothering*. Berkeley: University of California Press, 1978.

——. "Mothering, Male Dominance, and Capitalism." In *Capitalist Patriarchy and the Case for Socialist Feminism*, ed. Zillah Eisenstein. New York: Monthly Review Press, 1979, 83-106.

Christ, Carol. *Diving Deep and Surfacing: Women Writers on Spiritual Quest*. Boston: Beacon Press, 1980.

Christ, Carol, and Judith Plaskow, eds. *Womenspirit Rising*. San Francisco: Harper & Row, 1979.

Collins, Patricia Hill. *Black Feminist Thought: Knowledge, Consciousness, and the Politics of Empowerment*. New York: Routledge, 1991.

Cone, James. *Martin and Malcolm and America: A Dream or a Nightmare*. Maryknoll, N.Y.: Orbis Books, 1991.

Daly, Mary. *Gyn/Ecology: The Metaethics of Radical Feminism*. Boston: Beacon Press, 1978.

Davaney, Sheila, ed. *Theology at the End of Modernity*. Philadelphia: Trinity Press International, 1991.

Davis, Angela. *Women, Race, and Class*. New York: Vintage Books, 1983.

Dawe, Alan. "Theories of Social Action." In *A History of Sociological Analysis*, ed. Tom Bottomore and Robert Nisbet. New York: Basic Books, 1978, 362-78.

Dobash, R. E., and R. Dobash. *Violence Against Wives: A Case Against Patriarchy*. New York: Free Press, 1978.

Donovan, Josephine. *Feminist Theory*. New York: Frederick Ungar, 1985.

Durkheim, Emile. *The Division of Labor in Society*, trans. W. D. Halls. New York: MacMillan, 1933. Reprint, New York: Basic Books, 1984.

Ehrenreich, Barbara. *Fear of Falling: The Inner Life of the Middle Class*. New York: Pantheon, 1989.

Eisenstein, Zillah, ed. *Capitalist Patriarchy and the Case for Socialist Feminism*. New York: Monthly Review Press, 1979.

——. "Developing a Theory of Capitalist Patriarchy and Socialist Feminism." In *Capitalist Patriarchy and the Case for Socialist Feminism*, ed. Zillah Eisenstein. New York: Monthly Review Press, 1979, 5-40.

——. "Some Notes on the Relations of Capitalist Patriarchy." In *Capitalist Patriarchy and the Case for Socialist Feminism*, ed. Zillah Eisenstein. New York: Monthly Review Press, 1979, 41-55.

——. *The Radical Future of Liberal Feminism*. New York: Longman, 1986.

Ellison, Marvin. "Holding Up Our Half of the Sky: Male Gender Privilege as Problem and Resource for Liberation Ethics." *Journal of Feminist Studies in Religion,* vol. 9, nos. 1 and 2 (1993): 95-113.

Elshtain, Jean Bethke, ed. *The Family in Political Thought.* Amherst: University of Massachusetts Press, 1982.

Englehardt, Tris, and Dan Callahan, eds. *Morals, Science and Society.* New York: The Hastings Center, 1978.

Evans, Sara. *Personal Politics.* New York: Vintage Books, 1980.

Evans, Sara M., and Barbara Nelson. *Wage Justice.* Chicago: University of Chicago Press, 1989.

Fabella, Virginia, and Mercy Amba Oduyoye, eds. *With Passion and Compassion: Third World Women Doing Theology.* Maryknoll, N.Y.: Orbis Books, 1988.

Felder, Cain Hope, ed. *Stoney the Road We Trod: African American Biblical Interpretation.* Minneapolis: Fortress Press, 1991.

Ferm, Dean William, ed. *Third World Liberation Theologies: A Reader.* Maryknoll, N.Y.: Orbis Books, 1986.

Fish, Stanley. *Is There a Text in This Class? The Authority of Interpretive Communities.* Cambridge: Harvard University Press, 1980.

Flax, Jane. "Postmodernism and Gender Relations in Feminist Theory." *Signs* 12 (Summer 1987): 624-43.

Foster, Hal, ed. *The Anti-Aesthetic: Essays in Post-Modern Culture.* Port Townsend, Wash.: Bay Press, 1983.

Foucault, Michel. "What Is an Author?" in *Language, Counter-memory and Practice: Selected Essays and Interviews,* ed. and trans. Donald F. Bouchard. Ithaca, N. Y.: Cornell University Press, 1980.

———. *Power/Knowledge,* ed. and trans. Colin Gordon. New York: Pantheon, 1980.

———. *The History of Sexuality,* vol. 1 *An Introduction.* New York: Vintage, 1980.

———. *Foucault Reader,* ed. Paul Rabinow. New York: Pantheon, 1984.

Fox-Genevese, Elizabeth. *Feminism without Illusions: A Critique of Individualism.* Chapel Hill: University of North Carolina Press, 1991.

Frazer, Nancy. *Unruly Practices.* Minneapolis: University of Minneapolis Press, 1989.

Freire, Paulo. *Pedagogy of the Oppressed,* trans. Myra Bergman Ramos. New York: Continuum, 1986.

Friedan, Betty. *The Feminine Mystique.* New York: Dell, 1963.

Fulkerson, Mary McClintock. "Contesting Feminist Canons." *Journal of Feminist Studies in Religion,* vol. 7, no. 2 (Fall 1991): 53-73.

———. "Sexism as Original Sin: Developing a Theocentric Discourse." *Journal of the American Academy of Religion,* vol. LIX, no. 4 (Winter 1991): 653-75.

Gardiner, Judith Kegan. "Self Psychology as Feminist Theory." *Signs,* vol. 12, no. 4 (1987): 761-80.

Geertz, Clifford. *The Interpretation of Cultures.* New York: Basic, 1973.

Giddings, Paula. *When and Where I Enter: The Impact of Black Women on Race and Sex in America*. New York: Bantam, 1984.

Gilligan, Carol. *In a Different Voice*. Cambridge: Harvard University Press, 1982.

Gouldner, Alvin. *The Coming Crisis of Western Sociology*. New York: Basic Books, 1970.

Gutierrez, Gustavo. *A Theology of Liberation*. Maryknoll, N.Y.: Orbis, 1973.

Hanmer, Jalna, and Mary Maynard. *Women, Violence and Social Control*. Atlantic Highlands, N.J.: Humanities Press International, 1987.

Harding, Sandra. "The Instability of the Analytical Categories of Feminist Theory." *Signs* 13 (Spring 1984): 645-64.

———. *The Science Question in Feminism*. Ithaca, N.Y.: Cornell University Press, 1986.

———, ed. *Feminism and Methodology*. Bloomington: Indiana University Press, 1987.

Harrison, Beverly. *Our Right to Choose*. Boston: Beacon Press, 1983.

———. *Making the Connections*. Boston: Beacon Press, 1985.

Hartsock, Nancy. *Money, Sex, and Power*. New York: Longman Press, 1983.

———. "Foucault on Power." In *Feminism/Postmodernism*, ed. Linda Nicholson. New York: Routledge, 1990, 157-75.

Hauerwas, Stanley. "Understanding Homosexuality." *Pastoral Psychology* 24 (Spring 1976): 231-44.

Hauerwas, Stanley, Richard Bondi, and David Burrell. *Truthfulness and Tragedy*. Notre Dame, Ind.: University of Indiana Press, 1977.

Hauerwas, Stanley. *A Community of Character*. Notre Dame, Ind.: University of Notre Dame Press, 1981.

———. *Peaceable Kingdom*. Notre Dame, Ind.: University of Notre Dame Press, 1983.

Hauerwas, Stanley, and Alasdair MacIntyre, eds. *Revisions: Changing Perspectives in Moral Philosophy*. Notre Dame, Ind.: University of Notre Dame Press, 1984.

Hauerwas, Stanley. *Against the Nations*. Minneapolis: Winston Press, 1985.

———. *Character and the Christian Life*. San Antonio: Trinity University Press, 1975; reprint, 1985.

———. *Suffering Presence*. Notre Dame, Ind.: University of Notre Dame Press, 1986.

———. *Christian Existence Today*. Durham, N.C.: The Labyrinth Press, 1988.

———. "Hating Mothers as the Way to Peace." *Journal of Preachers* 11 (1988): 17-21.

Hauerwas, Stanley, and William Willimon. *Resident Aliens*. Nashville: Abingdon Press, 1989.

Hauerwas, Stanley. "The Testament of Friends." *The Christian Century* (February 28, 1990): 212-16.

———. *After Christendom*. Nashville: Abingdon Press, 1991.

———. *Unleashing the Scripture*. Nashville: Abingdon Press, 1993.

———. *Dispatches from the Front*. Durham, N.C.: The Labyrinth Press, 1994.

hooks, bell. *Ain't I A Woman*. Boston: South End Press, 1981.

———. *Feminist Theory: From Margin to Center*. Boston: South End Press, 1984.

———. *Talking Back*. Boston: South End Press, 1989.

———. *Yearning*. Boston: South End Press, 1990.

Horsley, Richard. *The Liberation of Christmas: The Infancy Narratives in Social Context*. New York: Crossroad Publishing, 1989.

Humphrey, William. *The Ordways*. New York: Knopf, 1965.

Hunter, Anne Marie. "Numbering the Hairs of Our Heads: Male Social Control and the All-Seeing Male God." Presentation to the American Academy of Religion. Kansas City, November, 1991. Photocopy.

Johnson, Elizabeth. *She Who Is: The Mystery of God in Feminist Theological Discourse*. New York: Crossroad Publishing, 1992.

Keen, Sam. *Fire in the Belly: On Being a Man*. New York: Bantam Books, 1991.

Keller, Evelyn Fox. *A Feeling for the Organism*. New York: W. H. Freeman, 1983.

———. *Reflections on Gender and Science*. New Haven, Conn.: Yale University Press, 1985.

Lasch, Christopher. *Haven in a Heartless World*. New York: Basic, 1977.

Lee, Jarena. "The Life and Religious Experience of Jarena Lee." In *Sisters of the Spirit: Three Black Women's Autobiographies of the Nineteenth Century*. William L. Andrews, ed. Bloomington: Indiana University Press, 1986.

Lessing, Doris. *Martha Quest*. London: Panther, 1972.

Lindbeck, George. *Nature of Doctrine: Religion and Society in a Postliberal Age*. Philadelphia: Westminster Press, 1984.

Loades, Ann, ed. *Feminist Theology: A Reader*. London: SPCK. 1990.

Lorde, Audre. *Sister Outsider*. Trumansburg, N.Y.: Crossing Press, 1984.

Luker, Kristin. *Abortion and the Politics of Motherhood*. Berkeley: University of California Press, 1984.

McAuliffe, Patricia. *Fundamental Ethics: A Liberationist Approach*. Washington, D.C.: Georgetown University Press, 1993.

McClendon, James Wm. *Ethics: Systematic Theology*, Vol. I.Nashville: Abingdon Press, 1986.

MacDonell, Diane. *Theories of Discourse: An Introduction*. Oxford: Basil Blackwell, 1986.

MacIntyre, Alasdair, and Stanley Hauerwas, eds. *Revisions: Changing Perspectives in Moral Philosophy*. Notre Dame, Ind.: University of Notre Dame Press, 1984.

MacKinnon, Catherine. *Toward a Feminist Theory of the State*. Cambridge: Harvard University Press, 1989.

Marx, Karl. *Early Writings*, ed. Quintin Hoare, trans. Rodney Livingstone. New York: Vintage Books, 1975.

Merchant, Carolyn. *The Death of Nature*. New York: Harper and Row, 1980.

Mitchell, Juliet. *Woman's Estate*. New York: Pantheon, 1971.

Moore, Henrietta. *Feminism and Anthropology*. Minneapolis: University of Minnesota Press, 1988.

Mosala, Itumeleng. *Biblical Hermeneutics and Black Theology in South Africa*. Grand Rapids, Mich.: William Eerdmans, 1989.

Newman, Katherine. *Falling from Grace: The Experience of Downward Mobility in the American Middle Class*. New York: Vintage Books, 1988.

Norton, Theodore Mills. "Contemporary Critical Theory and the Family." In *The Family in Political Thought*. Jean Bethke Elshtain, ed. Amherst, Mass.: University of Massachusetts Press, 1982.

Okin, Susan. *Justice, Gender, and the Family*. New York: Basic Books, 1989.

Ooskwi, Marzieh Ahmadi. "Honor." In *Ecumenical Decade 1988-1998: Churches in Solidarity with Women*. Geneva: World Council of Churches Publications, 1988.

Ortner, Sherry. "Is Female to Male as Nature Is to Culture?" In *Woman, Culture and Society*, eds. Michelle Rosaldo and Louise Lamphere. Stanford: Stanford University Press, 1974.

Pagels, Elaine. *Adam, Eve, and the Serpent*. New York: Random House, 1988.

Pateman, Carole. *The Problem of Political Obligation*. New York: Wiley & Sons, 1979; reprint, Berkeley: University of California Press, 1985.

———. *The Sexual Contract*. Stanford: Stanford University Press, 1988.

Plaskow, Judith. *Sex, Sin, and Grace*. Lanham, Md.: University Press of America, 1980.

———. *Standing Again at Sinai*. San Francisco: Harper & Row, 1990.

Plaskow, Judith, and Carol Christ, eds. *Weaving the Visions*. San Francisco: Harper and Row, 1989.

Pui-lan, Kwok. "Discovering the Bible in the Non-Biblical World." In *Lift Every Voice: Constructing Christian Theologies from the Underside*, eds. Susan Thistlethwaite and Mary Potter Engel. San Francisco: Harper & Row, 1990, 270-82.

Rasmussen, Larry. *Moral Fragments and Moral Community*. Minneapolis: Fortress Press, 1993.

Ringe, Sharon. "Reading from Context to Context: Contributions of a Feminist Hermeneutic to Theologies of Liberation." In *Lift Every Voice*, eds. Susan Brooks Thistlethwaite, and Mary Potter Engel. San Francisco: Harper and Row, 1990.

Rosaldo, Michelle Zimbalist. "Woman, Culture, and Society: A Theoretical Overview." In *Woman, Culture and Society*, eds. Michelle Rosaldo and Louise Lamphere. Stanford: Stanford University Press, 1974, 17-42.

———. "Moral/Analytic Dilemmas Posed by the Intersection of Feminism and Social Science." In *Social Science as Moral Inquiry*, ed. Norma Haav. New York: Columbia University Press, 1983, 76-93.

Rubin, Gayle. "The Traffic in Women: Notes on the 'Political Economy' of Sex." In *Toward an Anthropology of Women*, ed. Rayna Reiter. New York: Monthly Review Press, 1975.

Ruether, Rosemary Radford, and Rosemary Skinner Keller, eds. *Women and Religion in America,* vol. 1, *The Nineteenth Century.* San Francisco: Harper & Row, 1981.

Ruether, Rosemary Radford. *Women and Religion in America,* vol. 2, *The Colonial and Revolutionary Periods.* San Francisco: Harper & Row, 1983.

———. *Sexism and God-Talk.* Boston: Beacon Press, 1983.

———. *Theology and Practice of Feminist Liturgical Communities.* San Francisco: Harper and Row, 1985.

———. "The Western Religious Tradition and Violence Against Women in the Home." In *Christianity, Patriarchy, and Abuse: A Feminist Critique,* eds. Joanne Carlson Brown and Carole R. Bohn. New York: Pilgrim Press, 1989.

Russell, Letty. *Church in the Round: Feminist Interpretation of the Church.* Louisville, Ky.: Westminster/John Knox Press, 1993.

Saiving, Valerie. "The Human Situation: A Feminine View." In *Womanspirit Rising,* eds. Carol Christ and Judith Plaskow. San Francisco: Harper & Row, 1979, 25-42.

Say, Elizabeth A. *Evidence on Her Own Behalf: Women's Narrative as Theological Voice.* Savage, Md.: Rowman and Littlefield Publishers, 1990.

Schaberg, Jane. *The Illegitimacy of Jesus: A Feminist Theological Interpretation.* San Francisco: Harper and Row, 1985.

Schüssler Fiorenza, Elisabeth. *In Memory of Her.* New York: Crossroad, 1983.

———. *Bread Not Stone.* Boston: Beacon Press, 1984.

———, ed. *Searching the Scriptures.* N.Y.: Crossroad, 1993.

Scott, Joan Wallach. *Gender and the Politics of History.* New York: Columbia University Press, 1988.

———. "Deconstructing Equality-Versus-Difference: or, The Uses of Post-structuralist Theory for Feminism." *Feminist Studies* 14 (Spring 1988): 33-50.

Smith-Rosenberg, Carroll. *Disorderly Conduct.* New York: Knopf, 1985.

Soelle, Dorothee. *The Window of Vulnerability: A Political Spirituality,* trans. Linda M. Maloney. Minneapolis: Fortress Press, 1990.

Spelman, Elizabeth. *Inessential Woman.* Boston: Beacon Press, 1988.

Stanton, Elizabeth Cady. *Eighty Years and More, Reminiscences 1815-1897.* New York: Schocken, 1971.

———. *The Woman's Bible.* Salem, N.H.: Ayer Co., 1895; reprint Salem, N.H.: Ayer Co., 1988 (page references to reprint edition).

Swedish, Margaret. *Central American Reflections: A Handbook for Religious Witness.* Washington, D.C.: Religious Task Force on Central America, undated.

"Task Force on Issues of Vocation and Problems of Work in the United States, Presbyterian Church (U.S.A.)." *Challenges in the Workplace.* Louisville, Ky., 1989.

Taylor, Mark Kline. *Remembering Esperanza.* Maryknoll, N.Y.: Orbis Books, 1990.

Thistlethwaite, Susan. *Sex, Race, and God.* New York: Crossroad, 1989.

Thistlethwaite, Susan, and Mary Engel, eds. *Lift Every Voice: Constructing Christian Theologies from the Underside.* New York: Harper & Row, 1990.

Tracy, David. *Plurality and Ambiguity: Hermeneutics, Religion, Hope*. San Francisco: Harper and Row, 1987.

Trible, Phyllis. *Texts of Terror*. Philadelphia: Fortress Press, 1984.

Vaughan, Judith. *Sociality, Ethics, and Social Change*. Lanham, Md.: University Press of America, 1983.

Walker, Alice. *In Search of Our Mothers' Gardens*. San Diego: Harvest/HBJ Book, 1983.

Washington, Mary Helen. *Black-Eyed Susans/Midnight Birds*. New York: Anchor, 1990.

Weedon, Chris. *Feminist Practice and Poststructuralist Theory*. New York: Basil Blackwell, 1987.

Welch, Sharon. *Communities of Resistance and Solidarity: A Feminist Theology of Liberation*. Maryknoll, N.Y.: Orbis Books, 1985.

———. "Ideology and Social Change." In *Weaving the Visions*, eds. Judith Plaskow and Carol Christ. San Francisco: Harper & Row, 1989.

———. *A Feminist Ethic of Risk*. Minneapolis: Fortress Press, 1990.

Welter, Barbara. "The Cult of True Womanhood: 1820-1860." *American Quarterly*, vol. 18, no. 2 (Summer 1966): 151-74.

Werpehowski, William. "Justice." In *The Westminster Dictionary of Christian Ethics*, eds. James Childress and John Macquarrie. Philadelphia: Westminster Press, 1986.

Williams, Delores. *Sisters in the Wilderness*. Maryknoll, N.Y.: Orbis Books, 1993.

Yoder, John Howard. *The Politics of Jesus*. Grand Rapids, Mich.: William B. Eerdmans, 1972.

———. *The Priestly Kingdom*. Notre Dame, Ind.: University of Notre Dame Press, 1984.